FREE CHOICE
FOR WORKERS

FREE CHOICE FOR WORKERS

A HISTORY OF THE RIGHT TO WORK MOVEMENT

GEORGE C. LEEF

Jameson Books, Inc.
Ottawa, Illinois

Titles from Jameson Books are available at special discounts for bulk purchases, for sales promotions, premiums, fund raising or educational use. Special condensed or excerpted paperback editions can also be created to customer specifications.

For information and other requests please write
Jameson Books, Inc.
722 Columbus Street
P.O. Box 738
Ottawa, Illinois 61350

Mail Orders: 800-426-1357
Telephone: 815-434-7905
Facsimile: 815-434-7907
Email: jamesonbooks@yahoo.com

Printed in the United States of America.

Jameson Books are distributed to the book trade by MidPoint Trade Books, 27 West 20th Street, Suite 1102, New York, NY 10011 Bookstores please call 212-727-0190 to place orders.

Bookstore returns should be addressed to MidPoint Trade Books, 1263 Southwest Boulevard, Kansas City, KS 66103.

ISBN: 0-915463-97-0

6   5   4   3   2   1 / 09   08   07   06   05

In memory of my grandfather, George H. Leef,
who first got me interested in the importance
of freedom and its decline in America

CONTENTS

FOREWORD
BY STEVE FORBES

America suffers from a great many laws that should never have been passed—laws that are at odds with both the Constitution and with our tradition of individual liberty. Among the worst of that bad lot are laws covering labor relations.

Since the time of the New Deal, we have been shackled with statutes and administrative decrees that are designed to promote labor unions and collective bargaining. There is nothing wrong with either unions or collective bargaining, but in a free society, there is no justification for government intervention to promote them. A worker's decision to join a labor union to obtain the benefits of its representation should be individual and voluntary, just as we join civic groups or contract for services. There is no good reason why the law should turn that choice into a collective decision binding upon all workers and then sanction union contracts requiring the payment of union dues as a condition for holding a job. Unfortunately, that is how our law works. Millions of American workers are compelled to pay union dues or else be fired. We wouldn't tolerate a system like that in any other aspect of our society.

This intolerable state of affairs is due mainly to the National Labor Relations Act (NLRA), passed in 1935. If we could repeal or amend the NLRA to remove its most authoritarian features, the problem of compulsory unionism would be eliminated. Doing that, however, would be extremely difficult given the enormous political power of Big Labor, but steady progress is being made. Meanwhile, the battle goes on to add to the number of states—currently 22—which forbid union contracts making the payment of dues a condition for keeping a job.

Protecting their citizens from federally-authorized, compulsory unionism is the one and only area in which states are permitted to regulate labor relations. The crucial language is in Section 14(b) of the 1947 Taft-Hartley Act and consists of just 44 words: "Nothing in this Act shall be construed as authorizing the execution or application of agreements requiring membership in a labor organization as a condition of employment in any State or Territory in which such execution or application is prohibited by State or Territorial law." Big Labor has tried hard to get that part of the law repealed, and as this book recounts, came perilously close to doing so in 1965.

Since 1955, there has been one national organization devoted to passing Right to Work laws and defending the rights of workers to choose whether they want a union or not—National Right to Work (NRTW). If it hadn't been for the efforts of National Right to Work over the years, America today would be much less free and prosperous than it is. NRTW has held its finger in the dike against the expansion of legal powers that the chieftains of Big Labor have clamored for.

Alas, few people know how much they owe to this organization. Most Americans are unaware of the principled stance National Right to Work has always taken and the many battles it has fought to preserve the freedom of workers to say "no" to compulsory unionism. But with the publication of *Free Choice for Workers—A History of the Right to Work Movement,* author George Leef gives us a much-needed overview of the Right to Work movement. It's about time that we had a book on this important topic.

Besides chronicling the history of the Right to Work movement, Leef (a lawyer who thankfully devotes his time to public policy work) explains the legal morass we are in and how it came about. He also corrects many false impressions that people may have from hearing Big Labor's anti-Right to Work sloganeering. For example, union officials often say that Right to Work is anti-union. In fact, the movement was galvanized by railroad union members dissatisfied with the change from

voluntary to compulsory membership. Furthermore, by allowing workers an escape hatch if their unions become too arrogant and self-serving,
Right to Work laws are the best check workers have against abuse. Unions
serve workers better if members are free to drop out when they feel that
their interests are being neglected.

What I particularly enjoy about *Free Choice for Workers* is the way
Leef makes clear the philosophical connection between Right to Work
and belief in free markets and limited government. If you favor those,
as I do, it should follow that you also favor Right to Work. Not only is
Right to Work legislation consistent with the same individualist principles that underlie free markets and limited government, but our opponents' political machine is fueled by Big Labor's money. Leef shows that
much of the support for the Big Government agenda comes from compulsory dues extracted from union members—many of whom wouldn't
donate a penny to the candidates and causes favored by union bosses if
they could help it. In short, if you want to rein in the relentless growth
of government and restore the freedom we have lost, you should embrace
the Right to Work cause and put reform of our antiquated labor statutes
at the top of your priorities list.

Another mistaken impression that *Free Choice for Workers* demol-
ishes is the notion that Right to Work is a Big Business/Republican plot
against the average worker. The truth is that Big Business has rarely even
given lip service to the Right to Work movement; the financial support
for the National Right to Work Committee and its sister-organization,
the National Right to Work Legal Defense Foundation, has overwhelmingly come from donations by individuals and small businesses. As for
the Republican Party, the book surprisingly shows that Republicans have
often been the obstacle to Right to Work legislation. Quite a few elected
Republicans seem to believe that Big Labor will "go easy on them" if they
cave in on the matter of Right to Work. To me, that seems an exercise
in wishful thinking.

This book should be read not just for its blow-by-blow accounts of
the crucial battles Right to Work has fought over the years, but also
because it shows that in the United States, good ideas can still prevail

over bad ones. What it takes is to stick to your principles and communicate them clearly to the people. For almost fifty years now, that is exactly what National Right to Work has been doing.

THE PROBLEM OF COMPULSORY UNIONISM IN AMERICA

America's greatness is rooted in its commitment to freedom. Millions of people have come to these shores, often facing great hardship and danger, not because they believed that the streets were paved with gold, but because they understood that here they would escape from the unfree conditions of their homelands. In America, people could live their lives according to their own goals and convictions. In America, people did not have to bow to haughty authorities telling them what they must and must not do. In America, your life was your own. Uniquely, our Constitution and laws protected the liberty of individuals to peacefully go about their affairs as they thought best. That was the powerful beacon that brought people to America.

A crucial component of freedom is the freedom to say "No." Americans have always enjoyed the freedom not to associate with groups they do not choose to—groups whose values and actions they find incompatible with their own beliefs. We have the freedom to decline to join churches or civic associations as we please. We have the freedom to say "No thanks" to countless businesses that would like to sell to us. We are free to choose whether to accept or reject offers from countless contractors and professionals who would render us services. The people who run all those churches, businesses, and organizations understand that they have to take "No" for an answer when it is given. That's part of the freedom of America.

There is, however, a notable exception to the rule that Americans get to decide with whom they will or will not associate and do business.

Labor union bosses have long operated on the belief that they should be able to coerce people into joining them—or at least into accepting and paying for their services—whether they want to or not. Going far back into their history, one finds in them a repulsive streak of violence and authoritarianism, a ready willingness to use intimidation and coercion to accomplish their ends. We would be astonished if churches or businesses or professionals claimed to have the right to compel us to join, to do business with, or to pay for services from them. Labor bosses, however, not only make such a claim, but enforce it against millions of Americans.

Labor unions could, and sometimes do, function on a voluntary basis. Associations of workers who wish to collaborate for common goals are no more inherently coercive than are associations of people who organize in order to attain any other legitimate goal. Under American principles of freedom, workers have just as much right to form an organization to seek to advance their interests as do investors, environmental advocates, chess enthusiasts, or anyone else. The question is not the *ends* that people desire, but the *means* they employ. Anyone is free to join, for example, The Nature Conservancy, but is equally free to leave it at any time. Unfortunately, labor union autocrats have rejected voluntarism and act as though they are so important that people should be compelled to accept their representation and pay them money, whether they want to or not.

Because of laws written many years ago, the aggressive, domineering attitude of many union officials has been transformed into our nation's policy. Big Labor sought and obtained legal privileges and immunities enjoyed by no other kind of association or organization in America. As Professor Morgan O. Reynolds writes, "(U)nions are immune from taxation and the antitrust laws. They can compel a firm to bargain with them 'in good faith'—an undefined term—and make its private property available for union use. Unions represent all employees in a bargaining unit, whether all employees want that representation or not. And, by and large, unions are immune from payment of damages for personal or property injury in labor disputes."[1] This book will focus on one of those powers, namely the power to "represent" workers who do not want their representation and compel them to pay for it.

Millions of Americans—auto workers, school teachers, truck drivers, retail clerks, airline pilots, musicians, and many more—work under collective bargaining agreements negotiated by labor unions to which they have never consented. As a result of "agreements" forced upon employers in the past (and often decades ago), workers hired in many companies are told that they must pay dues to the legally certified union or else be fired. Workers are not asked, "Do you wish to join this union and have it represent you in dealings with the company?" Instead, the iron fist of coercion is thrust into their faces: "Pay up or lose your job." They are not permitted to choose to represent themselves or to have some other person or group act as their representative. Nowhere else in American life do we so radically depart from our founding philosophy of individual liberty as in the laws that make people into vassals of union bosses.

The power to compel workers to accept and pay for their services has a profound impact upon the nature of labor unions. Since they have a guaranteed income stream from compulsory dues, union officials know that they can act with impunity regarding the wishes of many of their "members." They can, for instance, use union funds to engage in polit ical advocacy that many workers find completely distasteful. They can invest members' pension money in risky ventures where the workers would never willingly sink a penny. They can indulge in lavish living for themselves, as was most recently revealed in the scandals involving the heads of the Washington and Miami teachers' unions. Power, as Lord Acton so correctly observed, tends to corrupt. It also attracts those who prefer to control and dominate others. Donald Richberg, a lawyer who was one of the architects of our set of labor laws and who later came to see the tremendous harm they were doing, hit the nail on the head when he wrote about our powerful labor monopolies, "unlimited power concentrated in few hands will be used irresponsibly for personal or collective aggrandizement rather than for the common interest...."[2]

Individuals who have sought to avoid subservience to union bosses have often suffered grievously for their simple desire to be left alone.

Some have lost their jobs. Some have endured threats to themselves and loved ones. Some have suffered property damage and bodily injury. Some have been killed. Union coercion against independent-minded people is an ugly and continuing stain on the fabric of a nation committed to individual liberty, freedom of contract, and freedom of association.

Since 1955, there has been one organization dedicated to the principle that Americans should not be compelled to support unions and accept their supposed services against their wills. That organization is the National Right to Work Committee. Almost unique among Washington policy groups, the Committee seeks no government money or power. Its sole reason for existence is to fight for a belief—the belief that we should be free to accept or reject labor unions, just as we are free to accept or reject churches, businesses, civic groups, and so forth.

The National Right to Work Committee is not a "pro-business" group. While some, mostly small, businesses give it voluntary support, big businesses have often sided against it in the battles over compulsory unionism. Nor is it an anti-labor group. Many of the Committee's most fervent supporters are one-time voluntary union members who have felt the sting of the union lash when they had the temerity to think and act for themselves, rather than as the union hierarchy demanded. The Committee's story is not business versus labor, but liberty versus coercion.

For half a century, the National Right to Work Committee has fought a David versus Goliath battle against the powerful forces of compulsory unionism in America. The fact that in so many of its fights, it has bested union officials who refuse to take "No" for an answer and stop at virtually nothing to advance their agenda, should give us optimism. Good ideas, when advanced with determination and conviction, can still defeat bad ideas.

NOTES

1. Morgan O. Reynolds, *Making America Poorer* (Cato Institute, 1987), p. 193.
2. Donald Richberg, *Labor Union Monopoly* (Regnery, 1957) p. vi.

CHAPTER ONE

HOW COMPULSORY UNIONISM INVADED THE LAND OF THE FREE

On August 7, 1997, Rod Carter was driving his route for United Parcel Service. Carter was a muscular young man who had played linebacker for the University of Miami on its 1987 national championship team and had briefly played with the Dallas Cowboys of the NFL. This was not an ordinary day, though, because he knew that he was doing something he had been told not to do—work.

Days before, the International Brotherhood of Teamsters had declared a strike against UPS after the company and the union failed to agree on a new contract. Top union officers ordered all drivers to cease working and support the strike, no matter what their personal circumstances. Carter, with a wife and young children to support, decided that he would remain on the job. He even spoke his mind in an interview on an evening news program, saying that, while he agreed that his colleagues had the right to strike if they wished, he would exercise his right to keep earning a paycheck.

The previous evening, Rod's wife had received an ominous phone call from someone calling himself "Benny." The caller asked if he had reached the home of Rod Carter, then hung up. She was very worried, but Rod was still determined not to bow down to intimidation. In a worried state of mind, he went to work that August 7.

Rod's morning routine was quickly shattered. As he was stopped at a red light, another vehicle with several men in it pulled alongside his truck. One threw a bottle at him and the group shouted racial epithets

1

and threatened to kill him. Rod continued his route despite the ugly incident.

Five hours later, while again stopped at a red light, a Jeep Cherokee suddenly pulled up behind Rod's truck. A burly thug jumped out and pulled open the door of the truck. Four more attackers quickly joined the first, drawing Rod from his vehicle. They began to punch and kick at him, overcoming Rod's considerable ability to defend himself. As the beating continued, a fifth attacker, Benigno "Benny" Rojas stabbed Rod five times in his chest with an ice pick. When the light turned, the thugs fled, leaving their victim on the pavement, dazed and bleeding. Rod Carter had been given his lesson: When the Teamsters bosses say you don't work, you don't work.

The thugs who had attacked Rod Carter were later arrested, but were bailed out by Teamsters officials. Attorneys for Rod Carter eventually found witnesses who stated that the president of Teamsters Local 769, Anthony Cannestro, had encouraged militants to threaten and harass non-striking drivers and promised them legal assistance if any should be arrested for crimes committed against non-strikers. Only one of the six assailants served any jail time for the brutal attack on Rod. Carter filed a civil suit against the union and, fearing the bad publicity of a trial, the union offered him a settlement—paid with money that came from the dues of other drivers. Some "brotherhood."

While the violence in this case is shocking, it is far from unique. Every year, thousands of American workers find themselves beset with intimidation and violence directed by union bosses who demand their obedience. Furthermore, millions are subject to forced unionism, whereby they must pay dues to union treasuries as a condition of employment. Unwilling just to offer their services to willing customers, as other organizations do, union officials have spread a net of fear and coercion over millions of workers to extract money and obedience in return for jobs. Most unions don't have so brutal a reputation as the Teamsters, but they are all united on this point: Workers should be *compelled* to support them—or else.

That net of fear and coercion, which now entangles so many, had its beginnings in the 1930s. How did it come about? Did Americans willingly surrender their right to work without first bowing down to labor union officials—or was it brazenly snatched away? We will see that the loss of freedom to say "No thanks" to unions has two roots:[1] federal legislation giving union officials special privileges and immunities, and[2] the Supreme Court's willingness to turn a blind eye to the Constitution.

LIBERTY AND THE LAW

In the early years of our nation, Americans were free to live their lives very much as they chose. The Constitution, as well as the constitutions of the states, carefully restricted the coercive power of government over the people, and gave none whatsoever to private groups. Americans had had enough of the heavy-handed rule of a monarch who treated them as resources for his empire and whose arrogant officials had no respect for their rights. Accordingly, our laws protected those rights against both the actions of individual criminals and the high-handed scheming of people who would use the power of government in order to bring about their particular vision of the social good.

Among the rights that Americans insisted upon were those of property, contract, speech, and association. A person's property was under his control—no one else had the right to trespass upon it, much less seize or destroy it. A person was free to enter into contracts as he thought best and equally free to decline to enter into them. A person was entitled to speak or write what he wanted on any subject without having to worry about official punishment for the expression of his opinions. And a person was free to choose to associate with others for any peaceful purpose, but he could not be forced to associate against his wishes.

Those rights were key elements in the common law—a set of fundamental rules that covered all of our relationships with others. The rules were neutral, giving no person or group any special legal privileges, embodying the image of justice blindfolded. Under the common law, there was no need for a special set of rules for labor relations because the law of contract and property rights was sufficient to handle any disputes that arose.

Following common law principles, workers were free to join labor organizations and seek to bargain as a group if they wanted to do so, but no one could be legally compelled to join or accept representation by any such group. Similarly, common law permitted employers to choose whether or not they would bargain with the representatives of a labor organization. Labor union officials could say or publish whatever they wanted about the benefits of having their services and the miserliness of employers, but employers were also free to disparage union promises and question the character or motives of the union leaders. (The laws of libel and slander applied equally, of course.) And crucially, no one was permitted to use violence or intimidation. In short, the law respected freedom all around.

THE GREAT DEPRESSION

As late as the 1920s, Americans were scarcely less free to enjoy life, liberty, and property than they had been when the nation was new. During the Great Depression of the 1930s, however, a chorus of voices intoned the supposed need for America to jettison its "old-fashioned" commitment to individual freedom, private property, and a market economy. Instead, declared many opinion leaders, we should follow the examples that had been set by more "progressive" European nations such as England, Italy, and Germany, and adopt central economic planning and welfare policies. Politicians reacted by enacting hasty, ill-advised, and constitutionally dubious legislation that greatly increased the scope of government regulation and whittled away at individual freedom—including the freedom to choose whether you wanted to join a union or not. The republic of George Washington, Thomas Jefferson, Patrick Henry, and the other Founding Fathers was radically transformed in the 1930s by the enactment of laws that would have astounded them.

The bitter irony in all of this is the fact that the Depression, far from being proof of a failure of capitalism and our system of limited government, was actually caused by bad policies of the federal government, particularly the Federal Reserve System. After it had triggered the financial calamity that struck in October 1929, manifesting itself in the stock market crash, the government then made things far worse with a great variety of laws and programs that were supposed to speed recovery, but only interfered with the economy's natural recovery processes. Professor Gene Smiley explains that:

> The Great Depression is often said to demonstrate the instability of market economies and the need for government oversight and direction. The evidence can no longer support such assumptions. Government efforts to control and direct the gold standard for national purposes brought on the depression. Once it began, government actions, particularly in the United States, caused it to be much longer and much more severe. When the contraction finally ended, government interference in U.S. markets made the recovery unbearably slow and in 1937–1938 brought on a "depression with a depression." The 1930s economic crisis is tragic testimony to government interference in market economies.[1]

Americans were thus seduced away from their great tradition of freedom and self-reliance because the enemies of that tradition managed to pin the blame for the Depression on it. That was like convicting an innocent bystander of a crime, and doing so based on the testimony of the culprit. But few people understood the causes of the Depression then (or even now) and they were desperate for solutions. So Congress passed numerous laws that were supposed to improve economic conditions, including the laws that deprive workers of the freedom to remain independent of labor unions—laws that remain on the books to this day.

RAILROAD LEGISLATION IN THE 1920S

Labor union officials had sought preferential laws even before the era of the Great Depression. The beginnings of the federal government's abandonment of neutral principles of law in labor relations began in the railroad industry in the 1920s.

During World War I, the federal government seized control of railroads from their owners. Heads of the railroad unions wanted that arrangement to continue after the end of the war, realizing that they would have more leverage if they dealt with the government rather than only with managers who represented the stockholders. They pressured Congress for a scheme called the Plumb Plan, whereby the government, the unions, and the railroad management would share in control of the industry. The Plumb Plan was rejected, however, and the railroads were returned to their stockholders. America stayed with its traditional policy of leaving employers and employees free to work out their contracts under the principles of common law—for the time being.

Federal regulation would soon return, though. The Transportation Act of 1920 established a Railroad Labor Board (RLB) charged with regulating labor relations in what was then the nation's largest industry. In 1922, the RLB sought to impose a regime of collective bargaining in which a union that received a vote of a majority of the workers would then have the authority to negotiate on behalf of *all* the employees in that class. We see here for the first time the glimmering of an idea that many union officials had desired for years—exclusive representation. The notion that a person could be *compelled* to accept another as his agent for any purpose was entirely foreign to America under common law, but union organizers believed that they would be able to corral far more workers into their ranks if they could make unionism a matter of majority vote rather than individual choice. The Supreme Court ruled in 1923 that the RLB had exceeded its authority in ordering the exclusive representation system and the idea that workers could be forced to accept union representation against their will was, temporarily, suppressed.[2]

In 1922, a very disruptive strike put pressure on Congress to do something to smooth out labor relations in the railroad industry. After years of legislative wrangling, Congress passed the Railway Labor Act (RLA) of 1926. The law stated that railroad workers had a "right to organize" and that management had a "duty to bargain" with designated employee representatives. While the statute did not adopt exclusive representation as railroad union officials wanted, the imposition of a legal "duty to bargain" was an ominous departure from common law principles of freedom of contract, which never forced anyone to bargain against his will. The RLA applied only to the railroad industry at the time (it has since been expanded to cover airlines as well), but in creating a mandatory "duty to bargain," it set the terrible precedent of giving union officials special legal privileges not enjoyed by other Americans.

At the onset of the Depression, with the exception of workers covered by the RLA, labor relations in America were still governed by the common law and its protections for individual rights. Workers could join unions and seek collective bargaining, but they were equally free to remain independent. Some employers chose to bargain with union representatives, but others did not. The law neither favored nor opposed unions and collective bargaining. It still performed its time-honored function of upholding the equal rights of all.

TRASHING THE COMMON LAW

It is often said that Herbert Hoover failed as president because he was a *laissez-faire* advocate who disdained governmental action needed to shore up the crumbling economy from 1929 to 1932. In fact, Hoover was very much an interventionist and one law that he signed was the 1932 Norris-LaGuardia Act. Norris-LaGuardia was a statute that gave labor union officials several things they wanted: a) agreements by workers that they would not seek to unionize would not be enforceable in federal courts; b) labor unions would be immune from liability for wrongful acts under the antitrust laws; and c) unions would not be subject to private damage suits or injunctions against their strikes in federal courts. Professor Morgan Reynolds succinctly explains the thrust of the law, writing that "The overriding object of the act was to allow unions to be freer of the constraints that bind businessmen and everyone else, thereby allowing unions more latitude to use their aggressive tactics."[3]

The anti-injunction provision was the centerpiece of the legislation. Union spokesmen had long complained that they were being thwarted in accomplishing their objectives because employers would hurry off to find a sympathetic judge who would issue an injunction—(an order to cease and desist)—against strikes. Sympathetic academics such as Professor Felix Frankfurter helped to convince many Americans that injunctions were unfairly suppressing workers in their attempts to improve their conditions. That view has since been shown to be erroneous. After a thorough study of all reported labor injunctions between 1880 and 1932, Professor Sylvester Petro concluded that injunctions were seldom issued except where there had been violence associated with a strike. "In case after case," he found, "conscientious and capable and liberal judges revealed how deeply they were troubled by the overwhelming threats to ordered freedom that the prevalent violence of the unions posed."[4] Unfortunately, President Hoover bowed to public sentiment and signed the Norris-LaGuardia Act, thereby weakening the common law protections against violence and property damage—for both employers and for employees who preferred to work when union bosses had ordered a strike. That the Norris-LaGuardia Act was a "success" from the standpoint of union officials cannot be doubted, since the number of strikes, often accompanied by violence, doubled from 1932 to 1933 and continued to climb in the following years.

Franklin D. Roosevelt's huge victory in the 1932 presidential election set the stage for a sea change in the law of labor relations. He had received enthusiastic backing from most union leaders during the campaign and they wanted favorable legislation in return. Also, FDR's "Brain Trust" consisted of men who were admirers of European collectivism where strong unions were regarded as socially beneficial. The only question was how far the new administration would go in overturning our legal traditions to make it easier to form unions and compel workers to join them.

One fallacious notion that dominated the Roosevelt Administration was that high prices caused prosperity. The Agricultural Adjustment Act, for example, was premised on the idea that prices would rise if production were curtailed and existing commodity stocks were destroyed. (Prices did rise, but instead of restoring prosperity, that simply made it harder for struggling people to get by.) Another application of the idea was that higher wages would help the economy by giving workers more purchasing power. Union officials naturally agreed, and contended that, by empowering them with new legal "rights" to organize workers and demand higher wages, the administration would thereby help to restore the nation's economic health. The centerpiece of the early New Deal was the National Industrial Recovery Act (NIRA). The architects of the NIRA were convinced that America's economic troubles were rooted in the competitive free market system and they believed that the nation needed to take "progressive" steps into a planned economy. Under the NIRA, that would be accomplished (or at least started) by replacing the "anarchy" of the free market with "codes of fair competition." The law required business and trade associations to first seek governmental approval as "true representatives" of their industries, and once approved, they could write their codes—which would have the force of law. In short, the law promoted business cartels. Competition, the deadly enemy of all efforts to fix prices by collusive agreement, would be choked off with the government's blessing. In the Brave New World of early 1930s America, businessmen could be punished for such brazen transgressions against the public welfare as selling a quart of milk for *less* than the official price.[5] The regimentation of business was supposedly justified by the overall economic benefits of keeping prices high, but prosperity cannot (and did not) come about as a result of artificially high prices.

Cartelization of business, of course, was only half of the game. The New Deal planners also wanted to see labor cartelized to offset the "power" of business. The NIRA declared that it was the public policy of the United States to favor collective bargaining. Every "code of fair competition" drawn up by industry groups had to state that "employees shall have the right to organize and bargain collectively through representatives of their own choosing, and shall be free from interference, restraint, [and] coercion of employers or their agents." Furthermore, the codes had to ensure that workers could not be required to join a company union as a condition of employment or to refrain from joining or organizing any other union.

While the NIRA undoubtedly gave a strong boost to unionization, it did not go as far as Big Labor wanted. It did not ban company unions, which frequently held the allegiance of workers when "real" unions tried to organize them. It did not give to majority unions the power of exclusive representation, thus preserving the liberty of workers who did not desire union representation to negotiate on their own. And it did not mandate that companies bargain with unions, leaving owners free to ignore them if they chose. To remedy those "shortcomings" of the NIRA, Senator Robert F. Wagner of New York introduced a new bill in March 1934. That bill would have greatly strengthened the position of Big Labor by prohibiting company unions, compelling employers to bargain with union representatives, and allowing the National Labor Board to issue injunctions against vaguely defined "unfair labor practices" by employers. The NLB would thus become a judicial body, but using evidentiary standards much less rigorous than would be required in a federal court. Wagner's 1934 bill didn't pass, but it was a portent of things to come. Union officials were not satisfied with the legal advantages they had already been given, and kept pushing simultaneously for more power for themselves and curtailment of the rights of employers and workers who did not desire unionization.

THE NATIONAL LABOR RELATIONS ACT

The year 1934 was marked by numerous violent strikes in which the heads of unions sought to compel management to recognize and deal with them. In many of the strikes, union leaders employed squads of outsiders to man picket lines and intimidate workers and suppliers. Those strikes, further disrupting an already weakened economy, were often cited as a reason for passing a new labor law that would bring "industrial peace." Such "peace" would be bought by caving in to Big Labor's demands for sweeping powers to force workers into union ranks and further undermine the ability of employers to resist their demands.

Senator Wagner introduced a new bill in February 1935 that went even further than had his 1934 bill. Democratic control of Congress had been strengthened by the 1934 elections. This time there would be no stopping the union juggernaut.

In an atmosphere of economic despair and widespread strike violence, Congress took very little time in debating Wagner's bill. The Senate passed it on a vote of 63 to 12 in May and the House passed a slightly amended version by voice vote in June. The differences were reconciled in conference and the final bill was sent to President Roosevelt, who signed it with much fanfare in early July.

Known as the Wagner Act or the National Labor Relations Act (NLRA), this legislation brought about a radical transformation of the law of labor relations in America. The common law was replaced with a comprehensive scheme of federal regulation that would, under the Constitution's Supremacy Clause, preempt any attempts by the states to establish their own labor relations statutes, or to maintain common law principles. That is the chief reason why Big Labor concentrated on Washington rather than the state capitals in its quest for power—if the federal government acted as they wanted, it would eliminate the possibility of state-to-state differences in labor law. Under the principles of federalism, the states should have had the freedom to determine labor relations policy for themselves, but the union bosses knew that if states had that freedom, some would refuse to go along with their coercion-laden schemes and thus become magnets for capital and labor. Big Labor, like other enemies of the free market, has always abhorred competition, whether among workers, companies, or governments. Establishing federal control of labor relations would ensure that there would be no competition in labor relations law.

The Wagner Act begins with a tendentious legislative finding that "inequality of bargaining power between employees who do not possess full freedom of association or actual liberty of contract, and employers who are organized in the corporate or other forms of ownership association substantially burdens and affects the flow of commerce, and tends to aggravate recurrent business depressions. . . ." That fundamental premise of the law is erroneous. Under common law, employees enjoyed just as much liberty of contract and freedom of association as did anyone else. But Big Labor wanted to be depicted as oppressed victims of a supposedly unfair legal system, and Congress and President Roosevelt were glad to oblige.

The language about burdening and affecting the flow of commerce was the "industrial peace" argument turned into constitutional cover:

Under Article I, Section 8, Congress has the power to "regulate interstate commerce." The drafters of the bill knew that Supreme Court precedents were against federal attempts to control the conditions of labor, since the *production* of goods was regarded as preceding *commerce* in goods and therefore not subject to congressional control. Senator Wagner and his allies wanted to protect the legislation from constitutional attack by contending that lack of unionization was ultimately responsible for the economic depression and Congress was therefore within its constitutional powers to unburden "the flow of commerce" by fostering unionization. It was a weak argument, factually and constitutionally, but ultimately it prevailed.

Based on the above "finding," the Wagner Act then declared that it is the "policy of the United States to eliminate the causes of certain substantial obstructions to the free flow of commerce ... by encouraging the practice and procedure of collective bargaining. ..." With that statement, the federal government declared that the law would no longer be neutral, but would instead side with Big Labor. The rest of the bill was designed to stack the deck in favor of unions, and against workers and employers who wanted nothing to do with them.

Big Labor's strategy has always been to use the control it has over many legislators to obtain through law and regulation what it cannot get through voluntary means. The Wagner Act was a gigantic step toward its goal of inserting itself as the middleman between employer and employee, no matter what their desires might be. Upon its passage, the dam that had protected individual rights was dynamited, and compulsory unionism rushed forth over the land.

WORKER FREEDOM OF CHOICE VERSUS "UNION SECURITY"

Legislation is often drafted with misleading language in order to make it more difficult for the people to figure out what is actually being done to them, thereby reducing opposition.[6] The Wagner Act is a classic illustration of this phenomenon. Section 7 of the Act states that "Employees shall have the right to self-organization to form, join, or assist labor organizations, to bargain collectively through representatives of their own choosing, and to engage in concerted activities, for the purpose of collective bargaining or other mutual aid or protection." That language sounds reasonable and seems to ensure that the law is simply giving workers freedom of choice regarding labor unions. But freedom of choice for workers was not the objective of the Wagner Act. It gave absolutely no legal protection to workers to *refrain* from participating in labor unions and collective bargaining. Moreover, it authorized "union security" measures that enable union bosses to make union membership a condition for obtaining and keeping a job.

Other kinds of associations may wish they could prevent dissatisfied members from dropping out; businesses may wish they could demand that customers continue to patronize them; professional service providers may wish they had a law that compelled clients to keep paying for services even if they were no longer wanted. Only labor unions, however, have had the nerve to seek "security" by making payment for their services mandatory—unless you're willing to lose your job.

Once a union has been recognized as the bargaining agent of the employees (how that occurs is discussed below), the union officials almost invariably seek to negotiate some form of "union security" with the company. That is, they want to make the company compel its employees to join or support the union even if they don't want to. It's a case of union officials obtaining security for *themselves* at the expense of freedom for the workers they claim to represent. The law aids them in getting employers to agree to such arrangements because it declares that an employer is guilty of an "unfair labor practice" if the management does not "bargain in good faith" with union officials. An employer who refuses to put his employees' freedom on the negotiating table and holds out against "union security" thus risks a costly battle with expert union lawyers. The threat of legal action over the failure to "bargain in good faith" (a concept unknown under common law) is an ace up the sleeve for union officials.

One kind of union security arrangement, both common at the time of the Wagner Act and approved by it, was the "closed shop" under which no person could be hired who was not already a union member. Another kind of union security arrangement is the "union shop," under which newly hired individuals must join the union within a short period of time after their hiring or be fired. Yet another is the "agency shop," under which employees must pay union dues whether or not they formally join the union. (The agency shop didn't come into use until the 1950s.) Thus, compulsory unionism is accomplished in America *indirectly*. The government doesn't force workers to accept and pay for union representation, but the law assists unions in strong-arming employers into agreements to fire any worker who won't pay the dues directed by union bosses.

What the different "union security" provisions have in common is that they ensure a steady flow of money into union treasuries from the workers, whether they are satisfied with the union's services or not. And to make that flow yet more secure, union officials also negotiate for an automatic dues check-off scheme that requires the employer to withhold union dues from worker paychecks and then turn the money directly over to the union—the same as income tax withholding. That not only saves the union the trouble of trying to collect from workers who may not want their representation, but also helps to hide its cost from them.

The closed shop was outlawed by the Taft-Hartley Act, which amended the Wagner Act in 1947. (Taft-Hartley will be discussed in Chapter 2.) But federal law still smiles on and facilitates union shop and agency shop arrangements that compel workers to pay for union representation even if they abhor unions and would never voluntarily pay a penny for their services. To call that "freedom of choice" is an Orwellian perversion of the English language.

EXCLUSIVE REPRESENTATION

Crucial to the Wagner Act's empowerment of union officials was its gift to them of the "right" of exclusive representation. Section 9(a) says, "Representatives designated or selected for the purposes of collective bargaining by the majority of the employees in a unit appropriate for such purposes, shall be the exclusive representatives of all the employees in such unit. . . ." Because of that provision, once a union has been certified as the bargaining agent for a group of workers, it has the power to bind *all of them* to a contract—even those who would rather represent themselves or prefer to be represented by a different union. Workers who may become dissatisfied with the union are not allowed to bargain on their own or seek some other representative more concerned with their interests. The law thereby gives unions monopoly status and tears away at another basic American liberty—the freedom to make your own contracts.

In giving monopoly power to union officials, the politicians ignored the wisdom of Justice Louis Brandeis, a long-time supporter of organized labor but an opponent of compulsory unionism. In a 1905 speech, Brandeis said, *"The union attains success when it reaches the ideal condition, and the ideal condition for a union is to be strong and stable, and yet to have in the trade outside of its ranks an appreciable number of men who are non-unionists. . . . Such a nucleus of unorganized labor will check oppression by the union as the union checks oppression by the employer."* Brandeis could foresee that exclusive representation would lead to arrogance and abuse by labor bosses, and that is exactly what we have seen repeatedly ever since the passage of the Wagner Act.

Monopolies rarely last very long unless government intervenes to prevent competition with them. Our general policy is to oppose monopoly, which is what antitrust laws are designed to do. But unions were exempted from antitrust law by the Clayton Act—another of the special favors the law has given them. Further, Section 9(a)'s exclusive representation provision deliberately gives monopoly power to a union that manages to get a majority of workers to vote in its favor. If workers were free to choose union representation when they wanted it, to drop the union's service when they became dissatisfied with it, and to say "No thanks" to unions altogether if they wanted to remain independent, union officials would have to operate on the basis of consumer sovereignty as all other service providers must. Exclusive representation is a unique legal privilege that allows union officials to treat the workers as a captive market to be exploited.

In the years directly following the passage of the Wagner Act, there was a dispute as to whether the exclusive representation provision was meant to prohibit individual bargaining, but in 1944 the Supreme Court settled the matter. In *J.I. Case Co. v. NLRB,* a group of employees approached the company, asking to separately negotiate their contracts, even though they were covered by a union collective bargaining contract. The Court held that. Although both sides wanted to do so, the company had violated the law by negotiating with the workers. Harkening back to the "industrial peace" justification for the government's policy of promoting collective bargaining, the Court said, "advantages to individuals may prove as disruptive of industrial peace as disadvantages. They are a fruitful way of interfering with organization and choice of representatives; increased compensation, if individually deserved, is often earned at the cost of breaking down some other standard thought to be for the welfare of the group."[8] That is to say, the freedom of individuals to peacefully strive to improve their circumstances may be forcefully prevented lest it get in the way of "the welfare of the group." A law more out of keeping with the ideals of the American Founders would be hard to imagine.

As the reader will recall, the preamble to the Wagner Act makes much ado about workers who do not possess "actual liberty of contract," but the exclusive representation provision creates the very problem that the law was said to solve. When workers are forbidden to bargain for themselves, they no longer possess liberty of contract. Nothing could more clearly show that in moving from the common law to the Wagner Act, worker rights were extinguished.

"INDUSTRIAL DEMOCRACY"

The Wagner Act established a new federal agency with authority to administer its provisions, the National Labor Relations Board (NLRB). Composed of five members— most of whom have been selected from the ranks of defenders and apologists for compulsory unionism—the NLRB has a number of regulatory and judicial functions, including oversight of elections to determine if a group of workers will have a union as their exclusive bargaining agent or not.

Once a substantial number of workers have shown their interest in holding an election—the rule being that at least 30 percent of the workers sign cards saying that they want an election—the NLRB must conduct one. In the election, the eligible voters in the "bargaining unit" (a group of workers the NLRB determines to have a strong commonality of interest) vote to determine whether they want to be represented by a specific union, or prefer to continue to have no union representation. A majority of the votes cast prevails and if the union wins, it is then certified as the exclusive bargaining agent for all the workers in the unit.

In this version of democracy, however, one choice is never permitted to the employees. They cannot vote for a union sponsored or supported by the employer because the law makes it an "unfair labor practice" for an employer to have its own labor organization or support one in any way. Before the Wagner Act, many firms had company unions in which the workers would choose representatives to meet with management to discuss the terms and conditions of employment. In the 1920s and 1930s, independent unions often failed in their efforts to secure worker support because they were content with their company unions. Union officials wanted a prohibition against company unions, claiming that workers could only receive "real" representation from an outside, adversarial union. Congress agreed and gave them what they wanted, making it an "unfair labor practice" for an employer to sponsor its own union. That prohibition fits in perfectly with the anti-competitive mindset of labor bosses. They don't want workers competing against each other; they don't want employers competing against each other; and they don't want to have to compete against any kind of rival organization.

Because of the prohibition of company unions, employers' freedom to manage as they think best is curtailed, and employees are restricted in their range of choice in representation. Moreover, by locking in adversarial unionism as the only permitted alternative to having no union at all, the law short-circuits the free market's powerful discovery process, which only works when people are free to experiment with different ways of doing things. America probably would have evolved better means of dealing with labor relations if it weren't for the law's prohibition against companies trying their own variations of industrial democracy.

The NLRB's election system may seem like a clean and simple exercise in democracy, but it isn't. Often, the process is tainted from start to finish with pressure to sign the cards and vote the "right way" by union militants. Furthermore, the rules of campaigning during the time prior to the election are stacked in favor of unionization. Union spokesmen can say virtually anything, but the employer must be extremely careful in what it communicates to the employees. If management says or does anything that might upset the "laboratory conditions" the NLRB wants for certification elections, it has committed an "unfair labor practice." This can lead to a new election at a later time, or even a declaration by the NLRB that the union will be certified even though it did not receive majority support.

What sorts of communications from employers are forbidden? Here is a sampler. The employer may not make any promises of benefit to the workers if they vote against the union. If a management spokesman were to say, "Once this election is over and the prospect of unionization is gone, we are going to give all of you a raise," he would have committed the unfair labor practice of "interfering" with the workers' right to organize. Union officials can promise everything, but the company may not promise anything. In fact, it may not actually confer a benefit either. To give the workers a raise during the campaign period, or to provide any other benefit—in one case, building a ball field the workers could use during break time—is "interference" that may invalidate the election.

Or suppose that the firm suggests to the workers that unionization might not be in their best interests. Pointing out the possibility that the plant might have to be closed in the event of a strike, or that the company's financial situation is too weak to afford the additional costs that union demands would bring, is forbidden. Such "threatening" statements are not allowed because they "interfere" with employee rights. The operative NLRB theory is that workers should want unionization and must be protected against employer actions or communications that might change their minds. Under the original Wagner Act, employers were not allowed to campaign against the union *at all*. Since the 1947 amendments, they are no longer under a complete gag rule, but still must be very careful not to step over an ill-defined line into the area of "interference."

The reader may be wondering, "But what about the First Amendment?" The Supreme Court has always turned a blind eye to what it calls "commercial speech," and employer communications on the undesirability of unionization fall into that category. The Court bends over backward to protect all manner of "symbolic speech," but permits the NLRB's rules to stifle *real* speech by employers.[9]

Not only does the employer lose freedom of speech, but his property rights are no longer respected either. Under the law, companies must make their property "reasonably" accessible to union organizers. Although organizers can be kept out of working areas, the law does not allow employers to exclude them from company property as trespassers. Furthermore, employers are required to violate the privacy rights of their employees by disclosing to the union organizers their names and addresses.

There is one more unusual feature of our "industrial democracy." If the majority of workers favor the union, it is certified as their bargaining agent *indefinitely*. Unlike our political system with its regular elections, unions do not have to face periodic re-elections. Most American workers who have union representation have *never* had the opportunity to vote on it themselves, since the union was certified before they were hired.

It is possible for workers to oust a union they no longer want to continue to represent them. That can be done through a decertification election. Decertification elections are relatively rare, for two reasons. (In 2002, for example, there were 2,587 certification elections, but only 433 decertification elections.) First, company management is not allowed to do anything to promote decertification; even suggesting the possibility openly would be the unfair labor practice of "interference." Second, few workers know about the possibility, and among those who do, not many also have the fortitude to risk anger and reprisals from union bosses for trying to end their domination. Despite the obstacles, decertification sometimes happens, but until it does incumbent labor bosses remain in control year after year, decade after decade.

Finally, unions can thrust themselves upon workers even without an official election. Nothing prevents a company from agreeing with a union to recognize it as the bargaining representative of its employees without going through an election. Unions today often pressure companies into bargaining with them through so-called "corporate campaigns." Corporate campaigns entail a long-term effort by a union to weaken the company through boycotts, adverse publicity, trumped-up litigation, and other tactics, which cease only when management agrees to its demands for bargaining and "union security." That can occur even if the workers have already voted against unionization! Many union bosses today admit that they concentrate on "organizing employers, not employees."

There really isn't much democracy in "industrial democracy."[10]

MANDATORY BARGAINING

Imagine that a stranger walked up to your house and when you answered the door, said, "I want to buy your house. Let's bargain over the sale." Taken aback, you reply, "My house isn't for sale." The stranger then says in return, "But you *must* bargain with me, and unless you do so in *good faith,* I will take legal action against you for violating the law." You would undoubtedly be flabbergasted. Whether you want to deal with this stranger or not should be entirely your own decision and the law should respect your right to deal or not to deal as you see fit.

Ordinarily, the law respects contractual freedom. You couldn't be forced to bargain with that stranger over the sale of your house, or with a telemarketer wanting to sell you magazines, or with a dentist who wants to do your kids' braces, or with anyone else. Freedom of contract means that you get to choose with whom you bargain.

But this is not so under the National Labor Relations Act. Once a union has been certified, the employer has a *legal duty* to bargain with the union over all terms and conditions of employment, and must do so in "good faith." Failure to do so is an "unfair labor practice," which the

NLRB, backed up by the power of the federal courts, can enforce. Under common law, an employer who did not want to engage in collective bargaining could say to a union representative, "I don't care if some or all of my employees want you to negotiate an agreement on their behalf. That just isn't the way I want to do business. I'll deal with each of them individually if they want, but I'm not going to bargain with you." The Wagner Act, however, took contractual freedom away from employers in order to put teeth in the law's "encouragement" of collective bargaining.

The law thus puts union officials in a commanding position. They have monopoly status as the sole legal representatives of the workers, backed up by a mandate that company management bargain with them over everything affecting the terms and conditions of employment. Thanks to the special privileges and immunities they have succeeded in wrangling from compliant legislators, they sit as nearly permanent middlemen between workers and their jobs, extracting money for services that may or may not be desired. The union truly becomes, as Professor Clyde Summers put it, the "economic government" of the workers,[11] Many workers do not want that extra "government," but cannot escape from it.

Summing up our survey of American labor law, it is authoritarian, coercive, and one-sided. Former federal judge Robert Bork put his finger on the problem when he wrote, "Our labor law, and the ideology that supports and suffuses it, encourages the organization of employees into fighting groups, and lets the wage bargain depend on the outcome of the fight. The rhetoric of union organization and struggle is the rhetoric of war."[12]

THE WAGNER ACT AND THE CONSTITUTION

In 1935 and 1936, legal experts thought it probable that the Supreme Court would strike down the Wagner Act when the first case under the new statute reached it. Long-standing precedents that had recently been reaffirmed indicated that the law would be struck down because it went beyond the powers of Congress to regulate interstate commerce.

In 1935, the Court had declared the National Industrial Recovery Act unconstitutional in *Schechter Poultry Corp. v. United States.*[13] In that case, the Court held that the NIRA involved an unconstitutional delegation of legislative power to the executive branch. It also ruled that congressional power to regulate interstate commerce did not extend to business practices in the *production* of goods. While Congress could regulate interstate *commerce,* the production of goods could be regulated only by state or local government. The Roosevelt administration had argued that business practices might have *some effect* upon the volume of interstate poultry sales and therefore should be regarded as falling under the reach of federal regulation, but the Court rejected that argument. If everything that might have *some effect* on interstate commerce were subject to federal control, the Justices reasoned, there would be virtually nothing that wasn't. The distinction between interstate commerce and intrastate commerce would thus vanish, a result that the drafters of the Constitution certainly did not intend.

In 1936, the Supreme Court decided another case involving New Deal regulatory legislation, the Bituminous Coal Conservation Act. That law attempted to regulate labor conditions in coal mines, setting minimum wages and maximum hours. A 6 to 3 majority of the Court declared it unconstitutional in *Carter v. Carter Coal Co.*[14] Justice Sutherland's opinion for the Court again distinguished between *production* and *commerce,* reiterating the holding in *Schechter* that Congress had no power to control the conditions of production. Sutherland then went on to make an important point about individual liberty. The Bituminous Coal Act also involved industry codes that a majority of companies could impose upon a minority and Sutherland's opinion struck right at the heart of the matter:

> The power conferred upon the majority is in effect the power to regulate the affairs of an unwilling minority. This is delegation in its most obnoxious form; for it is not even delegation to an official or an official body ... but to private persons whose interests may be and often are adverse to the interests of others in the same business.... (A) statute which attempts to confer such power undertakes an intolerable and unconstitutional interference with personal liberty and private property.

That language had direct relevance to the Wagner Act's scheme of compulsory unionism. By forcing a minority of workers who do not desire to be represented by a union to abide by a majority decision that gives that union—a private organization—control over key aspects of their employment, the Wagner Act did to employees exactly what Justice Sutherland said the government could not do to coal companies.

Based on *Schechter* and *Carter*, it seemed certain that the Wagner Act would be declared unconstitutional when the first test case reached the Supreme Court. Roosevelt easily won re-election in 1936, despite the fact that the country was still very much in the Depression after four years of the New Deal. He needed some scapegoats and pointed his finger at the Supreme Court for striking down key New Deal legislation, thereby interfering with his program for the nation's recovery. Shortly after his 1937 State of the Union address, FDR announced his famous "Court packing" plan to deal with a Court that insisted on reading the Constitution as it had been intended.

The Constitution says nothing about the number of justices who sit on the Supreme Court. While the number has traditionally been nine, it could be changed. Angered over the decisions in *Schechter, Carter,* and other cases, Roosevelt announced that he proposed to appoint one new justice for each current member of the Court who was over seventy years of age and had served for more than ten years. Under his plan, the Court would expand to fourteen members and the infusion of new, Roosevelt-picked justices would give him a majority. A bill to give the president the authority to appoint those new justices was quickly introduced, but ran into unexpectedly strong opposition even among Democrats and died in Congress.

The Court-packing plan succeeded in a different way, however. The first case testing the constitutionality of the Wagner Act reached the Supreme Court in 1936—*NLRB v. Jones & Laughlin Steel Corp.*[15] When the decision was announced in 1937, two members of the Court who in the *Schechter* and *Carter* cases had found the legislation beyond the authority of Congress, switched sides. Chief Justice Charles Evans Hughes and Justice Owen Roberts said that the Wagner Act's regulation of employment *was* within congressional authority under the Commerce Clause, a decision they reached by rejecting the precedents that distinguished between manufacturing and commerce. If steel mills were shut down by strikes, the Court said, the *flow* of commerce would be reduced and that was a sufficient *effect* on interstate commerce to give the federal government authority to regulate their labor relations. Here was the "industrial peace" argument again. Supposedly, giving in to compulsory unionism and monopoly bargaining would end the strikes and violence that were plaguing not only the steel industry, but many other important sectors of the economy. In a 5 to 4 decision that has been called "the switch in time that saved nine," the Court upheld the Wagner Act.

The four dissenters were not only true to the meaning of the Constitution, but showed remarkable prescience in writing, "Whatever effect any cause of discontent may ultimately have upon commerce is far too indirect to justify congressional regulation. Almost anything—marriage, birth, death—may in some fashion affect commerce." Since 1937, the United States has seen a torrent of legislation in which Congress regulates almost every facet of life on the grounds that it might have some indirect effect upon interstate commerce. We have *Jones & Laughlin Steel* to thank for opening the floodgates.

The Wagner Act was the great turning point where America departed from the path of neutral rules that protected the freedom of employers and employees alike, to the path of special privileges and immunities for union officials to force themselves upon both. Big Labor did not stop seeking special coercive legal powers with the approval of the Wagner Act. It continues to do so to this day. The change from laws that permitted voluntary unionism to laws that foster compulsory unionism has had terrible consequences for the nation ever since 1937.[16]

THE EROSION OF LIBERTY

At the time of the founding of the United States, no one had to face the loss of employment because he did not want to pay tribute to some group calling itself a union. No one had to accept any person or organization as his agent in contract negotiation if he did not want to. No one had to relinquish the use of his property to others unless he freely chose to do so. No one could be punished for deciding not to bargain with another. No one could be told what he could and could not say to his employees.

All of that freedom and more has been lost to Americans, taken away by the special-interest legislation demanded by union advocates during the Depression. Big Labor has never been content with the gifts of power it received in the 1930s, however. It has constantly sought more, using the vastly increased flow of dues money garnered through the special privileges granted by Congress to elect politicians who will do its bidding. For the last fifty years, worker interest in unions has been falling, but instead of trying to attract more members voluntarily, Big Labor's top brass has looked to politics to improve their fortunes. It is as if a failing restaurant went after laws to compel people to eat there, instead of improving the food and service.

Fortunately, many Americans have been willing to fight back against Big Labor's political juggernaut. The rest of this book will discuss the battle to cast off the net of compulsory unionism and restore freedom of choice for workers.

NOTES

1. *Pennsylvania Railroad v. Railway Labor Board,* 261 US 72 (1923).
3. Morgan O. Reynolds, *Making America Poorer,* pp. 19–20.
4. Sylvester Petro, "Injunctions and Labor Disputes, 1880–1932," 14 *Wake Forest Law Review,* pp. 345–6.
5. *Nebbia v. New York,* 291 US 502 (1934).
6. For an excellent and thorough discussion of the many tactics politicians use to increase the cost of opposing special interest legislation they want to enact, see Professor Charlotte Twight's book *Dependent on D.C.: The Rise of Federal Control Over the Lives of Ordinary Americans* (St. Martin's Press, 2002).
7. Louis D. Brandeis, "The Desirable Industrial Peace" (address, delivered April 25, 1905 to the Industrial Economics Department of the National Civic Federation. Available online: http://library.louisville.edu/law/brandeis/desirable.html.).
8. *J.I. Case Co. v. NLRB,* 321 US 332, 338 (1944).

9. For a vigorous critique of the legal distinction between commercial speech, which receives little or no constitutional protection, and speech that the courts do protect, see Professor Martin Redish's book *Money Talks* (NYU Press, 2001).

10. Not only is the process of union selection not very democratic, unions are often not democratic in their internal operations. As Lipset, Trow, and Coleman wrote in their book *Union Democracy,* "(A)n incumbent administrator (has) great power and advantage over the rank and file.... This advantage takes such forms as control over financial resources and internal communications.... The normal position of the trade-union member in modern urban society makes it likely that few individuals will ordinarily be actively interested in the affairs of the union.... The absence of membership participation facilitates the existence of one-party oligarchy.... Union leaders possess great power to do things which would never be approved if democratic choice were available." Seymour Martin Lipset, Martin Trow, and James Coleman, *Union Democracy* (The Free Press, 1956), p. 404.

11. Clyde Summers, "Union Power and Workers' Rights," 49 Michigan Law Review 805, 811. Professor Petro makes the same point, writing, "The NLRA delegates to majority unions a kind of power which can accurately be designated only as governmental in character." "Civil Liberties, Syndicalism, and the NLRA" 5 University of Toledo Law Review, 447, 504.

12. Robert Bork, "We Suddenly Feel that Law is Vulnerable," *Fortune,* December 1971, p.115.

13. *Schechter Poultry Corp. v. United States,* 295 US 495 (1935).

14. *Carter v. Carter Coal Co.,* 298 US 238 (1936).

15. *NLRB v. Jones & Laughlin Steel Co,* 301 US 1 (1937).

16. Professor Richard Epstein explains the *Jones & Laughlin* case, along with other constitutional blunders in "The Mistakes of 1937," 11 *George Mason Law Review* 5 (1988).

CHAPTER TWO

RIGHT TO WORK LAWS AND THE ORIGIN OF THE NATIONAL RIGHT TO WORK COMMITTEE

Big Labor's top brass had long wanted to stamp out freedom of choice for workers, and Congress and the Supreme Court had granted their wishes. By 1944, with the *J. I. Case* decision, the labor chiefs were sitting pretty on a throne of powers created for them by subservient politicians and timorous judges. They had unique legal privileges and immunities that enabled them to coerce workers and employers into the shackles of compulsory unionism. During and shortly after the end of World War II, however, Big Labor terribly overplayed its hand.

Despite the need for national unity during the war and the nearly-universal belt-tightening that the war effort entailed, Big Labor never stopped trying to augment its power and expand its forced-dues empire. During the war, union bosses ordered more than 13,000 strikes—many of them having nothing to do with wages and working conditions, but simply to expand their control over the labor market. A good example was the strike in 1943 against Montgomery Ward.

The company had had a contract with a union requiring the workers to pay their dues as a condition of employment. When that contract expired, however, Montgomery Ward's chairman, Sewell Avery, refused to continue enforcing it, thereby giving some 7,000 workers the freedom to choose whether or not to support the union. Avery's stand caused the union to order a strike, but he held firm against the forced union shop. A few months later, President Roosevelt stepped in, threatening to have the federal government seize the company if Avery didn't capitulate to the

27

demand for compulsory union membership. Montgomery Ward had just a small amount of defense-related business, but that was enough for the federal government to use its leverage to impose compulsory unionism on the whole workforce in order to ensure "labor peace." Still, Avery refused to force unionism on his workers. So on April 27, 1944, armed national guard troops occupied the Montgomery Ward headquarters in Chicago. Two steel-helmeted guardsmen forcibly removed the 70-year-old Avery from the building, carrying him out in his chair. Avery later told a reporter that forced unionism was "slowly leading the nation into a government of dictators."

Displays of raw greed and lust for power by labor bosses during the war caused many Americans who had previously thought of unions in a positive light to change their minds about them. The worst was yet to come, though. After the end of the war in August of 1945, Big Labor unleashed an unprecedented wave of strikes—often accompanied by violence—across the United States. In 1946 a record-setting number of strikes occurred, with a resulting loss of 116,000,000 man/days of work. The union "dictators" (as Sewell Avery put it) managed to corral many more workers, willing and unwilling alike, into union ranks, but in doing so they also angered millions of Americans. Commenting on the postwar national mood, lawyer Donald Richberg, one of the architects of the New Deal labor legislation, wrote, "There is no doubt that the overwhelming sentiment in Congress for a revision of the Wagner Act was generated in part by the exasperation with which a war-stricken people had watched the unions take advantage of war necessities to force unreasonable demands on private industry and government."[1]

THE FIRST RIGHT TO WORK LAWS

As Big Labor's domination over workers and the economy grew, people looked for some way of halting or at least slowing it through state legislation. The Wagner Act did much to promote compulsory unionism, but nowhere did it say that state governments could not shield workers against it. That small crack in the armor of the union juggernaut was to serve as the basis for a counterattack by Americans who believed that unionism should be a personal and voluntary choice. Opponents of compulsory unionism succeeded in getting referenda put on the 1944 general election ballots in Florida and Arkansas, asking the voters to approve laws that would make contracts that forced workers to choose between paying union dues and losing their jobs illegal. In both states, the voters approved the measures.[2] Those were the first "Right to Work" laws.

The term "Right to Work" originated on September 1, 1941, in an editorial written by William B. Ruggles, an editor with the *Dallas Morning News.* That was Labor Day, and Ruggles argued in favor of a constitutional amendment saying, "No person shall be denied employment because of membership in or affiliation with a labor union or because of refusal to join or affiliate with a labor union...." At several points in the editorial, Ruggles used the phrase "right to work." Subsequently, other proponents of voluntary unionism picked up the phrase as a shorthand description of their goals and it stuck. (Compulsory unionism advocates hate the term and when they use it at all, usually employ derogatory snicker quotes, as in *those so-called "right to work" laws.)*

In 1946, three more states added Right to Work protection for their workers—Arizona, Nebraska, and South Dakota. Six additional states did so in 1947—Georgia, Iowa, North Carolina, Tennessee, Texas, and Virginia. Big Labor looked on in horror and disgust as those states chipped away at its power to force workers into union ranks. Wanting to kill off the Right to Work movement, union bosses brought lawsuits against the Arizona, Nebraska, and North Carolina laws, contending with incredible gall, that Right to Work laws infringed upon *their* constitutional rights.

Those cases went through the courts of each state and reached the U.S. Supreme Court in 1948. The Court consolidated the Nebraska and North Carolina cases in *Lincoln Federal Labor Union v. Northwestern Iron and Metal.*[3] The Arizona case was handled in a separate opinion that did not materially differ from the decision in *Lincoln Federal.* Six justices joined with the Court's famed civil libertarian, Justice Hugo Black, in his opinion that demolished the arguments against Right to Work laws, and the other three justices issued concurring opinions. The tenor of Justice Black's view of the case is captured in this sentence: "There cannot be wrung from a constitutional right of workers to assemble to discuss improvement of their own working standards, a further constitutional right to drive from remunerative employment all other persons who will not or can not participate in union assemblies." Their effort to stop state governments from offering workers shelter from compulsory unionism had ended in ignominious defeat for Big Labor's top brass.

THE TAFT-HARTLEY ACT

In the elections of 1946, the Democratic Party suffered huge losses, with 56 House seats and 11 Senate seats shifting to the Republicans. As in any election, there were many reasons for the voting trends, but the fact that the Democrats were correctly seen as the allies of Big Labor—except in the South—was one of the key factors in the outcome. Control of both the Senate and the House went to the Republicans, most of whom had little sympathy for compulsory unionism. Thus, the conditions were propitious for revision of the Wagner Act when the new Congress convened in January 1947.

That spring, Senator Robert Taft of Ohio and Representative Fred Hartley of New Jersey introduced a bill to amend the Wagner Act in several ways. Their bill was easily passed, but then vetoed by President Truman, who had always depended on the support of union bosses throughout his political career. Congress mustered the two-thirds vote needed to override Truman's veto, however, and the Taft-Hartley Act became law on June 23, 1947. To this day, "Taft-Hartley" is a phrase that militant unionists utter with loathing.

WHAT TAFT-HARTLEY DID—AND DIDN'T—DO

From the vehemence with which union supporters denounce the Taft-Hartley Act, one might think that it had outlawed unions. It was called a "slave labor" bill, "union-busting," "class warfare," and much more. In fact, Taft-

Hartley's changes in the law were fairly minor and did little to impede the growth of unionization. (The high-water mark for unionism came six years later in 1953, when 36 percent of workers in the private sector were represented by unions; it has steadily declined since then, to about 9 percent today.) Congress might have restored the common law and constitutional rights of Americans by repealing the Wagner Act's coercive, one-sided meddling in employer-employee relations. Instead, the Taft-Hartley Act reiterated the national policy favoring collective bargaining and then proceeded to make several amendments to the statute. Compulsory unionism escaped the 80th Congress with nothing more than a few scratches.

First, Taft-Hartley established the Federal Mediation and Conciliation Service, with the objective of avoiding strikes through mediation and voluntary arbitration. Second, it authorized the President to seek an injunction against any strike that he regards as imperiling the national health or safety. Third, the law added a list of union unfair labor practices—under the Wagner Act, there was no such thing as a *union* unfair labor practice—including coercion, discrimination, and the use of secondary boycotts and picketing (tactics to pressure companies into agreeing to union demands by hurting other businesses that deal with them).

The most important provision in the Taft Hartley Act was the following language: "Nothing contained in the amendment made by subsection (a) shall be construed as authorizing the execution or application of agreements requiring membership in a labor organization as a condition of employment in any State or Territory in which such execution or application is prohibited by State or Territorial law." That new section, referred to as Section 14(b), was critical in preserving the authority of state governments to guard workers against union security agreements that made it mandatory for them to pay union dues as a requirement of employment.

While the Supreme Court's decision in the *Lincoln Federal* case obliterated Big Labor's argument that Right to Work laws were unconstitutional, Taft-Hartley revised Section 7 of the Wagner Act in a way that actually strengthened compulsory unionism. Following the 1947 revision, Section 7 reads:

> Employees shall have the right of self-organization, to form, join, or
> assist labor organizations, to bargain collectively through representatives
> of their own choosing, and to engage in other concerted activities for
> the purpose of collective bargaining or other mutual aid or protection,
> and shall also have the right to refrain from any or all such activities
> *except to the extent that such right may be affected by an agreement requir-*
> *ing membership in a labor organization as a condition of employment as*
> *authorized in section 8 (a).*[3] (Emphasis added.)

The Wagner Act had not acknowledged any right of workers to
refrain from union participation and Taft-Hartley's language does make
that right explicit—but then takes it away with the "except" clause. Using
that clause as the basis for a new attack on Right to Work laws, Big Labor
would have been able to argue that since it was clearly federal policy to
allow agreements "requiring membership in a labor organization," the
states could not enact any laws to the contrary. Therefore, the inclusion
of Section 14(b) was necessary to protect Right to Work laws against that
attack—and that is why 14(b) has been a key target of compulsory unionism advocates ever since.

Taft-Hartley was one of those all-too-frequent cases where Congress
tries to fix a problem it has created not by eliminating its initial blunder
(the Wagner Act), but instead by piling on regulations to supposedly rectify its bad effects. Federal labor law actually became more interventionist after the 1947 amendments, not less. Alas, Congress chose to rely on
yet more law to remedy the disastrous Wagner Act, when the right move
would have been to repeal it and restore freedom in labor relations.

THE "FREE-RIDER" ARGUMENT

Big Labor hates Right to Work laws because they are an escape hatch for
workers who don't value union services enough to want to support them
voluntarily. As we have seen, union officials are never content to try selling their services just to willing customers and respect the wishes of those
who say "No thanks." They want to make their position secure by forcing unwilling workers to make this decision: Your money or your job.

Most Americans see that choice as fundamentally unfair, so the proponents of compulsory unionism need to provide some fig leaf of justification for their coercion. The argument that union spokesmen usually give for compulsory union support (and for exclusive representation) is that workers should not be allowed to be "free riders." They contend that since unionization benefits all workers, all should therefore have to pay for it. If people were able to take a "free ride" on the "sacrifices" of union supporters, the argument goes, so many would be tempted to do so that the union couldn't accomplish any good for workers. Thus, they try to depict Right to Work laws as a way of allowing individual greed to triumph over the common good.

What that argument ignores is the fact that worker interests are not uniform. While some think that union representation will prove beneficial to them, others believe that the goals of the union officials would do them more harm than good. A recently hired worker, for example, may realize that if the union negotiates a large wage increase, he might enjoy that increase only until the company finds a way of economizing on labor. Last hired, first fired—and then what would the union do for him?

Or a veteran worker, who is highly efficient and compensated well for his productivity, may see that the notoriously inefficient union work rules would reduce his earnings. If he decides not to support a union that would depress his income and prevent him from dealing directly with the company, he isn't getting a "free ride" to benefits. Instead, compulsory unionism forces him to pay for his own victimization and loss of freedom.

Or a worker may regard the political activities of the union that "represents" him as philosophically repugnant. Union bosses give massive support in money, manpower, and assets to political candidates and causes that they like. Many workers, however, have different political views and hate to be compelled to fund candidates and causes they abhor. It isn't "greed" for a worker to stop paying for union representation if he concludes that it empowers the union hierarchy to use his own money in politically harmful ways.

Professor John Moorhouse of Wake Forest University contends that the real problem is not "free-riding" by workers who desire to remain independent of a union, but that they become "forced riders" by union security agreements:

> What seems more probable is that those who refuse to support the union (if given the opportunity) do so either because of genuine philosophical reservations or because they expect to suffer economically as a result of union action.... Only the individual can assess the subjective benefits of union membership; no outside objective measure of these benefits exists to be imposed on individuals without giving rise to unintended and detrimental side effects, e.g., rank and file apathy toward the union, corruption, and employer-union leadership discrimination against employees. Little attention has been focused on the welfare implications of the "forced rider." How do the benefits of unions accord the majority of their members compare with the costs imposed on a minority by forcing them to support the union?[4]

In a free society, people do many things that create benefits for others. But in the interest of preserving our individual liberty, we leave it up to each person to decide whether he will *voluntarily* support groups whose actions in some way benefit him. Union officials, however, want a different set of rules for themselves than apply to the rest of society. They want to be able to *force* people to support them and thereby avoid the trouble of having to *persuade* them that the union is deserving of their loyalty.

Finally, there is no basis for the argument's self-pitying premise that unions are so fragile that they will collapse unless all workers are forced to accept and pay for their services. In Right to Work states, unions continue to exist and bargain on behalf of workers, despite the fact that individuals can stop giving them financial support. The cry of labor bosses that they're rendered impotent unless they can represent everyone and make them pay for it is not the least bit convincing.

Union autocrats hunger for the "solidarity" that comes from being able to compel all to join and pay, but if their services are as beneficial as they claim, they should be able to succeed without the use of compulsion. In fact, union officials would probably act in a more responsible manner, placing the interests and concerns of their members first, if they had to worry about the prospect of people leaving if they became dissatisfied. With the captive membership that "union security" measures provide, union bosses can and often do act in ways that benefit themselves while squandering the workers' money and harming their interests. Far from threatening the existence of unions through "free-riding," Right to Work laws serve the beneficial function of providing some restraint on union boss arrogance and irresponsibility.

THE WEAKNESS OF TAFT-HARTLEY

Despite white-hot union rhetoric against the Taft-Hartley Act, it actually did little to rectify the fundamental wrongs of federal labor law. Permitting states to enact Right to Work laws—which under principles of federalism they should have been able to do anyway—only protects workers against "union shop" or "agency shop" agreements. They do nothing to shield workers from control by labor bosses in other respects. If a union is certified in a Right to Work state, it still has the power to negotiate for all workers under the exclusive representation provision of the law. Even though workers can't be fired for declining to support the union, they still don't have the freedom to negotiate for themselves when they believe that they can better serve their own interests. Nor do they have the freedom to individually prosecute grievances against the company. If the union decides not to represent a worker with a grievance, the Supreme Court has held that the individual is not allowed access to the courts on his own.[5] Right to Work laws therefore protect workers against having to *pay for union services,* but they do not shield them from union *control.*

The Taft-Hartley amendments also did little to remove the numerous violations of employer rights in the NLRA. The infringements upon employer freedom of contract, freedom of speech, and property rights that are essential to the scheme of "encouraging" collective bargaining all remain in the law. A provision that was intended to restore some freedom of speech by saying that employer communications could not be treated as evidence of an unfair labor practice unless they contain a "threat of reprisal or force or promise of benefit," only cured the most outrageous NLRB interpretation of the term "interference." Early on, the NLRB had forbidden employers to say *anything* critical of unions during a representation campaign. The new language leaves the NLRB considerable latitude to penalize speech that can be characterized as promising something to the employees or "threatening" them in any way. Employers still must be very careful what they say—not exactly the First Amendment ideal.

Nor did the addition of union unfair labor practices to parallel employer unfair labor practices change things much. Taft-Hartley amended the law to make it an unfair labor practice for union officials to "coerce or restrain" workers, or to cause an employer to discriminate against any worker (Sections 8(b)[1] and 8(b)[2]), but many do so anyway, knowing that they can usually get away with it. The sad truth is that Big Labor has repeatedly demonstrated its contempt for the law, taking a "see if you can catch us" approach. When brought before the NLRB on charges of unfair labor practices, unions often benefit from foot dragging and favorable interpretations of the law by sympathetic bureaucrats. The "economic government" of workers disdains the rules of the true government when they are inconvenient. By creating the list of union unfair labor practices, Taft-Hartley improved the *appearance* of the law far more than its *actuality.*

Finally, the Taft-Hartley amendments did nothing to allow Right to Work protection to be extended to workers covered by the Railway Labor Act. Hundreds of thousands of workers in the railroad and airline industries are outside the protection of state Right to Work laws because the RLA expressly permits compulsory union agreements.

The Wagner Act left American law like a ship listing heavily to one side—the side of union boss interests. The Taft-Hartley amendments merely shifted a few pieces of furniture back to the middle of the ship, barely affecting its list toward Big Labor. All the talk about the "union busting" Taft-Hartley Act is just propaganda intended to make people think that it instituted a terrible regime of oppression against labor unions. It most certainly did not.

Inadequate as it was in restoring freedom to American workers and employers, Taft-Hartley was nevertheless an important symbol. It was a rallying point for all Americans who had come to hate the bullying and arrogance of labor bosses, and showed that Big Labor's juggernaut *could* be defeated—much as the Battle of Bunker Hill had shown the patriots that they could stand and fight the supposedly invincible British redcoats. From 1947 to the present, the Taft-Hartley Act, and specifically its approval of state Right to Work laws, has given heart to those who oppose the heavy hand of union coercion.

Big Labor used its congressional muscle, which was much restored by the 1948 elections, to push for repeal of Taft-Hartley in 1949. A repeal bill sponsored by Representative John Lesinski of Michigan was vigorously promoted by President Truman, who even plugged for it in his 1950 State of the Union Address. Lesinski's bill was narrowly defeated, but the labor barons briefly licked their wounds and then proceeded as before to expand their empire.[6]

In 1951, labor's top brass succeeded in getting an again compliant Congress to amend the Railway Labor Act, permitting compulsory unionism in the industries that statute covers—railroads and also airlines. Back in 1934, they had demanded and gotten a provision written into the RLA that prohibited compulsory unionism as a means of breaking company unions. By 1951, the heads of railroad unions had organized and secured exclusive representation privileges on railroads with 95 percent of the nation's trackage. Now they were ready to lock in the employees, so they told their congressional puppets that it was time to remove the Right to Work provision from the RLA. Immediately, union negotiators in the railroads and airlines pressured the companies to cave in to union shop agreements, thus forcing thousands of workers to choose between union membership and their jobs. Only a few firms had the will to resist the demands that they strong-arm their workers into union ranks. Aided by this legislative victory—again relying on politics to achieve what it couldn't get through voluntary means—Big Labor continued to grow.

VIOLENCE IN KANSAS

One of the many battles between big labor and worker freedom in 1953 took place in Wichita, Kansas. The mighty Teamsters Union had set its sights on "organizing" taxi-cab companies across the nation and called a strike in Wichita when the cab companies resisted demands that they agree to compulsory union shop contracts. When the companies continued to operate, drivers who stayed on the job were targeted by union toughs—mostly out-of-town Teamsters Union experts in violence—just as if Wichita were a war zone. Rocks, bottles, "stink bombs," paint, and even gasoline bombs were thrown at cabs by lurking union terrorists. The dispatch office of one company was dynamited. Firebombs were thrown at the homes of drivers who had the courage to defy the strike orders. Their wives received threatening phone calls day and night. The Wichita police were no match for perpetrators of the guerilla war that Teamsters were waging against fellow Americans who had chosen to work rather than "honor" the union's picket lines.

On the night of December 12, 1953, cab driver Deering Crowe responded to a call for a ride. The two "customers" he picked up directed him to a quiet area outside of town. They were taking him into a trap. Another car pulled up behind the cab. Six union thugs got out and attacked Crowe, mercilessly whipping him with chains and screaming, "This will teach you to be a scab!"

Just two days before the attack, Deering Crowe had been examined by a doctor, who determined that a growth on his jaw was a malignant tumor that could be surgically removed. The repeated blows to his face had burst the tumor. After Crowe was found and taken to a hospital, the surgeons decided that they had to postpone the operation because of his numerous wounds and weakened condition. By the time they could operate on the tumor, it was too late to stop the spread of the cancer. Crowe lived for nearly a year, in and out of hospitals, but no treatments worked. He died in November 1954, leaving a widow and two children. His killers were never brought to justice.

The beating of Deering Crowe coincided with a non-violent battle also taking place in Kansas—the debate over a Right to Work bill in the legislature. During his struggle for life in 1954, Crowe served as a compelling spokesman for the Right to Work cause. In his April 28, 1954, testimony before the Kansas Legislative Council Committee on Labor and Industrial Relations, Crowe put the matter very simply: "I figure that in the state of Kansas and in the United States, we ought to have the privilege of working and making a living for ourselves regardless of the union."

A young man who supported Right to Work was Reed Larson. Following his graduation from Kansas State University, he had been hired as an engineer by the Coleman Company of Wichita—well known for its line of lanterns and other outdoor products. Larson had been with Coleman for six years and had entered the firm's executive training program. He felt certain that he would make his career with the company. Larson was also active in several civic organizations, including the Junior Chamber of Commerce, for which he served as statewide president in 1953–54. In that capacity, he had traveled all around the state and had come into contact with people whose experiences with union bosses and their tactics were shocking.

One of them was Louis Weiss, who owned Spencer-Safford Loadcraft, a business in Augusta, Kansas that manufactured truck trailers. Weiss had negotiated a contract for his employees with the United Auto Workers (UAW), but he refused to concede to the demand for a compulsory union shop. When Weiss told the union agents that he would not fire any of his employees merely because they wouldn't pay dues to the UAW, he was astounded at their reply. They were willing to give up the entire wage and benefit increases they had negotiated if Weiss would give in on their demand for compulsory union membership. When Weiss still would not give in, the union bosses called a strike against Spencer-Safford, led by imported union toughs. Through threats, often aimed at the families of workers, union militants were able to keep many of the employees off the job, but Weiss continued to operate as best he could. (Remember that Taft-Hartley made it an unfair labor practice for union bosses to engage in coercion against workers, but those words in a statute book meant nothing to those who ordered the beating of Deering Crowe and the intimidation of Louis Weiss's employees.) The strike against his company convinced Weiss that the ultimate objective of the union bosses was not the welfare of the employees, but their own revenue.

In 1954 Right to Work was an important issue in the campaign for the Republican nomination for the governorship of Kansas. In that contest, George Templar, a strong advocate of Right to Work legislation, was running against Fred Hall, who refused to take a stand publicly on the issue, but had ties to the organized labor hierarchy in Kansas. Larson, well-known in the state for his active civic leadership, appeared in television ads for Templar.

A deep believer in individual liberty, Larson was naturally drawn to the Right to Work battle. He could see no reason why anyone should be forced to join a union and pay for its representation if he didn't want to. He was appalled at the violence that labor bosses were bringing to America, violence that he had seen first-hand in Wichita. And he detested the idea that workers like those at Louis Weiss' trailer business could be victimized by union officials in their pursuit of compulsory dues. For those reasons, Larson agreed to leave his career with the Coleman Company to organize a campaign to pass a Right to Work statute in Kansas, accepting the position of executive vice president of the newly-formed Kansans for the Right to Work in September 1954.

The next spring, Reed Larson guided the Right to Work bill to passage by the Kansas legislature, only to have it vetoed by Governor Fred Hall—despite his promise to Larson that he would sign the bill if it reached his desk. Hall's attempt to remain on the good side of Big Labor backfired however. Hall was denied re-nomination for the governorship in 1956. He would later become a mouthpiece for union bosses as they fought Right to Work ballot measures in 1958.

Larson had visited Deering Crowe in his hospital room just a few days before he died. Cancer had reduced Crowe to a living skeleton, but he encouraged Larson to continue the battle against compulsory unionism. No encouragement was needed, but his visit with the dying man left Reed Larson with a painfully vivid memory of union brutality.

THE RIGHT TO WORK MOVEMENT COALESCES

By the early 1950s, many Americans were coming to the same conclusion that Reed Larson had: Big Labor's drive for power threatened both the vitality of the economy and the foundations of representative government. One of them was Donald Richberg. This former advocate of compulsory unionism wrote in his 1957 book *Labor Union Monopoly: A Clear and Present Danger,* "Instead of being a movement of workers banded together for the protection and advancement of their interests in a free economy, the labor movement has now become a political movement with the objective of establishing a socialist labor government in control of the economic and social life of the nation."[7] He added, "the sincerity and good intentions of some of the builders of labor monopoly do not lessen the dangers of the power complex they have helped to establish."

And from the speeches of top union officials, it was clear that the "labor movement" was now about more than just wrangling for wage and benefit increases—it was about changing the fundamental nature of the country. For example, Walter Reuther, head of the United Auto Workers, said that "We as American trade unionists have much to learn from the European experience as regards mobilizing our labor political strength for social gains at the political level." Big Labor's grand strategy was for the United States to mimic the "progressive" welfare states of Europe with their extensive government regulation, stifling both liberty and private property rights.

Hiding behind a smokescreen of professed concern for the welfare of American workers—people whom they would assault and even kill if they rejected unionism's supposed benefits—the union bosses were busily assembling a political machine they intended to use to control the economic and political life of the nation. In 1955 AFL-CIO president George Meany announced that the union movement was shifting its focus away from the nation's plants and factories and to Congress and the state legislatures. (In truth, Big Labor had depended on favors from government since the 1930s, so what Meany actually meant was that his forces would concentrate even *more* on getting their way through lobbying.) A few Americans dedicated to the ideals of liberty and free enterprise now realized that they needed a national organization of their own to combat the cancerous spread of Big Labor's power. With union officials incessantly pushing for new laws to augment their power and cast their net of coercion over more and more workers, it was imperative to have some national organization that would fight back. That was the idea behind the creation of the National Right to Work Committee.

RAILROAD WORKERS REBEL AGAINST COMPULSORY UNIONISM

Life is full of unexpected consequences. One of the unexpected consequences of the 1951 amendment to the Railway Labor Act authorizing compulsory unionism was a revolt by many railroad workers. To the surprise of union officials, who expected the workers to quietly go along with mandatory union membership, many employees who had been voluntary union members rebelled. They established a group to fight against this attack on their rights as Americans called the National Committee for Union Shop Abolition (USA). It was founded August 5, 1952, with the assistance of the National Labor-Management Foundation. The President of the National Labor-Management Foundation was Maurice Franks, himself a former railroad labor leader, and Franks was named General Counselor to USA. The Chairman of USA was William T. Harrison, an employee of the Louisville & Nashville Railroad.

Thousands of railroad workers and some in the airline industry signed petitions circulated by USA calling for the abolition of the union shop in all industries, "as an unfair labor practice, un-American in principle and totally unnecessary to the growth and development of sound and honest unionism." Unfortunately, those petitions fell mainly on deaf ears in Congress. There was no going back to voluntary unionism once the union autocrats had given their orders. While USA started off with much fanfare and widespread support from railroad union members, it faded quickly.

In 1954 a group of small business owners joined forces with USA movement and organized a coalition of employers and employees called the National Right to Work Committee. A key leader in the forging of this coalition was Whiteford Blakeney, a founding partner in the Charlotte, North Carolina law firm of Blakeney, Alexander & Machen. A true southern gentleman deeply committed to the principles of freedom, Blakeney stitched together the disaffected railroad workers of USA with a group of small business owners who shared their aversion to compulsory unionism and feared the growing power of Big Labor. Those business owners included: E.S. Dillard, president of the Old Dominion Box Company, also located in Charlotte; Robert Englander, president of Gary Steel Products of Lynchburg, Virginia; P.M. French, president of Southern Manufacturing Company of Nashville, Tennessee; and Nathan Thorington, president of Thorington Construction Company of Richmond, Virginia. Key representatives from the employee movement were S.D. "Duke" Cadwallader, a former Baltimore & Ohio Railroad conductor, and USA Chairman William T. Harrison.

THE BIRTH OF THE NATIONAL RIGHT TO WORK COMMITTEE

In a press release on January 28, 1955, the National Right to Work Committee announced its existence. The release was signed jointly by E. S. Dillard, who would serve as Chairman of the Board, and former Representative Fred Hartley, as President. Under the motto, "Americans Must Have the Right, But Not Be Compelled, to Join Labor Unions," Dillard and Hartley made it clear that the Committee was not an anti-union organization and "would defend a man's right to join a union voluntarily just as vigorously as it opposed his being forced to do so against his will." The single objective of the organization, the press release emphasized, would be to establish the principle that Americans should be free to choose union membership, but never be forced into it.

With the formation of the National Right to Work Committee, there was finally an organization committed exclusively to the objective of ridding all Americans of the scourge of compulsory unionism. Compared to its Big Labor adversaries, it had but a tiny budget and staff, but Blakeney, Hartley, Dillard and the other backers knew they had something that the advocates of union coercion would never have—a good cause.

In a separate statement accepting the presidency of the new organization, Fred Hartley stated that "compulsion is the cancer of the labor movement, and if allowed to continue and grow it will have disastrous consequences for organized labor and for the entire country." He went on to explain: "The goal of the union leaders who are advocating compulsion is clear. They want monopoly control of all jobs. They want compulsory submission of all workers to government by the unions."

The press release set forth the Committee's program of action:

1. To carry on a national educational campaign aimed at public understanding of compulsory unionism and the threat it poses to the freedom of all of us;
2. To encourage and support both employers and employees who are resisting the adoption of union shop and other compulsory unionism provisions in labor-management contracts;
3. To assist workers who are already fighting, through the courts and otherwise, to avoid discharge from their jobs under union shop contracts because they personally do not want to join a union;
4. To provide information and material for the various state groups fighting compulsory unionism; and
5. To serve as a clearing house and information center for all who are active and concerned over this matter.

This was a tall order, considering the enormous political and financial resources at the disposal of labor bosses who were looking forward to continuing expansion of their forced unionism empire. David was striding out to fight Goliath.

THE FUNDING PROBLEM

The initial funding for the Committee came from contributions by USA members and the businesses owned by Dillard, French, Thorington, Englander, and a few others.

But running a national organization on the scale necessary to combat Big Labor would require a large and steady revenue stream. Dillard and his fellow organizers were optimistic that they would soon receive large cash infusions from major companies. Unfortunately, they had misjudged the management of America's business giants. Most of them were "gray flannel suit" types with no particular interest in fighting for a principle. Some had already capitulated to Big Labor and couldn't be seen as supporting the Right to Work movement without arousing the kind of trouble that union bosses were so good at causing. Others had succumbed to the prevalent idea that compulsory unionism was the wave of the future. And it did not help that President Eisenhower's Secretary of Labor, James Mitchell, had in late 1954 denounced the Right to Work movement—even though the Eisenhower White House promptly put out a statement saying that Secretary Mitchell was only speaking for himself.

Letters soliciting financial support from big business went unheeded. Phone calls weren't returned. The funds on hand were running out fast.

Unwilling to give up, the Committee's founders took stock of the situation. The managers of big business were apparently indifferent to Right to Work, but polls consistently showed that the great majority of Americans opposed compulsory unionism. The conclusion was obvious: If the Committee was to maintain the fight for worker freedom, it would have to harness the sentiments of grassroots America. Thus was born America's first broad-based direct-mail fundraising campaign. Instead of targeting large donors—big business and foundations—the Committee went after individuals and small firms in a massive direct-mail effort. That campaign was a remarkable success. Donations began to pour into the Committee's headquarters from small businesses and individual citizens all across America. Most of the donations were checks for $5, $10, or $25. Thanks to those people, the Committee was able to pay its bills and stay in the fight. But the fundraising effort did more than that—it demonstrated the potential of going to the grassroots to generate political pressure on officeholders, a tactic that the Committee would use again and again in the years to come.

THE AMERICAN WAY AND SHOWDOWN

In its educational efforts, the Committee made very effective use of two films, each about half an hour in length, explaining the evils of compulsory unionism. The first, entitled *The American Way,* had been made by Kansans for the Right to Work in 1954, and featured Louis Weiss recounting the vicious, ten-month strike the UAW had aimed at his company over the single issue of compulsion. With Weiss's narration, the film also depicted various acts of violence and intimidation for which labor bosses had become notorious, such as demanding that farmers bringing crops to city markets must pay for union men to drive through the city and unload. Eventually, the Teamsters' bosses dropped the small amount of actual work performed and simply made the farmers pay them for the privilege of doing their own work. In a plain, homespun fashion, "The American Way" was an excellent tool for arousing righteous indignation at the arrogance and immorality of union bosses.

Another film, made early in 1958 by Kansans for the Right to Work, was *Showdown.* The star of *Showdown* was the legendary movie director Cecil B. DeMille, who had personally encountered the sting of compulsory unionism.

Throughout his Hollywood career, DeMille had belonged to two unions, the Screen Directors Guild and the American Federation of Radio Artists. In 1944, however, the latter union imposed a one-dollar assessment on all members. The money collected would be used to fund its opposition to a ballot initiative in California that would have made closed shop agreements illegal. DeMille did not believe in compulsory unionism and refused to pay the dollar. Consequently, he was suspended from membership, which in turn meant that he had to be fired from his job with Lux Radio Theatre—a job that had paid him the enormous sum of $100,000 per year. In 1948 when Representative Hartley's House Education and Labor Committee held hearings on compulsory unionism, DeMille was among those who testified to its abuses.

"Showdown" featured DeMille explaining his own encounter with union bosses who denied him the right to work because of his stand on principle. It also contained scenes showing the powerlessness of ordinary workers to voice their objections to the decrees of labor bosses once union membership becomes mandatory. In his trademark velvety tones, DeMille summed everything up, "Right to work is not against labor; it is not for management—it is for the individual worker's freedom of choice."

THE DEFEATS OF 1958

In 1958 Right to Work supporters in six states used the initiative process—legislation by direct vote of the citizens—to place Right to Work measures before the electorate. A key reason for the optimism that those proposals would win was the ongoing Senate investigation into the links between organized labor and organized crime. Throughout 1957 and 1958, Arkansas Senator John McClellan's special committee had uncovered a cesspool of corruption and illegality and the findings caused many Right to Work supporters to assume that the voters would be ready to give workers the freedom to say "No" to union bosses. Sadly, things did not turn out that way at all.

In five of the six states, Big Labor was able to demagogue the issue with great success, scaring voters with ridiculous claims, such as the assertion that, if Right to Work passed, spendable income for workers would decline. Union voter registration drives, advertising, and get-out-the vote efforts swamped the initiatives. Of the six states—California, Ohio, Washington, Colorado, Idaho, and Kansas—only in Kansas did the initiative succeed. To put it in military terms, it was a case of attacking without adequate preparation (only in Kansas had there been significant previous discussion of the Right to Work issue) and using the wrong kind of troops (ballot initiatives play into union campaign strengths). The 1958 experience haunts the movement to this day.

That sole victory in Kansas occurred in a state where the case for Right to Work had already been strongly made in the legislature's passage of a Right to Work bill in 1955. Governor Hall had vetoed that bill, but important groundwork had been laid. The issue of compulsory unionism had been widely discussed and debated throughout the state. Most voters understood it and were not swayed by the scare tactics and outright lies that Big Labor always employs against Right to Work. Kansans for the Right to Work, headed by Reed Larson, produced and made effective use of *The American Way* and *Showdown.* Despite a last-minute union effort to confuse voters by placing ads in newspapers saying, "Vote Against Union Domination—Vote No on Amendment 3" (a "Yes" vote was in favor of passing Right to Work), the measure won handily—395,000 in favor and 310,000 against.

In the other five states, however, Right to Work forces were badly beaten. In California and Washington, the vote was almost two to one against the proposal. In Colorado, it was three to two. Even in lightly-unionized Idaho, where Right to Work backers were sure of victory, the outcome was a shocking 5,000 vote defeat. But the worst battering was in Ohio.

Led by Hersh Atkinson, executive director of the State Chamber of Commerce, Right to Work advocates brashly decided to try for a quick victory in that heavily unionized state. They were buoyed by the defeat that had been handed to a UAW-backed initiative two years earlier that would have increased unemployment compensation dramatically. Failing to see that it is usually easier to defeat ballot initiatives than to pass them—confused or doubtful citizens tend to vote "no"—Atkinson and his allies pushed to get Right to Work on the ballot, much to the horror of many Ohio Republican politicians. The most notable of them was Senator John Bricker, a prominent conservative who was running for re-election. Bricker was afraid that it would hurt his chances if he said anything about Right to Work and tried desperately to avoid the issue.

Atkinson, however, held control of the faucet for a great amount of campaign funding and told Bricker that unless he publicly endorsed the Right to Work initiative, the faucet would be shut off for his campaign.

Bricker chose to endorse the Right to Work measure, but did so unenthusiastically.

Having Right to Work on the ballot was like waving a red flag at the union bull. Big Labor poured vast resources into defeating the initiative, using all the fear and demagoguery their campaign consultants could muster. Panicked by the huge union propaganda barrage, Ohio voters crushed the Right to Work initiative. The referendum was defeated by more than two to one and Bricker narrowly lost his Senate race. Bricker blamed Right to Work supporters for his loss and remained bitter towards the Right to Work movement for the rest of his life.

The 1958 debacle caused many Republicans to conclude that they should have nothing to do with Right to Work—that the issue was political poison. The Chairman of the Republican National Committee, Meade Alcorn, denounced Right to Work in a speech before the National Association of Manufacturers at the Waldorf-Astoria Hotel in New York. Things *were* handled badly in Ohio and the other states where the Right to Work initiatives were defeated, but it didn't follow that Right to Work was a political albatross.

Republican candidates also did poorly in states where Right to Work was not an issue. They lost badly in Ohio, where Right to Work was on the ballot, but they also did poorly in other midwestern states where it wasn't. In fact, the Republican congressional vote fell less in Ohio in 1958 compared to the previous mid-term year of 1954, than it did in Wisconsin, Indiana, and Iowa, where Right to Work was not an issue.

In California, Senator William Knowland was defeated in his bid for the governorship, but he did not blame the loss on his support for Right to Work. Far more important, he said, was the strong nationwide Democratic trend. A comparison of the vote totals for Knowland, who supported Right to Work and Goodwin Knight, the Republican candidate for the Senate who opposed it, shows that there was very little difference between them. Republican Party officials, however, who were looking for a scapegoat for their disastrous results, eagerly pinned the blame on Right to Work. To this day, many Republicans quake in fear at the thought of voicing support for Right to Work and wish that the Committee would stop putting them on the spot with its questionnaires.

It was, and still is, a bum rap. The correct conclusion should have been that Right to Work is an issue too easily demagogued to have a good chance of passing in a *referendum* in most states. It requires a long-term legislative strategy. That doesn't mean that the issue itself is dangerous. Decades of polling have shown that, by a wide margin, most Americans oppose compulsory unionism. As we will see in coming chapters, voters are much more likely to turn against politicians who slavishly bow to Big Labor's wishes to get rid of Right to Work than they are to reject those who stand for it. Running on a pledge to give workers the freedom to choose to join a union or not is certainly *not* political poison.

The 1958 debacle also caused many people to conclude that the Right to Work movement was dead. If it couldn't even win in a state like Idaho, what chance did it have in other states that didn't already have Right to Work laws, much less in Congress? Furthermore, the 1958 elections brought to Washington solid Democratic majorities in both the House and the Senate and it seemed possible that Big Labor might finally succeed in ramming through a bill to repeal Section 14(b). Whether President Eisenhower would sign it was doubtful, but the Committee hoped desperately that he would not be put to the test.

Besides a new Congress coming to Washington in 1959, a new executive director for the National Right to Work Committee was installed. Knowing that it needed help from a proven winner, the Board asked Reed Larson to leave his Kansas home and reinvigorate the national movement in Washington. Two members of the Committee's Executive Board, Duke Cadwallader and Nate Thorington, telephoned Larson to offer him the huge challenge of trying to revive the struggling movement. They told Larson the sad truth about the Committee's financial situation. The bank account was down to only a few thousand dollars and there was no guarantee that staff salaries could be paid for more than a month. This was a chance for Larson to really make a difference in a cause to which he was deeply devoted, but at the risk of financial hardship for his family. With two small children and a third on the way, it was a tough decision, but devotion to the cause won out. Larson's experiences in Kansas—the vicious intimidation of workers and their families, union bribery and corruption, the memory of Deering Crowe on his deathbed, and more—had seared into him a fierce determination to oppose Big Labor's quest for domination. He and his wife, Jeanne, and their daughters were soon on their way to Washington.

With Larson's guidance, the Committee revived and grew. The headline of an April 1961 story in *The Wall Street Journal* told the tale: "Right-to-Work Drive, Left for Dead in 1958, Aims for a Comeback." The writer noted that the Committee was reaching new peaks in members and revenue, and was launching fresh campaigns in several states. "Mr. Larson suggests that part of the current resurgence results also from dogged, little-noticed campaigning in the past two years to dispel the notion that the movement was through. He and [Committee president William T.] Harrison logged thousands of miles as they traveled the country 'carrying the freedom message,' as the group's national newsletter headlined a recent Harrison trip," said the reporter.[8]

If the autocrats of Big Labor thought they would roll to victory over Section 14(b) in 1959, they were in for an unpleasant surprise. Senator McClellan's investigation into the problem of corruption in organized labor continued and newspaper headlines repeatedly trumpeted the findings of shady links between organized labor and the mob. On television, Americans saw labor bosses sweating—and invoking the Fifth Amendment—under questioning. Senator McClellan's chief counsel, Robert F. Kennedy, dug especially deep into the dark underside of the Teamsters union. Big Labor was thrown on the defensive when Senator McClellan introduced legislation designed to crack down on its abuses. Congress passed the bill and President Eisenhower signed it. Known as the Labor-Management Reporting and Disclosure Act (LMRDA), McClellan's bill was, like Taft-Hartley, an instance of trying to solve the problems inherent in compulsory unionism with still more federal regulation. LMRDA has never done much to thwart corruption.[9] At least, however, the attention it focused on union corruption prevented a bill to repeal Section

14(b) from making any progress. Not until 1965 would Big Labor mount a serious effort for its goal of making compulsory unionism the law in all fifty states.

TAKING ON THE COMMITTEE FOR ECONOMIC DEVELOPMENT

On December 9, 1961, the Committee for Economic Development (CED) released with considerable fanfare a 158-page study entitled *The Public Interest in National Labor Policy.* At that time, the CED was an especially prestigious organization with more than two hundred of America's top business leaders on its Board of Trustees. Since its founding in 1942, the CED had put out a stream of studies and reports, supposedly representing the enlightened views of America's most respected business leaders. But the "National Labor Policy" report, on pages 151–52, urged that Right to Work laws be abolished by federal statute, explaining, "Because our national labor policy is predicated on the trade union as the exclusive representative of all the members of the bargaining unit and because we feel that the participation of all members of the bargaining unit would improve the quality of such representation, we urge the elimination of the right of states to go beyond the restrictions contained in the federal law."

A strange thing about the publicity attending the release of "National Labor Policy" was that it made no mention of that explosive recommendation. Nowhere in the extensive summary of the report was its call for the abolition of Right to Work laws discussed. The National Right to Work Committee came to the conclusion that the CED staff and the "independent study group" that had prepared the study were attempting to create a "sleeper"—a call for the repeal of Section 14(b) and expansion of compulsory unionism, ostensibly coming from a prestigious business organization, to be hauled out for strategic use at some later time. Did the leadership of the CED really support this attack on Right to Work? Reed Larson was determined to find out.

First, he put out a press release on December 14, spotlighting the duplicity of the CED. "The bulk of the 158-page report camouflages a concession of total power to union professionals, a concession they have vigorously sought for many years. . . . On this vital issue of voluntary versus compulsory unionism, which affects every aspect of our political and economic freedom, the CED report lines up squarely on the side of the union professionals." Then he wrote to the chairman of the CED, Donald K. David, asking that he or some other spokesman for the organization publicly repudiate the report's call for repeal of Section 14(b). In reply, David said that the CED regarded the report as the work of the "independent study group" that had written it and that it did not necessarily express the opinions of the CED trustees and members. That argument was preposterous. The personnel of the "independent study group," which included such well-known compulsory unionism apologists as Harvard professor John T. Dunlop and University of Pennsylvania professor George Taylor, had been chosen by the CED. The report had been printed, distributed, and publicized with CED funds. To the reading public, it clearly seemed to represent the official position of the CED that national labor policy would be improved by forcing unionism on millions of workers who didn't want it.

Larson then sent a letter to all of the CED trustees, asking for their views on the report. He also wrote to the Committee's "Key Man" corps of active opponents of compulsory unionism in all 50 states. That really stirred up a hornets' nest.

Many of the CED trustees wrote back to Larson, saying that they did not support the call for repeal of Section 14(b) and hadn't known about it. Only two defended the report. Numerous businessmen who were CED members wrote to Donald David to express their outrage over the report. Typical was a letter from E. B. Germany, President of Lone Star Steel in Dallas, saying, "I cannot believe that men such as these will sit idly by and permit such a colossal hoax as this 'impartial inquiry' to be foisted on the American people." An editorial by Edward Maher, Vice President of the National Association of Manufacturers published in NAM News called upon CED member firms to "make it emphatically clear that this study does not represent their views."

Even though no CED trustee publicly disavowed the "National Labor Policy" report, the internal repercussions within the CED were severe.

On May 16 Donald David gave a speech in Washington in which he defended the CED's publication of "independent" reports, but announced that it had formed a new committee of businessmen to write another study on labor policy. That didn't mollify enough of the trustees and members who were angered over the fact that, as writer William F. Rickenbacker put it, "the names and money and prestige of the nation's top businesses were used by the CED staff to distribute a report calling in effect for compulsory unionism."[9] In June, Mr. David was replaced as chairman of the CED. His successor, T.V. Houser, former chairman of Sears, announced that the CED would no longer publish "independent studies."

Had it not been for the timely intervention of the National Right to Work Committee, the forced unionism advocates on the CED staff would have gotten away with their "sleeper." However, the Committee rang the alarm bells and this effort at hiding a call for compulsory unionism in a premier business group publication went for naught.

THE BATTLE IN THE AEROSPACE INDUSTRY—1962

The Eisenhower Administration had been mostly indifferent toward Right to Work, but the election of President John F. Kennedy in 1960 ushered in an administration that was downright hostile. Having received heavy support from Big Labor in the campaign, Kennedy was eager to push an agenda that promoted compulsory unionism. The first major battle came in 1962 over the issue of union shops in companies involved in the production of missiles for the nation's defense—the aerospace industry.

In 1962, there were five major firms in the industry—Douglas Aircraft, General Dynamics, Ryan Aviation, Lockheed Aircraft, and North American Aviation. All had union contracts with both the United Auto Workers and International Association of Machinists (IAM), run by Walter Reuther and Al Hayes respectively. On May 16 they opened negotiations with the five companies, with one of their major demands being the imposition of the union shop. The companies had long resisted the demands of union bosses that all workers must pay dues in order to keep their jobs, but if that resistance could be broken, it would mean an additional inflow of some $1,500,000 per year in money to union treasuries. Reuther and Hayes were licking their lips at the prospect.

By July, bargaining had reached an impasse. The companies were prepared to agree to a package of wage and benefit increases, but were adamantly opposed to giving in on the demand for the union shop. Therefore, on July 10 Reuther and Hayes announced that they would call strikes at the companies unless they capitulated on that issue. The nation faced the prospect of a strike that would hamstring production of vital defense material, all because two union bosses were insistent that all workers must pay dues to them.

On July 16, Douglas Aircraft caved in and agreed to the UAW-IAM demand for an "agency shop" contract. The next day, the Kennedy Administration began to apply its leverage to the other firms. It held control of Defense Department contracts that covered the great majority of the business done by the five companies, and Secretary of Labor Arthur Goldberg made it known that the Administration wanted to see the Douglas agreement followed by the other firms. The implication was clear—either go along with compulsory unionism or else face the possibility that Defense Department contracts will stop coming your way.

At this point, the Committee entered the battle. On July 17, Reed Larson released a public letter sent to the President of Douglas Aircraft, arguing that he should reconsider his capitulation to forced unionism, which would mean that more than 10,000 of his employees would have to pay union dues or be fired. Larson called on Douglas to reject the "agency shop" and "all other coercive devices of monopoly unionism." Three days later, the Committee began organizing opposition to forced unionism throughout the industry. With the Committee's help, Cecil Mitchell, a member of the Board and an employee of Lockheed who supported *voluntary* unionism, formed a group called Aerospace Workers for Freedom. This group began placing ads in California newspapers calling on citizens and other workers to—as the ad said in bold type— "Help Us Fight This Shakedown!" Seeing resistance at the negotiating table and now defiance by workers, Reuther and Hayes declared that the strike would begin on July 23.

On July 22, President Kennedy announced that he had asked Reuther and Hayes to postpone the strike (which they had agreed to do) and also that he would appoint a three-member "Fact Finding Board" to study the aerospace dispute and recommend a settlement. This step ignored the mechanisms in place under the Taft-Hartley Act for the resolution of key national labor disputes; moreover, Kennedy's choice of chairman, Professor George Taylor, was a well-known proponent of compulsory unionism.

Immediately, the Committee attacked the extra-legal process and especially the Taylor appointment. On July 24, Reed Larson wrote to President Kennedy that he should reject Professor Taylor, who would be a "prejudiced judge" in the matter. Kennedy didn't withdraw his appointment, but the nation had been alerted to the fact that the deck was being stacked in favor of a settlement that would benefit the union bosses and take freedom of choice away from aerospace workers.

By early August, the Committee had a team of veteran opponents of compulsory unionism in place in California. Duke Cadwallader and Lafe Hooser, railroad union men as well as President and Vice President of the Committee, assisted aerospace workers in organizing their resistance against the union shop. They established a field office in Santa Monica from which to lead the fight. The first target was the "agency shop" deal Douglas had struck with Reuther and Hayes. On August 8, 22,000 Douglas employees in California and Oklahoma received letters from the company that bluntly informed them they would have to begin paying a "service fee" of $5 per month to the union in order to keep their jobs. That same day, Secretary of Defense Robert McNamara announced that Douglas had been awarded a $141 million contract for the Saturn missile project.

The Taylor Board met with the resisting companies in August and September, trying to pressure them into caving in to the demands of the union bosses. But despite the fact that Douglas had received an enormous, prized contract shortly after its capitulation, leaders of the four firms refused to follow suit. On September 11, Professor Taylor made his report to President Kennedy. In it he called for a union shop contract, but dependent on an election by the workers. His plan, approved by the union heads, stated that if two-thirds of the workers voting approved of the union shop arrangement, it would be adopted. Reuther and Hayes were confident of their ability to engineer an election "victory" that would mean dues money from thousands of additional workers.

In a press release the next day, the Committee attacked the Taylor formula and the President's use of his office to promote it. "Basic constitutional keystones," the release said, "protecting the property and personal liberty of every citizen, are jeopardized by Federal Government action. Billions of dollars of tax money (in defense contracts) constitute the ultimate instrument to enforce the wishes of the President." The whole business of imposing compulsory unionism by majority vote should be unacceptable in a free society, but here was the President of the United States backing a plan calculated to force thousands of workers who had said "No thanks" to unionism into the clutches of union bosses.

President Kennedy held a news conference on September 13, during which he issued an ultimatum to the four hold-out aerospace firms to accept the Taylor proposal. If they didn't, Kennedy said, they would be responsible for a strike that would jeopardize the nation's defense. Somehow, the responsibility of the UAW and the IAM escaped the President. By September 19, the pressure from the White House, with the personal intercession of President Kennedy, finally caused North American Aviation to capitulate to the Taylor plan. Shortly thereafter, General Dynamics and Ryan did so also. The Committee put out a scorching press release on September 20, attacking President Kennedy for using "the White House as a 'bargaining room' and the $50 billion national defense budget as a 'blackjack.' He has done this, not in the public interest, but in the interest of his personal political fortunes." But the die was now cast— would unionism be forced upon thousands of aerospace workers?

Owing to the presidential arm-twisting, Taylor's Board set elections to resolve the needless compulsory unionism dispute. The first would be October 19 in the North American plants, with General Dynamics on

October 23 and Ryan on November 1. The UAW and IAM went into top gear, plastering the plants and local papers with pro-union shop advertising. But from its temporary California headquarters, the Committee and the thousands of workers who did not want to be forced into paying union dues fought back with their own handbills and advertisements. Union "election squads" tried to intimidate members of the worker group Aerospace Workers for Freedom from exercising their rights to distribute literature opposing the union shop plan. They weren't able to stop those determined Americans from making their case against compulsory unionism, however.

When the ballots were counted at North American, the result was a shock to the union autocrats: more than 40 percent of the workers defied their wishes and voted against the union shop plan. Despite all their pressure, a significant number of union members had joined with the non-members in opposing compulsion and denying them the two-thirds vote needed under the Taylor plan. The results were the same at General Dynamics and Ryan—the union shop lost.

In a press release, the Committee said that the election results weren't "a victory for freedom, but rather a defeat for compulsion. Freedom suffers any time a vote is permitted on compelling free men to accept compulsion."

The 1962 aerospace fight over compulsory unionism was the first of many where the Committee's involvement helped preserve freedom against long odds. The next would come three years later.

NOTES

1. Donald Richberg, *Labor Union Monopoly: A Clear and Present Danger,* p. 58.
2. The Right to Work laws in the various states are not identical, but the crucial feature is always a prohibition against agreements that require a worker to be terminated from employment for refusal to pay union dues. Typical is this language from North Carolina's statute: "Any agreement or combination between any employer and any labor union or labor organization whereby persons not members of such union or organization shall be denied the right to work for said employer, or whereby such membership is made a condition of employment by such employer, or whereby any such union

or organization acquires an employment monopoly in any enterprise, is hereby declared to be against the public policy and an illegal combination or conspiracy in restraint of trade or commerce in the State of North Carolina." (N.C. Gen. Statutes, Section 95–79).

3. *Lincoln Federal Labor Union v. Northwestern Iron & Metal,* 335 U.S. 525 (1949).
4. John C. Moorhouse, "Compulsory Unionism and the Free Rider Doctrine," *Cato Journal,* vol. 2 (Fall 1982), p. 628.
5. See *Republic Steel v. Maddox,* 379 US 650 (1965) and *Vaca v. Sipes,* 386 US 171 (1971).
6. The story of the effort to repeal Taft-Hartley is told in Irving G. McCann's book *Why the Taft-Hartley Law* (The Committee for Constitutional Government, 1950).
7. Richberg, p.vii.
8. "Right-to-Work Drive, Left for Dead in 1958, Aims for a Comeback," *Wall Street Journal,* April 19, 1961, p.1.
9. The Labor-Management Reporting and Disclosure Act was supposed to deter union corruption by requiring more disclosure of its finances. Predictably, however, the reporting requirements were written vaguely enough that unions can comply without saying with specificity where their funds come from and how they are spent. Recent attempts by Secretary of Labor Elaine Chao to strengthen the reporting system have, of course, been denounced by labor leaders such as AFL-CIO president John Sweeney as "politically motivated."
10. William F. Rickenbacker, "CED: Tycoon Trap?" *National Review,* February 26, 1963, p. 156.

CHAPTER THREE

THE BATTLE OF MIDWAY
UNDER THE CAPITOL DOME

Politics often has a lot in common with military campaigns. Following the attack on Pearl Harbor that had left the U.S. Navy a gravely weakened fighting force, the Japanese commander, Admiral Yamamoto, planned a knock-out blow. He assembled a vast armada of warships that outnumbered the depleted American forces in every category—destroyers, cruisers, battleships, and especially aircraft carriers. Those ships, he was confident, would defeat the remnants of the U.S. Navy that had escaped destruction at Pearl Harbor. Behind his huge fleet of warships sailed troop transports carrying the forces that would occupy a key island—Midway—that would then become the advanced Japanese base for the conquest of the great prize of Hawaii. If he could take Hawaii, Yamamoto knew, it would be almost impossible for the Americans to interfere with the planned Japanese seizure of the entire western Pacific, including Australia.

The Americans knew they were badly outnumbered, but Midway *had to be held*. Under the command of Admiral Raymond Spruance, the U.S. fleet sailed out to meet the Japanese. On June 4, 1942, the Battle of Midway was fought, and against long odds the U.S. Navy soundly defeated the Japanese, sending four of their carriers to the bottom. In shock, Yamamoto turned his fleet around and sailed back to Japan. The Americans had held the crucial outpost, dealing his plans for domination of the Pacific a tremendous blow. Of course, the Japanese did not give up their desire for conquest, but they had missed their best chance when everything was in their favor.

61

The military situation in the Pacific in early 1942 was much like the political situation in the United States in 1965. The Right to Work forces in Congress were badly depleted and most observers expected that their key outpost—Section 14(b)—would quickly fall. Big Labor intended to use its massive political power to wipe out the hindrance of Right to Work statutes, and then move along with its agenda of dominating the political and economic landscape. The union bosses were sure of victory, but just as at the Battle of Midway, events turned out in a way that was most unexpected.

THE 1964 ELECTION

Senator Barry Goldwater of Arizona was the Republican nominee for the presidency in 1964, but his campaign was doomed from the start. Democratic attacks on his policies and character were amplified by a hostile media. His defense of constitutionalism was portrayed as extremist and racist. Scare tactics were used to mobilize key voting groups such as the elderly, minorities, and union members to vote for Democratic candidates, most of whom were backed by Big Labor. In the November election, Goldwater carried only his home state of Arizona, plus South Carolina, Georgia, Alabama, Mississippi, and Louisiana. President Lyndon Johnson won in a landslide with over 60 percent of the popular vote, and carried with him to victory many Democratic House and Senate candidates.

The new Congress would have the largest Democratic majorities since the New Deal—295 to 140 in the House and 68 to 32 in the Senate. While some of the Democrats were southerners who could be counted on to defend Section 14(b), some of the Republicans were of the sort who believed that they could appease the labor bosses by siding with them on big issues. Undoubtedly, the correlation of forces in the 89th Congress was heavily against the preservation of Right to Work, and Big Labor knew that it was time to move in for the kill. Repeal of Section 14(b) was its top political priority in 1965.

Moreover, President Johnson, although from a Right to Work state—Texas—had enjoyed overwhelming support from union bosses during the 1964 campaign, and he was not about to let his backers down. In his 1965 State of the Union Address he announced his support for the repeal of Right to Work. His actual words, however, were typically vague. Rather than saying that he wanted to repeal the law that allows states to prohibit compulsory unionism, he said that he favored "changes in Taft-Hartley, including 14(b)." Johnson went on to explain his reason for wanting to make "changes" this way: "I will do so hoping to reduce the conflicts that for several years have divided Americans in various states of our union." More clouded, evasive language would be difficult to imagine. Johnson's words made it sound as if state to state variations in law were a divisive force that somehow set the citizens of one state against those of another. That suggestion was absurd—there was no "conflict" between, say, Right to Work Arizona and non-Right to Work California—but the confusing rhetoric fit in with the long-standing pattern of enemies of Right to Work. They wanted to hide the truth of their position from the people, knowing that popular sentiment was strongly against them.

Bills to repeal Section 14(b) had frequently been introduced in Congress before and had failed. But it seemed almost inevitable that in 1965, Big Labor's goal of clearing away that obstacle to their unchallenged control over American workers would finally be realized.

OPENING SHOTS

A bill to repeal Section 14(b) was quickly introduced. H.R.77 was sponsored by reliable Big Labor crony Representative Frank Thompson of New Jersey. Fortunately, the repeal of 14(b) was not at the top of the long list of bills that President Johnson most wanted—his "Great Society" legislation. That gave the Right to Work Committee a little time to shore up its defenses, and Reed Larson put that time to good use.

Despite the Democratic landslide in 1964, polls consistently showed that a strong majority of Americans favored Right to Work laws and opposed compulsory unionism. So if Big Labor's politicians in Washington were going to repeal 14(b), they would be going against the desires of a large number of their constituents. That fact dictated the Committee's strategy: It would have to make certain that voters back home were informed of what was going on in Congress and that they raised their voices in protest. Right to Work leaders figured that Big Labor would try to get the repeal bill through Congress with as little publicity as possible. Therefore, the Committee immediately set about to put it in the spotlight and draw as much attention as possible to the impending destruction of the key outpost in the battle against compulsory unionism.

The plan of defense centered on the following:

- Organization of the Citizens Committee for the Preservation of Taft-Hartley, a broad-based group that would concentrate on nothing else.
- Organization of Union Members Against Compulsory Unionism, a special task force to demonstrate clearly that union officials did not speak for all American workers or even all union members in their efforts to wipe out Section 14(b).
- Organization of Women for Right to Work, a task force that would show the important interest of women in keeping Right to Work alive.
- The Committee produced and distributed 10,000 citizen-leadership "defense kits"—manuals for the organization of grassroots action at the local level—to convince fence-sitting members of Congress that support for repeal would harm their re-election prospects.
- The Committee began producing a steady stream of news releases to make sure that the repeal forces could not quietly sneak the bill through, to detail public reaction against repeal, and to answer the false statements made by Right to Work opponents.
- The Committee expanded its monthly newsletter and more than doubled its circulation within months.
- The Committee provided regular "insider" briefs to 1,000 key opinion leaders in all 50 states.
- The Committee produced and distributed a documentary film that

explained why Right to Work was important; it was offered free to more than 1,000 major TV stations, and 100 aired it.

- The Committee deluged newspaper editors with detailed suggestions for editorials, including clippings from other papers to show them what others were saying about the battle over Right to Work.
- The Committee sent numerous letters to 900 of the nation's larger newspapers to ensure that the pro-14(b) side would have forceful representation in their letters-to-the-editor section.
- The Committee expanded its speakers' bureau so it could present the Right to Work philosophy to as many civic groups as possible.
- At every opportunity, the Committee emphasized that it was a nonpartisan coalition of Americans from all walks of life who are united in their opposition to compulsory unionism and pointing to the fact that the president of the National Right to Work Committee, Duke Cadwallader, had been a railroad union member for 24 years.
- The Committee dispatched staff members to meet with editors and editorial writers at dozens of major daily newspapers, generating near-unanimous opposition to repeal of Section 14(b); among America's 1,500 daily papers, only four editorialized for repeal. Even the *New York Times* and *Washington Post* opposed repeal.
- It intensified its fundraising effort, nearly doubling its budget in 1965 over 1964, nearly all of the money coming from individual and small business contributions averaging less than $50.

With all those efforts humming, the Committee's office was an amazing beehive of activity throughout 1965 and into 1966. *It had to be if there was to be any chance of saving Section 14(b).*

THE OPINION RESEARCH POLL

An additional move that the Committee made in 1965 was to commission a poll by the nationally known organization Opinion Research Corporation of Princeton, New Jersey. Confident that the great majority of the American people sided with Right to Work, the Committee wanted fresh and authoritative evidence. The poll included questions that looked at every angle of the issue.

The poll's results were no surprise. Opinion Research concluded that by a margin of 64 percent to 14 percent, Americans favored retaining Section 14(b); by a margin of 61 percent to 24 percent, Americans said they would vote in favor of a Right to Work law in their state if they had the chance; and by a margin of 70 percent to 21 percent, Americans believed that a worker should not be fired just because he would not join a union. Those and other responses made it crystal clear that the people did not like compulsory unionism and strongly suggested that politicians who disregarded their beliefs could face trouble when they ran for re-election.

The poll results were not ready until late in 1965, but when the report was complete, the Committee used it like a squadron of dive-bombers against the repeal forces. It showed beyond a shadow of a doubt that Americans were in favor of Right to Work.

DEFEAT IN THE HOUSE

Big Labor's forces chose to begin in the House of Representatives, evidently concluding that they would get the more conservative House out of the way first, then coast through the more liberal Senate. Representative Frank Thompson of New Jersey led the attack on Section 14(b) by holding hearings on H.R. 77 in his House Subcommittee on Labor beginning June 1, 1965. That subcommittee was so stacked against Right to Work that not a single member of either party was willing to defend 14(b). To ensure that there would be one representative who would support Right to Work witnesses, asking questions that needed to be asked to expand upon their testimony, Representative Ed Gurney of Florida, a member of the full Labor Committee, sat in on the hearings.

Thompson wanted to railroad the bill through and had a parade of union officials to testify in favor of it. Reed Larson was among the few opponents of repeal allowed to testify, and he pointed out that the repeal

forces were ignoring the desires of the American people. "By every measure of public opinion—newspaper polls, public opinion surveys, congressional polls, editorial reaction—by every measurable evidence of
public sentiment, Americans want 14(b) preserved," he said. But Thompson would take no testimony from any of the numerous union workers
who had come to Washington seeking to have their voices heard in favor
of Right to Work. Thompson just wasn't interested in allowing them to
speak—Union members against compulsory unionism wasn't the right
message! Not only did he refuse to permit any of them to testify, but
when asked about his treatment of those people in a newspaper interview, he contemptuously dismissed them as "shills for the National Right
to Work Committee," implying that no union member could genuinely
oppose compulsory unionism. But how could he possibly know their
motives without permitting a single pro-14(b) worker to speak? The
episode is typical of the carefully cultivated but false idea that labor union
bosses speak for the entire "working class" and that there must be something wrong with a worker who disagrees with them.

Thompson's subcommittee voted H.R. 77 out on June 8 and the full
House Committee on Labor and Education swiftly pushed it along two
days later.

What was the hurry? The repeal forces knew that Reed Larson's testimony was correct. The tide of public opinion *was* strongly against them.
Newspaper editorials were blasting them daily. For example, on May 26
the *New York Times* wrote, "If the elimination of 14(b) is the only contribution Congress can make toward a more balanced labor law, it will
be better advised to leave the law alone." The May 20 *Philadelphia Inquirer*
had said, "It is one of the remarkable anomalies of our times that people who cherish their designation as 'liberals' should be in the forefront
of those pressing for compulsory unionism." Several papers pointed out
the blatant inconsistency of the administration's push for strengthened
civil rights legislation while at the same time promoting a bill that would
deprive millions of American workers protection for their rights. The
June 2 *Cincinnati Enquirer* put the matter this way: "And since Mr. Johnson has spoken up so eloquently for the right of minorities to plot their

own destinies without accepting dictation from the majority, it is diffi-cult to believe that his heart is in elimination of a section of the Taft-Hartley Act that seeks to accomplish the same objective."

With editorials like those ringing in their ears and sacks of letters pouring in from constituents who did not want to see Right to Work protection eliminated, the House members favoring repeal had good rea-son to worry about their standing with the voters back home. The Com-mittee's full-court press was putting enormous pressure on the politicians, especially those from Right to Work states, not to cave in to the union bosses. Big Labor lobbyists, however, worked hard to keep them in line, reminding nervous members that union backing had gotten them where they were. They apparently even went so far as trying to buy a vote in a special election to fill a vacant House seat in South Carolina. The Demo-cratic candidate, Preston Callison, told a newspaper reporter that he had been offered a $10,000 campaign contribution from the AFL-CIO if he would promise to vote in favor of the repeal of Section 14(b). (Callison, however, lost the special election to Floyd Spence, an unshakable Right to Work champion.)

Right to Work supporters were briefly cheered when, in mid-June, the chairman of the House Labor and Education Committee, Represen-tative Adam Clayton Powell of New York, stated that he would oppose immediate floor action on the bill until legislation was enacted to elim-inate racial discrimination by labor unions. Powell, a long-standing civil rights proponent, was acutely aware of the problem of discrimination against blacks by many unions. Solving that problem might delay H.R. 77 indefinitely. Unfortunately, Powell's principled stand was short-lived. Democratic Party leadership quickly pressured him into abandoning his opposition, which he did on June 17.

Efforts by the Committee to defeat the repeal bill in the House were complicated by a rift between Democratic and Republican opponents. In 1965, the House Republicans had voted to oust their long-time leader, Representative Charlie Halleck of Indiana, replacing him with Gerald Ford of Michigan. That move had greatly upset powerful Virginia Demo-crat Howard Smith, usually known as Judge Smith. He was so annoyed that he refused to cooperate with the Republican "young Turks" in fighting the repeal effort. In an effort to patch up the coalition against repeal, Reed Larson drove one of the "young Turk" Republicans, Representative Bob Griffin of Michigan, to meet with Judge Smith and a group of pro-Right to Work lobbyists at Smith's home in Alexandria on a Sunday afternoon. Griffin, co-author of the Landrum-Griffin Act, was the leader on labor issues among the "young Turk" Republicans. The meeting was done clandestinely because Griffin feared for his political future if word got out that he would cooperate with Judge Smith in fighting Big Labor on this issue. But the meeting failed to soften Judge Smith's contemptuous attitude toward the new Republican leadership and he refused to exercise his considerable influence among southern Democrats to oppose the bill.

The final vote in the House came on July 28 and the outcome was very much in doubt. Would enough union-backed congressmen stay "bought" for H.R. 77 to pass? Or would the avalanche of adverse reaction to the bill and the way it had been handled cause enough of them to back away from Big Labor's crusade against Section 14(b)? Quite a few House members had not yet declared which way they would go. Reed Larson sat in the gallery as the votes were recorded, focusing on those who were still uncommitted. He recalls that "When two Tennessee Democratic congressmen voted against us, I knew we were gone." The result was 221 in favor of the repeal bill, 203 against.

While the Committee never endorses political candidates, it always makes sure that voters know where their elected representative stand. Immediately after the House vote, it published the official tally along with Reed Larson's prescient comment that "A refusal to heed overwhelming public demands to reject repeal of 14(b) will result in a congressional house-cleaning in the 1966 elections." Nevertheless, Big Labor was halfway to its dream of wiping out Right to Work laws.

THE BATTLE IN THE SENATE
The House vote was very discouraging for the Committee, since Big Labor's hold on the Senate was thought to be even stronger. There was

no chance at all of getting enough support to defeat the bill in an up or down vote. The one and only hope was to keep it from being voted on. In the House of Representatives, time allowed for floor debate on bills is limited, but under the rules of the Senate, debate can go on indefinitely—the filibuster. A filibuster can be broken, however, if enough Senators vote to cut off debate in a "cloture motion." In 1965, it required a two-thirds vote to invoke cloture—67 Senators. Therefore, the battle came down to this: Could Right to Work advocates keep at least 34 Senators supporting a filibuster? If not, Section 14(b) would be gone within days and Big Labor would soon begin to corral thousands of workers who did not want to choose between paying union dues and losing their jobs.

The Committee's strategists knew that they could count on a block of twenty Democrats from Right to Work states. But would fourteen Republicans be willing to go along? A few of them were hopeless, like Jacob Javits of New York. He had no sympathy for Right to Work. Others were from states where Big Labor was strong, and the myth of Right to Work's role in the 1958 election was fresh. Even if they supported Right to Work in principle, many Republicans held the fallacious view that by voting to please union officials on this issue, they might reduce Big Labor's opposition to them when they ran for re-election. Besides, why go out on a limb for Section 14(b) if your own state was not a Right to Work state? Finding fourteen Republicans who would stick with the filibuster would not be easy.

The southern Democrats were willing to filibuster the repeal bill, but they pointed out to Committee leaders that they had engaged in an ill-fated filibuster against the 1964 Civil Rights Act and had gone down to defeat in an unpopular cause. If they were to lead the filibuster against H.R. 77, it would hurt Right to Work by making it seem as though the discredited enemies of the civil rights legislation were the primary friends of Right to Work. If the filibuster were to succeed, it was imperative that the Committee find a northern Republican to lead it. There was only one candidate for the job—Senator Everett McKinley Dirksen of Illinois.

GETTING TO YES WITH SENATOR DIRKSEN

Everett Dirksen, the Republican leader in the Senate since 1959, was a man of great oratorical skill and sharp wit.[1] He had sided with President Johnson on the 1964 Civil Rights Act, helping to get the bill through the Senate despite the filibuster against it. Although Illinois was not a Right to Work state, Dirksen was philosophically opposed to compulsory unionism and would later publish a law review article arguing that compulsory unionism ought to be regarded as unconstitutional.[2] But when Reed Larson approached him about leading a filibuster, he demurred.

"I'll make a speech and I'll vote with you," he told Larson, "but you can't filibuster this issue. Filibusters succeed only when they can enlist broad grassroots opposition to a bill. I'm afraid that Section 14(b) is a lost cause. The ordinary people in my state of Illinois know little about it and care less. On the other hand, the labor unions have fired up their membership. In a day or two, the letters and phone calls would be pouring in from local unions and the filibuster would collapse."

Larson realized that he had a tough sales job ahead of him. He *had* to persuade Dirksen. But when he argued that there really was strong opposition to the repeal of 14(b), Dirksen shook his head and sighed. "I wish I could agree with you, but I can't," he replied.

Disappointed, Larson left Senator Dirksen's office and headed back to the Committee's headquarters on Connecticut Avenue. When he got there, he went to see Information Director Hugh Newton, and asked him to compile all the supporting editorials and cartoons he had collected from newspapers nationwide. The staff had been working hard to keep up with the waves of material and the stack Hugh handed him was over 3,000 pages! Larson grabbed the large bundle and hurried back to see Senator Dirksen again.

"Senator, if you don't think this is a grassroots issue, then take a look at these," Larson said, putting the stack of papers on his desk. Somewhat reluctantly, Dirksen looked through a sampling of the material. After a few minutes, he looked up.

"I must say that there is much more support for 14(b) than I had realized," he said.

Larson thought he could close the deal with the Senator.

"So will you lead the filibuster?" he asked.

To Larson's dismay, Dirksen again shook his head and said, "No, I won't—because I don't think there are enough votes in the Senate to sustain it."

Larson thanked Dirksen for his time and then left to get more help to close the deal. That help would have to come from the Committee's allies in the Senate. The conservative Democrats had organized an informal committee composed of six members, three from each party, to fight the repeal bill: Democrats Sam Ervin of North Carolina, Willis Robertson of Virginia, and Richard Russell of Georgia, and Republicans Carl Curtis of Nebraska, Wallace Bennett of Utah, and Paul Fannin of Arizona. Larson called to let Senator Ervin know that his group needed to pay a visit to Senator Dirksen and convince him that with his leadership, the filibuster would not be broken. Ervin said that he would set up an appointment to see Dirksen.

Next, Larson gathered together Right to Work's key allies in Washington—staff members and lobbyists with associations that were also against repeal of 14(b)—and prepared to mobilize grassroots support for the filibuster they were hoping for. The Senate would soon begin floor debate on H.R. 77. The bill had been rammed through the Senate Rules and Labor Committees in late June with exactly the same high-handed disregard for the opinions of ordinary working Americans as Representative Thompson had shown, with the unusual step of beginning the hearings even before the final vote in the House. Therefore, it was imperative that the Committee be ready to show that the filibuster was not just a group of die-hard Southerners trying to talk the bill to death. The country had to see that a wide swath of public opinion was in favor of keeping Section 14(b). From polls, it was clear that that was the case. If a filibuster began, Big Labor would undoubtedly activate its base to pour out calls and letters demanding an end to debate and passage of the bill. Larson was determined to create an avalanche of support for the hoped-for filibuster that would overwhelm the efforts of the union bosses against it.

The Committee prepared new press releases to send to newspapers around the country, as well as radio and television stations to explain why a filibuster was justified, and also to provide them with refutations of Big Labor's inevitable misinformation and red herring arguments. To keep public opinion with Right to Work, it was important to contain Big Labor's inflammatory rhetoric as much as possible to its own publications and keep it out of the general media. To do that, the Committee was going to keep editors supplied with better reasoned material.

On the day of the scheduled meeting between the "Committee of Six" and Senator Dirksen, the Committee put its team on alert. One person was stationed in the office of each of the six Senators, ready to put the pro-filibuster operation into effect as soon as Dirksen agreed to lead it. *If he agreed.*

Larson himself went to Senator Curtis' office. The Senator told him, "Sit at my desk. I'll call you when we have Dirksen's answer."

The wait was agonizing. Larson sat at Senator Curtis' desk for hours, staring at the telephone as afternoon shadows lengthened across the lawn outside. For it to take so long, he reasoned, Dirksen must be resisting the persuasive efforts of the six, just as he had resisted his own. What if the call, when it finally came, was to say that the effort had failed? Without the strength of Senator Dirksen, a filibuster would almost surely fail and that would mean that all the state Right to Work laws would be wiped out. The movement would have to start from scratch again, a terribly depressing prospect.

Late in the afternoon, the phone on Senator Curtis's desk rang and Larson answered instantly. Senator Curtis said to him, "It's going to take a little longer than we'd thought. As a matter of fact, there's no need for you to hang around. We'll be here for a while. However, I want you to know that things are going *very well.*"

Limp with relief, Larson headed back to his office. The publicity campaign would have to wait until the next day, but with Senator Dirksen apparently in on the filibuster, Right to Work was still in the ball game. It would be a hard game. Big Labor still might win, but Right to Work now had a fighting chance.

THE FILIBUSTER

Senator Dirksen had been won over. The "Committee of Six" convinced him that with his leadership, they could hold at least 34 votes and that the preparations for the filibuster had been made. Dirksen followed his instinctive dislike of compulsory unionism and agreed to lead the filibuster against H.R. 77.

In 1965, a filibuster required that those Senators opposed to calling for a vote on a bill had to keep the floor and speak continuously, unlike the contemporary Senate where a "filibuster" doesn't require round-the-clock speaking, but only a showing that a sufficient number of Senators are opposed to a vote—the so-called "filibuster lite." On October 4, 1965, the day set for floor debate on the repeal bill, Dirksen led a team of 27 Senators who were prepared to speak against it incessantly. There were numerous Senators in the "uncommitted" camp and no one knew for sure how they would go when the cloture vote inevitably came.

When President Johnson learned that Senator Dirksen was going to lead a filibuster against the repeal of 14(b), he called to cajole him.

"You wouldn't do that to me, would you Ev?" he asked.

"I'm going to do it and the debate will be long and formidable. It could last until Christmas," Everett told him.

President Johnson wailed to Everett, "I thought you were my friend."

"I am," Everett replied. "But remember why Brutus rose against Caesar—'not that I loved Caesar less, but that I loved Rome more.' Well, I love my country more."[3]

Senator Dirksen led off the filibuster with a ringing endorsement of the freedom of Americans to work without having to pay a union for the privilege of doing so. "Is there a more fundamental right than the right to make a living for one's self and for one's family without being compelled to join a labor organization?" he asked. Senator Wallace Bennett of Utah summed up the controversy beautifully with these words, "Good unions don't need repeal of Section 14(b), and bad unions don't deserve it." Senator Spessard Holland of Florida said, "In my opinion, it is morally wrong to deprive a man of his right to earn a living because he refuses for reasons of conscience or any other reason to join or pay money to any private organization as the price for his right to work." Senator Harry Byrd of Virginia linked Right to Work with the basic purpose of government, saying, "My basic objection is that repeal of 14(b) would betray and overthrow a fundamental liberty for which this country was founded and which our form of government was designed to protect." For a full week, the Senate chamber resounded with such impassioned arguments in favor of maintaining Section 14(b)'s shield against compulsory unionism.

During that week, the Committee's campaign to rouse public sentiment against compulsory unionism hit full stride. Newspaper editorials were strongly against repeal of 14(b) and citizens were registering their opinions directly with a flood of letters, telegrams, and phone calls to Senators' offices. The fence-straddlers in the Senate took the nation's pulse and discovered that it was strongly against the repeal of Right to Work.

On October 11, the Senate Majority Leader, Mike Mansfield of Montana, called for a cloture vote to shut off debate and bring the bill to a vote. To the shock of the labor bosses, he didn't even come close, with only 49 Senators voting for cloture, far from the 67 needed. Mansfield then allowed the debate to go on for another two weeks while the anti-Right to Work forces tried to regroup. Big Labor's lobbyists twisted senatorial arms as hard as they could, but it was no use. The Committee had made sure that the voice of America was heard on the question of compulsory unionism, and the message had been received loud and clear in Washington. Enough of the fence-straddling Senators had concluded that their political futures would be in jeopardy if they voted against Section 14(b). On October 27, Senator Mansfield ran up the white flag and pulled H.R. 77 off the floor. Big Labor's supporters, however, vowed to renew the battle in early 1966. Then they went back to the drawing board to figure out why, with all their political clout, they couldn't knock out Section 14(b).

Over the congressional recess, union heads and their lobbyists, fearful that the golden opportunity to crush Right to Work was fading away, applied pressure to the Democratic leadership to try again. President Johnson was well aware that the public opinion battle had been lost, but nevertheless included in his 1966 State of the Union address a call for "repeal of Section 14(b) of the Taft-Hartley Act to make labor laws in all our states equal to the laws of the 31 states which do not have Right to Work measures." That was a disingenuous argument, of course, trying vainly to cast the effort to repeal 14(b) as another part of the fight for equality.

Senator Mansfield once again brought H.R. 77 to the floor on January 24, 1966. Senator Dirksen accepted the challenge, saying, "We will fight to the end. And there is no amicable compromise possible. There is no sweetener for 14(b). Our job will be difficult, but my notion is that we have gained ground since last year."

When the filibuster resumed, the Committee was ready with a powerful new ship to add to its fleet—the Opinion Research poll showing deep opposition to compulsory unionism and the repeal of Section 14(b). Information Director Hugh Newton made maximum use of the results, plastering ads showing the public's feelings in the Washington newspapers, including *Roll Call,* a weekly publication on politics that is widely read in Congress. Copies of the *Roll Call* ad were then sent to 1,000 key Right to Work supporters around the country, urging them to distribute the copies locally. The complete report, along with a press release summarizing it, was sent to the nation's 200 largest papers five days in advance of the actual release date so they could have editorials ready. It was also sent early to key columnists and to the Senators who were supporting the filibuster.

The date set for the release of the report was January 31. Unfortunately, a massive blizzard struck Washington that day. It literally shut down the town and the scheduled news conference had to be cancelled. Still, the report and news release were hand-carried through the snow to more than fifty major news outlets in Washington. The Committee pulled out all the stops, realizing that the information in the Opinion Research report could break the back of the effort to repeal Section 14(b).

As a result of the report and its distribution, there was a new flood of commentary in the media on the need to retain 14(b). The filibustering Senators also made great use of this fresh material supporting their cause. When Senator Mansfield called for a cloture vote on February 8, Senator Dirksen was proven right. Right to Work had gained ground. This time, 48 senators voted against cutting off debate. After one more failed cloture vote on February 10—the number of anti-cloture votes had risen to 49—Mansfield gave up the campaign. Like the Japanese admirals after Midway, Big Labor dejectedly turned its fleet around and sailed away—for the time being.

EPILOGUE—THE ELECTIONS OF 1966

Reed Larson's prophecy that Right to Work would be a cutting issue in the 1966 congressional elections was exactly right. Especially in the Right to Work states, votes by Representatives and Senators in favor of repealing Section 14(b) were used by their opponents with deadly effect. Illustrative of the strength of the Right to Work issue was the race in Arizona between Congressman George Senner and his challenger, Sam Steiger. Senner had vigorously supported the effort to repeal Section 14(b) and had flatly stated that even if his vote bothered his constituents, the financial and campaign assistance he would receive from the labor bosses would offset it. Mailings from the Committee helped to let Senner's constituents know just how he felt. On Election Day, Steiger, a strong Right to Work backer, breezed to victory with 63 percent of the vote.

Thirty-nine House members who had voted for repeal of 14(b) were defeated in primaries or in the general election, and Big Labor's candidates also did poorly in open seat contests. According to a post-election analysis done by *U.S. News & World Report,* Big Labor's strength in the House dropped by 49 seats.[4] The union bosses also lost votes in the Senate as a result of their campaign to repeal Section 14(b). Senator Ross

Bass of Tennessee, who had sided with the union bosses, wasn't even able to win re-nomination in 1966. His Senate seat was won by Howard Baker, Everett Dirksen's son-in-law and an opponent of compulsory unionism. In 1970, two more anti-Right to Work Democrats from Right to Work states, Ralph Yarborough of Texas and Albert Gore Sr. of Tennessee, also went down to defeat—Yarborough losing in the primary and Gore in the general election.

If some Republicans mistakenly concluded in 1958 that fighting for Right to Work was political poison, many Democrats discovered in 1966 that throwing their lot in with the union bosses to impose compulsory unionism was a long drink of hemlock.

The 1965 battle over Section 14(b) was one of epic proportions. Big Labor had enormous political superiority in Congress, and was backed by a popular president who fully supported its agenda. Right to Work defenders fought tenaciously to hold the outpost of 14(b) and made every shot count. The Committee's leadership made brilliant use of its strongest weapon—public opinion—to convince wavering legislators that a vote to repeal 14(b) would be going against a strong tide of voter sentiment. As had been the case with the 1962 aerospace fight, the only thing that saved freedom of choice for tremendous numbers of American workers was the National Right to Work Committee's staunch defense of their freedom.

NOTES

1. Dirksen's most famous quip, regarding congressional spending habits, is "a billion here, a billion there—pretty soon you're talking real money."

2. Everett M. Dirksen, "Individual Freedom Versus Compulsory Unionism: A Constitutional Problem," 15 *DePaul Law Review* 259 (1966). In that article, Dirksen argued that the freedom to work without joining a union should be protected under the Ninth Amendment. He concluded "(O)ur best hope for outlawing compulsory unionism in America must lie with our courts and their recognition of the Constitution as a shield between the working man and the union

officials who seek to force him to join a union or pay tribute as the price of keeping his job. We can only wait in anticipation of that bright Monday morning when the Supreme Court will at last announce the restoration of this important principle of civil rights which has been so long and so sadly ignored."

3. Louella Carver Dirksen, *His Finest Hours,* p. 197.
4. *U.S. News & World Report,* Nov 21, 1966.

CHAPTER FOUR

GOING POSTAL—DEFENDING GOVERNMENT EMPLOYEES FROM FORCED UNIONISM

T he labor union movement originally was aimed exclusively at workers in the private sector—plumbers, auto workers, longshoremen, and so on. Neither the American Federation of Labor nor the Congress of Industrial Organizations gave any thought to trying to extend their reach into *government* employment. As late as 1959, the president of the combined AFL-CIO, George Meany, said, "it is impossible to bargain collectively with the government."

That attitude changed abruptly in the 1960s. Big Labor's top brass realized that they were overlooking a gold mine of workers who might become union dues payers. Predictably, they were not content to rely on persuasion to get more workers to join voluntarily. They turned to their favorite political tactics in an effort to force government workers into union ranks, just as they had with millions of private sector workers. And when they did so, they aroused the National Right to Work Committee. Protecting workers against compulsory unionism in government employment is every bit as important as protecting workers against it in the private sector. In this chapter, we will look first at the fight over "reform" of the Post Office in 1969 and 1970, and then at the continuing battle against efforts by labor union officials to force their representation on unwilling government employees—while making them pay for it.

THE NIXON ADMINISTRATION AND POSTAL REFORM

If people thought that the election of Richard Nixon to the presidency in 1968 meant the National Right to Work Committee wouldn't have to devote its time and resources to fending off Big Labor's onslaughts and could concentrate on expanding worker freedom, they were soon proven wrong. Right at its beginning, the Nixon Administration began pushing for changes in the U.S. Post Office. Improvements in the postal service were no doubt needed, but to get them the government was willing to permit compulsory unionism for tens of thousands of workers who had chosen to remain free of union control.

The inefficiency of the Post Office was legendary. Throughout most of its history, the Post Office had been a money-losing operation, with annual operating deficits often reaching 20 percent, which Congress then had to make up out of tax revenues.[1] Union-negotiated work rules prevented efficient use of labor. Under President Johnson, the Commission on Postal Organization (named the Kappel Commission after its leader Frederick R. Kappel) had studied the Post Office and concluded that it was "not capable of meeting the demands of our growing economy and expanding population." The Kappel Commission recommended that the Post Office be restructured as a self-supporting government corporation.

Upon assuming the position of Postmaster General under President Nixon, Winton Blount had gone to work on a package of reforms that embraced the recommendations of the Kappel Commission, transforming the Post Office into the United States Postal Service and allowing for the privatization of some aspects of postal operations. If that had been all that was involved, the Committee would have had no interest except to applaud any increase in postal efficiency. But that was not all that was involved. In order to make the baby steps toward privatization in the plan acceptable to Big Labor chieftains—(especially AFL-CIO head George Meany and the president of the National Association of Letter Carriers, James Rademacher)—Blount had agreed to give them something they craved—compulsory unionism for postal employees and a foothold to install compulsory unionism throughout the federal government. The Post Office was the largest civilian employer in the United States, with some 750,000 workers. Of them, about 20 percent had chosen not to join a union, a right that was protected under Executive Order 10988 issued by President Kennedy in 1962[2] and had been reiterated by

President Nixon's Executive Order 11491 just months earlier in 1969. Meany and Rademacher were drooling over the prospect of collecting union dues from the 150,000 postal employees who had declined to associate with them—an annual windfall of some $6 million. Baby steps toward privatization in return for a giant step for union coercion? The labor bosses liked the deal.

NO HIDING THE UGLY TRUTH

Blount initially tried to hide the fact that his reform package contained this capitulation to Big Labor. When he testified before the House Post Office and Civil Service commission, he stated, "We do not propose a union shop under our reform legislation." Blount, however, was being disingenuous in uttering those reassuring words. When the details of the legislation—H.R. 11750 sponsored by Representative Thaddeus Dulski of New York—became public, it was evident that while Blount was correct in saying that his reorganization plan did not directly impose a union shop on postal workers, it would have cleared the way for its early imposition on the entire postal system. The executive orders protecting workers against forced unionism would be scrapped, and Meany and Rademacher knew that it wouldn't be long before the managers of the quasi-private postal corporation caved in to their pressure for compulsory unionism for all postal employees.

Post Office officials tried putting up a verbal smokescreen with a vague and confusing letter saying that just because the plan made compulsory unionism *possible* among postal workers, that didn't mean it would necessarily be put into effect. The National Right to Work Committee, however, was not confused or pacified by those verbal gymnastics and immediately swung into action. On July 9, Reed Larson wrote to Blount, criticizing his willingness to make postal employees choose between supporting a union and losing their jobs. Two days later, the Committee fired off a letter to President Nixon, urging him not to issue an Executive Order that would allow the firing of federal employees on the grounds that they refused to support a union. In its July 24 newsletter, the

Committee raised the alarm to its membership about the looming threat to worker freedom of choice. The fight was on.

One of the sad facts about Congress is that so many bills, of such length and complexity are introduced that legislators do not have time to read them. That had been the case with H.R. 11750. Accepting at face value the assurances from the supposedly friendly Nixon Administration that the bill did not impose a union shop, many Right to Work backers in the House had signed on as co-sponsors of the bill. Once the Committee pointed out that the bill carried the seeds of compulsory unionism, however, they quickly dropped their sponsorship. Still, there was abundant support from Big Labor's numerous House allies and the Nixon administration continued to push the plan. This was despite the fact that the 1968 Republican platform stated, "We pledge to protect federal employees in the exercise of their right, freely and without fear of penalty or reprisal, to form, join or assist any employee organization or to refrain from any such activities." In its newsletter dated September 25, 1969, the Committee asked pointedly, "Mr. Nixon, do you recall this pledge?"

In November, Secretary of Labor George Schultz weighed in on the Right to Work side, saying that "A person should not have to be a member of any organization to be able to work for the government." Unfortunately, he was only speaking for himself. The Nixon Administration remained committed to postal reform, and Blount was unshakable in his convictions that: 1) his reforms would be blocked by Big Labor lobbying unless he gave them the union compulsory shop, and 2) his reforms were so beneficial that it was worth setting a precedent for the eventual forced unionization of millions of government employees, in the postal service and elsewhere. Reed Larson and his team at the Committee remained equally unshakable in their conviction that this was a deal with the devil. It had to be stopped.

By the winter of 1970, Nixon and Blount realized that opposition was mounting to the original postal reform bill, so they got behind a new bill, H.R. 15430, introduced by Representative Glenn Cunningham, a Nebraska Republican. The bill was quickly analyzed at the Committee, and it was apparent that it was a case of merely rearranging the deck chairs on the Titanic. Try as it might, the Administration could not hide the stench of compulsory unionism in its proposal. Agreeing with the Committee that the new bill was just as unacceptable as the old, Representative H.R. Gross of Iowa, a legendary watchdog for imprudent legislation, wrote to the Committee, saying, "As a long-time foe of compulsory unionism, I scarcely need to tell you that I share your opposition to H.R. 15430, H.R. 11750, or any other legislative proposal which might force all postal employees to join a union."

The Committee's efforts at arousing opinion against Big Labor's attempt to dragoon unwilling postal workers into their ranks was paying off, just as it did in the 1965 battle against repeal of Section 14(b). Nationally syndicated columnist James J. Kilpatrick wrote, "Whatever Congress does in this regard will provide a precedent, of sorts, for teachers, trash collectors, police, firemen, nurses and countless other public employees. Here, at least, in public employment, the Right to Work has to be preserved absolutely; it can't be put on the table as an issue to be bargained away." In the nation's newspapers, editorials and cartoons were stressing the importance of keeping compulsory unionism out of government employment. Pressure against this disastrous deal was building up fast.

The Committee's work in defeating the postal reorganization bill was complicated, however, by the fact that the bill enjoyed the support of several very influential business groups in Washington, most prominently the U.S. Chamber of Commerce. The Chamber, under the leadership of Arch Booth, was a respected and influential advocate for the business viewpoint. Pro-business members of Congress kept responding to the Committee's arguments against the bill by saying that it couldn't really be so bad because the Chamber was supporting it. Reed Larson realized that unless the Chamber's position could be swung to opposition, the chances of keeping compulsory unionism out of the federal government were dim. So long as this major business organization supported the "reform" bill, there was no chance of mobilizing the opposition needed to stop it.

Larson knew from years of watching the Chamber that the Washington office would speak for the entire membership on issues where the interests of the business community were not in doubt. But on controversial matters, the national organization would poll its local chambers, which numbered some 3,500 in 1969. In order to confirm the position that the national leadership wanted to take in support of Blount (who had been Chamber president just two years earlier), Booth framed the issue in such a benign manner that local support was a foregone conclusion. Consequently, local chambers began to register their support for the bill.

According to the Chamber's bylaws, however, the polling had to take place over a 30-day period, and a local chamber could change its vote up to the last minute. So the Committee launched a counterattack, obtaining a list of local chamber members and sending them a letter to explain the true nature of the bill and its dangerous consequences. The letter was signed by W.B. Camp, a former treasurer of the U.S. Chamber who had served as chairman of its Right to Work subcommittee until it was abolished. When they read the letter, many Chamber members were shocked at the Administration's sell-out and the Chamber's willingness to help push it through. Many local chambers changed their vote on the postal reorganization bill, with some also expressing their dissatisfaction with the national leadership and threatening to withdraw membership in the U.S. Chamber.

To increase the pressure, the Committee also sent a letter to its own membership, which began with this attention-grabbing sentence: "Guess who George Meany just enlisted as a national ally. The U.S. Chamber of Commerce!" Many of the recipients of the letter were also members of the Chamber, and they added their voices to the swelling chorus of protest.

A staff member of the U.S. Chamber's office in Washington who was friendly to the Committee reported that at a staff meeting soon after the mailing went out, Arch Booth stomped into the meeting brandishing a thick sheaf of papers.

"You know what these are?" he asked.

No one spoke.

"These are resignations from the Chamber of Commerce! All the result of a mailing from the National Right to Work Committee. Why can't you people write letters like Reed Larson?"

Booth was shaken. What had seemed like a minor concession that would attract little attention had suddenly turned into a very divisive issue that would cost the Chamber a significant amount of support. And in the last ten days of the 30-day polling period, there was a flood of letters and telegrams into the national office, changing previous "yes" votes and expressing strong opposition to the postal reorganization bill as long as its language opened the door to compulsory unionism. Despite his longtime friendship with Blount, Booth had no choice but to bow to the will of his membership and announce that the Chamber had changed its position and would oppose the bill in its current form.

After turning around the U.S. Chamber, the Committee found it less difficult to sway other business groups in Washington, most of which had followed the Chamber's lead in endorsing the postal "reform" bill. With support from the business lobby evaporating, many members of Congress finally began listening to the arguments against it.

Lastly, the Committee contacted a list of 25,000 big contributors to Republican candidates—the people who would be crucial to the financing of re-election campaigns in 1970. The letter, signed by Representative Ben Blackburn of Georgia, pointed out that the Nixon/Blount plan would have a negative impact on the Republican Party. By paving the way for compulsory unionism in the postal service, the plan would bring millions of dollars of new money into Big Labor's coffers, money that would of course be used to defeat Republican candidates. When those big donors called their Senators and Representatives to protest the reorganization bill, their pleas could hardly be ignored.

THE POSTAL STRIKE

Despite the fact that Postmaster Blount's postal reform measures had been blessed by AFL-CIO president George Meany ("a new benchmark in labor relations," he had ominously described them), many local postal unions were horrified that the proposed reorganization would mean losing their comfortable status in a government monopoly. Anger among militant unionists had been boiling for months when, on March 17, 1970, it erupted into an illegal strike, the first ever against the federal government. The 2,500 members of Letter Carriers Branch 36, covering Manhattan and the Bronx, voted to strike that day by a margin of three to two.

Once the walkout began in New York, it quickly spread throughout the nation. By March 21, fully a third of the nation's postal workers were on strike. Nine of the ten largest post offices were shut down. "The impact was immediate and crushing; huge parts of the business sector ground to a halt," writes Murray Comarow, who had served both on the Kappel Commission and in the Nixon Administration.[3] The strike was illegal and government lawyers quickly sought and obtained injunctions against it, but court orders proved to be useless. Union bosses, who never seem to have trouble exerting discipline over workers who want to work during a strike, could not exert any discipline over local unions that went on strike when they were supposed to be working. President Nixon declared a national emergency on March 23 and announced that he would call up the National Guard to get the mail moving again. Two days later, the militants in New York called off the strike and it quickly collapsed around the nation.

Far from aiding their cause, the strike hardened opinion across the U.S. that Big Labor must not be allowed to have its way. Editorials and cartoons in newspapers large and small criticized the strike and the idea that compulsory unionism should be an ingredient in postal reform. As always, the Committee made sure that the members of Congress knew how unpopular compulsory unionism was with the American people.

REPRESENTATIVE HENDERSON STEPS IN

All the while, the Committee had been working hard to build congressional opposition to the Nixon/Blount plan. It found a friend in Representative David Henderson, a Democrat from eastern North Carolina who had represented its Third District since 1961. Henderson was the second-ranking member of the House Committee on Post Office and the Civil Service and an opponent of compulsory unionism. North Carolina was a Right to Work state and protecting against compulsory unionism was a much higher priority with many of his constituents than was a dubious improvement in postal service. Henderson could see that Blount's reorganization plan would almost inevitably lead to a union shop for the new postal service, which would quickly lead to the spread of forced unionism in federal employment. He decided to prevent that from happening.

In June 1970, Henderson and the ranking Republican on the Committee, H.R. Gross, led a bipartisan coalition in adding an amendment to H.R. 17070 to guarantee that postal workers would not be subject to a union shop under the new organization. Immediately, Postmaster Blount and Big Labor declared that the amendment was unacceptable. It would sink the carefully crafted deal they had put together. The Henderson amendment had to be stricken from the bill or postal reorganization would become impossible—or so they said.

But when the House voted on the bill on June 17, it voted by a lopsided margin in favor of the Henderson/Gross Right to Work amendment. No doubt, the memory of the 1966 elections was in the minds of many members who did not want to run for re-election that fall with the millstone of a vote in favor of forcing unionization on postal workers around their necks. On the House floor, Representative Henderson said that without his amendment, the bill "would result in a situation where a federal civil service employee has to join or pay dues to a union or lose his job. This is absolutely and completely contrary to the concept of freedom to choose which all federal employees have historically enjoyed." He concluded his remarks by saying, "I can see absolutely no justification for including compulsory unionism in the package." The amended bill passed the House the next day with the overwhelming margin of 359 to 24.

Speaking for the Committee, Reed Larson said, "Congressmen David Henderson and H.R. Gross deserve the highest praise from American citizens who believe in freedom of choice. These distinguished Congressmen provided the key leadership in corralling the resounding vote against compulsory unionism." They did deserve Larson's praise, but if it hadn't been for the intervention of the Committee in the early stages of the postal reform debate, the legislation would have sneaked through with the ticking time bomb of union shop negotiability in it. As the nationally syndicated columnist Ralph de Toledano wrote on July 24, 1970, "On Capitol Hill, members of the House and Senate knew that it had been the Right to Work Committee's David who had brought down the AFL-CIO and the Administration Goliath."

Passage of the House bill with the Right to Work amendment did not end the matter, however. The Senate passed its version of postal reform that contained the Administration's language inviting Big Labor to bargain over the union shop. Whenever the House and the Senate pass bills that contain different language, a conference committee must then be convened to work out the differences. The House then voted 225 to 159 to instruct its conferees that the Right to Work provision *must* be included in the final bill.

In the conference committee, the House stood its ground. The Senate conferees agreed to keep Representative Henderson's Right to Work amendment. The legislation received final passage in both chambers and President Nixon signed the postal reforms into law on August 12. The nation got postal reform without surrendering the rights of 150,000 postal workers to remain independent of Meany and Rademacher and without opening the floodgates to compulsory unionism in federal employment.

The vision of Postmaster Blount, President Nixon, and others that the Post Office caterpillar would be transformed into the United States Postal Service butterfly was never realized. Three decades later, postal service remains inefficient and mailing costs escalate faster than the rate of inflation.[4] At least, however, Congress held the line against compulsory unionism. As labor law expert D. Richard Froelke writes, "By banning compulsory unionism in the Postal Service ... Congress clearly advanced the principle of 'individual liberty.'"[5]

BIG LABOR'S CONTINUING QUEST FOR FORCED UNIONISM AMONG GOVERNMENT EMPLOYEES

The percentage of the American private-sector labor force that is represented by a labor union has been steadily falling for decades. From its peak in 1953 of 36 percent, it has declined to just 9 percent today.[6] Aware that this decline belies its claim that unionism is so beneficial and popular with workers, the AFL-CIO began a much-publicized campaign in 1995 to increase union organizing. That campaign failed to arrest the slippage in Big Labor's "market share," however.

The reason for the declining fortunes of unionism in the private-sector stems largely from the fact that you can't avoid competition there. Competition always tends to drive down prices that are too high, whether it's the price of a consumer product or the price of labor. That fact has had a tremendous impact on private-sector labor unions. The United Steelworkers Union, for example, used to be one of the nation's largest and most powerful, negotiating very hefty compensation packages for its members in the 1950s, 1960s, and 1970s. But competition for the steel-producing giants eventually arose from foreign sources, and from American "mini-mills" that were much more efficient than the huge steel mills where the USW compelled union membership and whose work rules hamstrung productive efficiency. Those huge mills could not meet the competition, in part because of production inefficiency resulting in high labor costs—56 percent higher than the average compensation for man ufacturing businesses.[7] Now most are shut down and membership in the USW has plunged from a high of over one million workers in 1975 to just 445,000 in 2001. That is why union bosses don't like competition. To the extent that they are able to drive compensation for workers above market levels, they create the opportunity for other producers to enter the market who are not saddled with inefficient work rules and the resulting high labor costs. Those competitors then start taking business away from the unionized firms. The inescapable force of competition in the private sector makes Big Labor's hold there insecure.

In contrast, unionism in the *public sector* avoids the "problem" of competition. Government employees usually perform functions that are exclusive to government, such as fire protection. But even when there are private sector alternatives—as, for example in the delivery of packages—the ability of government to cover its higher costs out of tax revenues means that the existence of competition is not a direct threat to the union bosses. Unlike the steel mills that went out of business, local, state, and federal operations manned with unionized workers will continue on unless and until voters pressure politicians to economize by contracting out or privatizing the service. Naturally, union bosses fiercely resist all moves in that direction. It is much easier for them to stop competition in government employment than it is for them to stop it in the private sector.

Because government employment is so much less subject to the pressure of competition, Big Labor has devoted much of its effort over the last three decades to picking the low-hanging fruit of federal, state, and local government workers. As Ralph de Toledano writes, "Big Labor realized that it could extend its hold only by the direct intercession of government, as it had since its initial expansion in the days of the New Deal. The logical direction, therefore, was the government itself, which the political power of the AFL-CIO could threaten via its captive senators and representatives. Government, whether federal, state, or local, controlled one-sixth of the nation's jobs."[8] Therefore, Big Labor strives incessantly to expand government. Virtually every bill that creates new government offices and programs receives its lobbying support. A growing governmental workforce, in turn, means for union officials a growing roster of dues-payers. And more dues money supports further lobbying for the expansion of government—a vicious cycle as far as taxpayers are concerned. As Max Green states in his book *Epitaph for American Labor*, "America's public-employee unions do more than flex political muscle for self-interested reasons; they present an objective intellectual case for increasing government spending. The Public Employee Department (PED) of the AFL-CIO, to which all unions that represent public employees belong, argues, for instance, that 'private investment cannot take place without public investment leading the way.' ... In line with this thinking, the PED holds that there can hardly be too much government spending."[9]

A recent example of union pressure for more public-sector employment and unionization is seen in the battle over airport security in 2001–02. The failure of privately-employed airport security personnel on September 11, 2001, to detect box cutters the hijackers managed to sneak aboard the four airplanes, was used as leverage by Big Labor and its congressional allies to demand that airport security be taken over by the federal government, naturally employing workers who might become union members. Even though there is no reason to believe that government employees are any less mistake-prone than are private employees (indeed, because it is so notoriously difficult to fire government employees, they have less incentive to be diligent on the job than do employees of private companies), backers airport security federalization prevailed. Georgia's Democratic Senator Zell Miller writes of that battle, "With the nation looking to us to beef up national security, Senate Democrats fought tooth and nail to block the new department solely to appease the federal employees union, which was ranting and raving and foaming at the mouth about job protection."[10] The deal that was eventually struck between the Bush Administration and Big Labor's allies in Congress did not allow for collective bargaining, but the labor bosses are content to wait for the time when they will be able to get that. Security still leaks like a sieve, as was demonstrated in October 2003 when a college student smuggled box cutters aboard a plane to show how poor the system is. Nevertheless, Big Labor got what it wanted—more workers employed by the government.

The National Right to Work Committee has never been opposed in principle to unions among government employees, so long as it is entirely voluntary. On many occasions, however, it has had to fight against attempts by Big Labor to force union membership or representation on workers who don't want any part of it. Since defeating the attempt to impose the union shop on postal workers in 1970, the Committee has repeatedly beaten back similar gambits in Congress that would deliver government employees into the clutches of the union bosses.

BIG LABOR GOES AFTER GOVERNMENT EMPLOYEES

In 1973, one of Big Labor's most dependable politicians, Representative William Clay of Missouri, introduced a bill entitled the "National Public Employment Relations Act." In a brazen affront to our system of -

federalism under the Constitution, Clay's bill (H.R. 8677) would have dictated to the states the details of their relations with employees, just as the NLRA dictates to private employers the details of their employment relationships. We have seen that the NLRA was an intrusion into the sphere of private decision-making that could be held constitutional only by a misreading of the Commerce Clause. Representative Clay's "National Public Employment Relations Act" would have been even more of a root and branch attack on the Constitution, for it would have destroyed the idea of state sovereignty. The Tenth Amendment plainly reads, "The powers not delegated to the United States by the Constitution, nor prohibited by it to the States, are reserved to the States respectively, or to the people." Clay and his friends in the councils of the public employee unions—especially the militant American Federation of State, County, and Municipal Employees—hoped to pass the bill and then benefit from a tortured, politically expedient decision by the Supreme Court such as they had gotten from the Court in *Jones & Laughlin Steel* and other cases. The labor chieftains would use their loyal troops in Congress to get the bill passed and their slick lawyers to glide it past the Supreme Court. The result: a vast expansion in the number of forced-dues payers. That was their plan, at least.

The preamble to the Clay bill cleverly made repeated reference to the alleged need for "amicable settlement of disputes." In truth, prior to President Kennedy's Executive Order 10988—which, although prohibiting compulsory unionism in federal employment, greatly encouraged the formation of unions of government workers—there had been very few disputes with government employees. At the federal, state, and local levels, most jobs had been covered by civil service rules and the employees were quite content to work under them. The "disputes" that the bill meant to "amicably settle" were almost wholly the result of illegal strikes by government employee unions, such as those that rocked New York City in the late 1960s. Using illegal and indeed life-threatening actions by union bosses as the pretext for legislation that would vastly increase their power showed stupendous arrogance, but that is nothing new where Big Labor is concerned.

Clay's bill was written to give state and local government employee unions all the leverage they needed to force themselves upon workers whether they desired union affiliation or not. (A similar bill would have put federal employees under the same kind of regime, designed to make unionization swift and sure.) Unlike the NLRA, which at least pays slight lip service to the right of workers to desist from unionization, this legislation would have only recognized the "right" to unionize, no matter what state or local law might say to the contrary, with no recognition of any corollary right to remain independent of unions. Moreover, the bill would have established a regulatory agency called the National Public Employment Relations Commission (NPERC) and given it sweeping, open-ended authority. Big Labor expected to dominate the Commission, just as it has for the most part dominated the NLRB, and use its authority to push its agenda.

One way that it would do so would be in deciding when to impose unionization. Under the bill, a union would not even have to win an election in order to be certified as exclusive bargaining representative. All that would have been necessary was an allegation backed by "credible evidence" that a majority of workers desired to be represented by a union. Compliant personnel at NPERC could simply have taken the word of a union organizer that a majority of workers wanted his union. And once a union had been declared, the government would be obligated to deduct from employees' paychecks the dues and fees that the union brass demanded as the price for their "services." If enacted, the Clay bill would have made it as easy as pie for government employee unions to rope vast numbers of workers into their domain without the least concern for their individual desires.

The Committee took H.R. 8677 as a very serious threat to not only the liberty of millions of state and local workers across America, but also to the very nature of our system of government. If it became law, state and local government would no longer have been independent of federal control and able to serve as "laboratories of democracy" as James Madison put it. In fact, they would have been under the heels of union officials, since the Clay bill created an *unlimited* scope for collective bargaining. State and local officials would have had to bargain with militant union leaders over practically every aspect of government. Like children on Christmas Eve, the union bosses' heads danced with visions of the new powers they would have and new dues-payers they would corral if they could ram the bill through.

The Clay bill put the National Right to Work Committee on a war footing. The alert went out to members to write their representatives and senators, urging opposition to the bill. When it came up for a hearing on October 11, 1973, Reed Larson testified, "If the union bosses get their way, our government services will be controlled, and we do mean controlled, by the same people who are demonstrating so clearly in Michigan their public spiritedness and dedication to the public." He was referring to the widespread teacher strikes in early 1973 in Michigan, in which more than 650,000 children were kept out of school due to strikes. Those strikes were over the "non-negotiable" demands of the Michigan Education Association that all teachers be compelled to pay agency shop fees to the union as a condition of holding a job.

Big Labor did not get its wish in 1973. Thanks in large measure to the Committee's spotlighting it, Clay's bill didn't even get through the House. But the union bosses are nothing if not persistent when it comes to their demand that all workers must pay them money. After the 1974 elections, which in the wake of the Watergate scandal had brought many new pro-union Democrats into Congress, the labor barons lit their cigars and prepared for a new assault on the freedom of America's public employees. President Gerald Ford, who had succeeded to the White House following Richard Nixon's resignation, was not thought to be sympathetic to compulsory unionism, but the union bosses know that bills can be passed over a presidential veto. Taft-Hartley and Section 14(b), after all, became law when Congress mustered the two-thirds vote needed to override President Truman's veto. Union-backed politicians dominated in the House and Senate. Maybe the 94th Congress would be able to reprise the 80th, but in reverse.

Believing that it would, Ralph Flynn, spokesman for the union lobbying group Coalition of American Public Employees told *Time* magazine that passage of Big Labor's cherished public employee unionization legislation was "certain" in 1975.[11] To put added pressure on Congress to give in to their demands, the militant heads of government employee unions promised more strikes against the public service. Knowing that the upcoming year would be one of grave danger, Reed Larson told Committee supporters in January, "We have more than two-thirds of the American people on our side, but union lobbyists have a shockingly high number of Congressmen under their thumbs. We CAN win, but it will require a massive effort."

1975: THE UNIONS TAKE THEIR SHOT

On more than one occasion, Big Labor has proven to be its own worst enemy. Public employee unions *did* engage in numerous strikes in 1975. In cities large and small, from New York to California, fires went unfought, garbage went uncollected, and students went without teachers. But just as German bombing of England in 1940 hardened the resolve of the British people not to give in, so did those strikes harden the resolve of the American people that the labor oligarchs should not have their way. Even liberal newspapers editorialized that it was a bad idea to give the union officials the power they craved. On August 23, 1975, for example, the *New York Times* criticized San Francisco Mayor Joseph Alioto for surrendering to union demands, writing that he "reinforced the conviction that unions in control of vital public services can compel the community to capitulate by holding a strike gun to its head." The Times called the trend "a death knell for democracy."[12] And on September 7, *The Boston Globe* acknowledged a growing consensus among liberals and conservatives that public employee unionization had gone far enough. Liberals, said the *Globe,* were having "second thoughts about some major trends in public hiring and management—the introduction of collective bargaining and, in some cases, binding arbitration, in addition to the job advantages already conferred by Civil Service."[13] The Committee put such editorials to good use in its campaign to arouse the public against Big Labor's legislative offensive, just as it had done a decade earlier when Section 14(b) had been spared from the chopping block.

Most of Big Labor's politicians shrank back into silence as public outrage over strikes against the citizenry multiplied. The opponents of compulsory unionism, on the other hand, had a field day. Representative Ed Derwinski of Illinois said in the Congressional Record, "Bad as this compulsion is in the private sector, it seems to me that the extension of compulsory collective bargaining laws to the public sector is inconceivable. It would not only be violently incompatible with a sovereign, responsible government, but would be incompatible with everything this country stands for."[14] Representative Charles Grassley of Iowa observed, "No other organization in American society seeks the extraordinary, special privileges that labor unions seek through the coercive powers of the union shop and captive membership. If allowed to grow unchecked, these special privileges will turn America—the land of the free—into America—the land of the fee."[15]

On June 24, Right to Work forces received a tremendous piece of news. The Supreme Court handed down its much-anticipated decision in the case *National League of Cities v. Usery*. In 1974, Congress had extended the coverage of the Fair Labor Standards Act, which regulates many aspects of employment such as minimum wages and overtime pay, to state and local government workers. The National League of Cities immediately brought a test case, arguing that under the Constitution, Congress had no authority to control the employment policies of state and local governments. Big Labor knew that much was at stake in the case, since a ruling in favor of the National League of Cities would throw a very large wrench in the gears of its plan to take over millions of workers at one fell swoop. If the Court held that Congress could not force states and localities to abide by the Fair Labor Standards Act, it probably could not shove compulsory collective bargaining down their throats either. Therefore, top lawyers for Big Labor weighed in on the case with *amicus curiae* (friend of the court) briefs intended to persuade the justices that the Constitution's division of powers between the levels of government nevertheless allowed the feds to tell state and local governments how to pay their workers. Several attorneys general from states dominated by Big Labor, such as Michigan's Frank Kelly, also tried to get the Court to give them a friendly "interpretation" of the meaning of federalism. On the other side, the redoubtable Professor Sylvester Petro

submitted an *amicus* brief arguing that it would be constitutional van-
dalism to allow Congress to tread upon the prerogatives of state and local
government.

The Court's opinion, written by Justice Rehnquist, was a severe setback for the union bosses. It held, 5 to 4, that the authority of Congress
did not extend to controlling the employment policies of state and local
governments. Rehnquist wrote that Congress could not "force directly
upon the states its choices as to how essential decisions regarding the
conduct of integral governmental functions are to be made."[16] That holding would surely doom the Clay bill or anything like it that Congress
might pass. Big Labor's chieftains denounced the decision. But it was
clear that at least until they could replace one of the five constitutional-
ists on the Court with a justice who would render more "politically correct" decisions, their dream of imposing compulsory unionism on state
and local workers through puppets in the U.S. Congress was dead.

Union militants had badly overplayed their hand, and the Supreme
Court had slammed the door shut on attempts by Congress to dictate
how state and local governments must deal with their employees. Nevertheless, Representative Frank Thompson decided to hold hearings on
a package of bills that Big Labor's chieftains wanted. One was his own
H.R. 77 (by coincidence bearing the same bill number as his ill-fated bill
to repeal Section 14(b) in 1965), which was essentially the Clay bill, speed-
ing along forced unionism for millions of state and local government
workers. There were other bills that the union bosses wanted, including
repeal of the Right to Work provision of the 1970 Postal Reorganization
Act, and a bill that would have allowed for the forced unionization of
the federal government's civilian workforce. In the early November hearings, Reed Larson testified against the bills for the Committee, pointing
out that the Supreme Court's decision in *National League of Cities* meant
that H.R. 77 would be a patently unconstitutional intrusion into the
sovereignty of state and local governments. As for the other bills, he
observed that they deprived federal workers of long-standing rights to
choose whether to join a union or not, rights that the great majority of
the American people thought they should retain.

That package of bills was stopped dead, never coming even to a vote in the House. Freedom for government workers to say "No" to forced unionism was thus preserved—for the time being.

ETERNAL VIGILANCE IS THE PRICE OF FREEDOM

Thomas Jefferson said that eternal vigilance is the price of freedom. The ongoing struggle between Big Labor to extend compulsory unionism to government employees and the Committee's efforts to prevent that from happening underscores the truth of Jefferson's saying. The labor bosses shrugged off their setbacks in the mid-1970s and have mounted periodic attacks against freedom of choice for public employees since then. Each time, the Committee has alertly foiled them.

In 1997, for example, a coalition of 165 Republicans and Democrats in the House signed on to H.R. 1173, a bill to make union representation mandatory for fire fighters and policemen across the nation. The bill would not only have deprived workers of their freedom to decline to participate in labor unions, but would have also saddled state and local taxpayers with hundreds of millions of dollars in additional costs each year due to its mandate of monopoly bargaining. Furthermore, the likelihood of strikes by these guardians of the public safety would have been greatly increased. That has been the experience in states and localities that have already caved into the demands of labor bosses for monopoly bargaining—even though police and firefighter strikes are still illegal, they frequently occur anyway once militant public employee unions enter the picture. After calling an illegal strike, union officials usually demand an amnesty for themselves and the strikers in the negotiations to end the strike, and the public authorities, eager to get things back to normal, usually give in. H.R. 1173 would have extended the folly of some states and localities by making it a national requirement. Forcing all governments to copy the mistakes of a few is hardly what federalism is about, but Big Labor has never cared about that.

The Committee jumped on H.R. 1173 right away, reminding members of Congress and Right to Work supporters of the disastrous consequences of monopoly bargaining in the past. Two such examples were the 1974 Baltimore police strike with its widespread looting and violence, and the 1975 Kansas City fire fighter strike, during which union militants actually prevented firemen who remained on duty from being able to fight fires. President Clinton would have gladly signed the bill as a favor to his Big Labor supporters, but H.R. 1173 could not withstand the scrutiny and history lessons that the Committee provided. The bill never made it out of committee.

Big Labor just won't take "no" for an answer, either from individual workers or from the U.S. Congress. In 2000, the monopoly bargaining bill returned, this time labeled H.R. 1093. The bill, co-sponsored by Representatives Bob Ney (R-Ohio) and Dale Kildee (D-Michigan) gathered 247 backers in the House—more than enough to pass it if the bill could be brought to a floor vote. Representative Ney disingenuously explained that the bill would merely extend "collective bargaining privilege for union officials who aren't currently so empowered under federal labor law." The problem, of course, is that the federal government has no moral or constitutional authority to "empower" union officials by overriding the desires of citizens of states and localities for public safety personnel who owe their allegiance to the people, rather than to union bosses.

Furthermore, passage of H.R. 1093 would have undermined state Right to Work laws by taking police and fire fighters out from their protection. The bill gave the Federal Labor Relations Authority, a constitutionally dubious entity created by an executive order issued by President Carter in 1979, power to "establish collective bargaining procedures for public safety employers and employees in States that do not substantially provide for such public safety rights and responsibilities." Big Labor knew that sooner or later, the "procedures" dictated by their allies in the bureaucracy would give them monopoly bargaining "rights" over individuals who preferred not to pay unions for the privilege of keeping their jobs.

Finally, enactment of H.R. 1093 (the so-called "Public Safety Employer-Employee Cooperation Act") would have been a disaster for small towns that rely upon volunteer fire fighters. Under the authoritarian rules of the International Association of Fire Fighters (IAFF), members are not permitted to do any volunteer service. Passage of the bill therefore would have meant that localities that had relied upon volunteer fire departments would have to switch to the IAFF brand, at a substantially higher cost. It was the same old story: Union bosses wanting to gain power and money at the expense of worker freedom and the taxpayers' wallets.

With its combined Republican and Democratic backing, H.R. 1093 looked as though it had a good chance of passing the House. It might have been stopped in the Senate, but the Committee takes no chances. It put out the alert to its members that they should notify House Speaker Hastert and House Majority Leader Armey that they opposed this attack on Right to Work protection for public safety employees. The Committee also launched a media blitz in key states to let the public know that if the bill became law, they could be facing the menace of monopoly bargaining with militant union bosses who had in the past engaged in many illegal strikes. That timely intervention stiffened the backbone of the House leadership—the bill was stopped cold without a vote in the House Education and Labor Committee.

Then, in 2001, the Ney-Kildee bill came back, like a sequel to the sequel of a bad horror movie. Just two days after the September 11 terrorist attacks on America, union lobbyists convinced Senators Ted Kennedy and Hillary Clinton to ram the bill through a closed-door Senate hearing without any testimony. Once the bill was through committee, Senate Majority Leader Tom Daschle (from the Right to Work state of South Dakota) tried to sneak the bill through the Senate without a recorded vote. Thwarted in that attempt, Daschle, who had given his commitment to the head of the IAFF that he would get the bill passed, tried a little Halloween trick. On October 31 he attached it as an amendment to a massive appropriations bill for the Departments of Labor, Health and Human Services, and Education. It is not uncommon for members of Congress to sneak through bills that would not pass on their own merits by hitching a ride on other legislation and Daschle thought he could pull it off. And it might have worked had it not been for the vigilance and swift action of the Committee.

Working with Senator Don Nickles, a forced-unionism opponent from Oklahoma, the Committee organized opposition to Daschle's amendment, threatening a filibuster until the amendment was removed. Daschle counted noses and found that he only had 56 senators with him—four short of the 60 needed to stop a filibuster. His little trick yielded no treat for the union bosses.

Public employees of all kinds will remain the top target for Big Labor. Currently, 33 states have Right to Work protections for public employees and the union bosses would dearly love to extinguish those laws at one fell swoop in Congress. Up to the time of this writing, the Committee has succeeded in blocking all such power grabs, and will continue to be the vigilant sentry on guard against future attempts to impose compulsory unionism on federal, state, and local employees.

NOTES

1. Murray Comarow, "The Demise of the Postal Service," available online: www.cosmos-club.org/journals/2002/comarow.html.
2. Although Executive Order 10988 stated that federal employees would not be compelled to join a union, it was meant to give a strong boost to government employee unions by establishing procedures like those of the NLRA, whereby if a majority votes in favor of a union, it becomes the exclusive representative of all.
3. Ibid.
4. See Douglas K. Adie, *Monopoly Mail* (Transaction Publishers, 1989). Professor Adie writes, "Since reorganization, the postal managers have been no more successful in negotiating changes in inefficient work rules and the introduction of labor-saving innovations than before reorganization." p. 10.
5. D. Richard Froelke, "Labor Market Outcomes of Postal Reorganization," in *Mail @ the Millenium,* ed. by Edward L. Hudgins (Cato Institute, 2000) p. 79.
6. Leo Troy, *Beyond Unions and Collective Bargaining* (M. E. Sharpe, 1999) pp. 9–10.

7. Aaron Schavey, "The Ailing Steel Industry Needs Less Government Intervention, Not More," *Heritage Backgrounder* #1519, February 22, 2002.

8. Ralph de Toledano, *Let Our Cities Burn,* (Arlington House, 1975), p. 36.

9. Max Green, *Epitaph for American Labor,* AEI Press, 1996, p. 37.

10. Zell Miller, *A National Party No More,* Stroud & Hall, 2003, p. 194.

11. *Time* magazine, December 16, 1974, p. 31.

12. "Frisco Follies," *New York Times,* August 23, 1975.

13. *The Boston Globe,* September 7, 1975.

14. *Congressional Record,* July 17, 1975.

15. Ibid.

16. *National League of Cities v. Usery,* 426 U.S. 833 (1976).

CHAPTER FIVE

THE BRAWL OVER "COMMON SITUS" PICKETING

I n the preceding chapter, we saw that in 1975 Big Labor failed to achieve one of its most sought-after goals—a federal law to impose compulsory unionism on millions of state and local workers. Two reasons for that defeat were the hard lobbying of the Committee against the legislation and the Supreme Court's *National League of Cities* decision, both of which took the wind out of Big Labor's sails. But there was also a third reason. The union strategists had decided to go after a different prize, one that they figured they had a better chance of getting. They set their sights on passage of a bill to legalize *common situs* picketing in the construction industry.

The issue was really very simple. In the construction industry, there are often several different subcontractors working simultaneously at a building site. After winning the job, the main contractor will engage subcontractors to do parts of work that fall within their particular specialties, such as plumbing, electrical, painting, and so forth. Those subcontractors might be unionized operations, or they might not be.

Union bosses, as we have previously observed, hate competition. In the construction industry, they hate the competition from non-union (or "merit shop") contractors who often can get work done for less because they don't have to deal with union work rules that notoriously retard efficiency. Union shop contractors usually have to hire more workers than necessary because the union rules demand strict job classifications. Under those classifications, when one worker is finished with his job, he has to sit idly by while another worker continues with the next step, even if it is something the first could easily do. That's where the common union refrain, "Hey, that's not my job," comes from. Construction unions defend such rules as safety measures, but the truth is that they have nothing to do with safety and everything to do with ensuring the maximum number of union dues payers are on the job. It is simple profit maximization for union treasuries.

Due to those time-wasting rules, merit shop contractors often underbid their unionized rivals. So how do the union contractors respond? Instead of adjusting their high-cost way of operating so as to meet the competition, union bosses and the companies that have caved in to their demands for compulsory union membership usually resort to politics to eliminate competition as much as possible. For example, the federal government and many states have enacted "prevailing wage" laws at the behest of unionized construction. Those laws state that workers on government construction projects cannot be paid less than what bureaucrats determine is the "prevailing wage," and that amounts to the union scale. Prevailing wage laws are just a price fixing scheme designed to offset the competitive advantage that merit shop contractors have, and thereby secure most if not all of the lucrative government business for less efficient unionized firms. It's the same old story with union bosses—force rather than competition.

In private-sector construction, a tactic that the union bosses had employed in their efforts to drive away non-union competition was to picket an entire work site if a merit shop contractor was chosen for any part of the work. If, for example, a merit shop contractor came to a hotel construction site to put up dry wall, the union officials would order all of their workers to stop working and picket the site in order to "protest" the inclusion of non-union men. That was "common situs" picketing. It would shut down the whole construction site, since people know that crossing a union picket line is almost invariably met with violence or retribution in job referrals by the union hiring hall. Such picketing obviously had nothing to do with wages or working conditions, but was aimed entirely at securing union monopolization of the construction industry.

Union officials used common situs picketing as long as they could legally get away with it, but it was declared to be an unfair labor practice by the Supreme Court's ruling in *NLRB v. Denver Building & Construction Trades Council* in 1951.[1] In that case, the Court held that strikes and picketing ordered by labor bosses simply to keep general contractors from doing business with any non-union firms was an unfair labor practice, a violation of Section 8(b)[4], which was added to the law by Taft-Hartley. Deprived of their favorite competition-suppressing tactic, the heads of the construction unions saw their share of the market slide year after year. Merit shop contractors underbid them to win more and more of the construction business. Over the decade from 1965 to 1975, the percentage of construction work done by union contractors fell precipitously, from 75 percent to 50 percent. High-cost, inefficient union contractors were facing the prospect of gradual extinction, at least in the private sector.

Trying to reverse its fortunes, Big Labor struck back with its favorite tool—political action—and its favorite politician—Representative Frank Thompson. Thompson introduced H.R. 5900 on April 10, 1975, a bill to amend the National Labor Relations Act so as to permit common situs picketing. As usual, the bill was given an innocuous description, "a bill to protect the economic rights of labor in the building and construction industry by providing for equal treatment of craft and industrial workers." But few people who knew anything about Big Labor were fooled, and certainly not the staff at the National Right to Work Committee. They could easily see the intent of the bill was to trample upon the rights of non-union construction workers by allowing union bosses to shut down an entire building site simply because the general contractor chose to deal with a subcontractor who didn't force his employees to join a union. Dropping the "equal rights" façade, Representative Thompson frankly admitted that the bill's goal was to keep non-union workers off construction jobs.

Far from securing "equal treatment for craft and industrial workers," H.R. 5900 was another in the long line of special interest legislation designed to give union officials unique privileges under the law. Section 8(b)(4) of the NLRA prohibits unions from engaging in secondary boycotts and picketing, which is to say that they must confine their economic attacks to parties with whom they actually have a dispute and may not inflict damage on others in order to pressure the primary party. What Big Labor wanted for the construction industry was special treatment so that it could inflict harm on parties with whom it had no legitimate dispute—the merit shop contractor and the site owner—just so it could realize its goal of stamping out competition from contractors who wouldn't bow to their demands for forced unionism and dues payments.

PRESIDENT FORD APPOINTS AN ENEMY OF RIGHT TO WORK

It was no surprise that Big Labor wanted the common situs picketing bill. What was a surprise was that President Gerald Ford should appoint a Secretary of Labor who was a long-time enemy of Right to Work. President Ford had chosen John T. Dunlop to be his Secretary of Labor in 1974—the same John T. Dunlop who had helped write the infamous 1961 Committee for Economic Development paper that advocated the repeal of Right to Work laws. The selection of Dunlop was strange in that Ford, during most of his years in the House of Representatives, had generally been friendly toward Right to Work. Dunlop, on the other hand, was a notorious compulsory unionism ideologue. The choice of Dunlop wasn't as surprising as it might seem, though. As House Minority Leader, Ford had supported the Nixon Administration in its cave-in on compulsory unionism in the postal reorganization battle in 1970 ("That's my job," he told Reed Larson) and upon becoming President, he evidently concluded that his political position would be strengthened by appearing to cooperate with Big Labor. The selection of John Dunlop as Secretary of Labor was another in the long line of failed Republican appeasements of union officials. (And as usual, the appeasement didn't work—in 1976, Big Labor went all-out to defeat Ford and elect Jimmy Carter.)

Dunlop had long been one of Big Labor's favorite academics. Whenever it wanted another special legal favor from Congress, he was one of the "expert" witnesses it would schedule to testify, knowing that he would come up with some high-sounding justification for the latest union power grab. Ford could hardly have chosen a Secretary of Labor more deeply opposed to Right to Work if he asked George Meany to make the selection. As an illustration of Dunlop's fanatical commitment to compulsory unionism, shortly after becoming Secretary of Labor, he participated in a boycott of the new Labor Department cafeteria, simply because the facility didn't compel its workers to be union members! With that astoundingly biased attitude, it was clear that Dunlop was going to be a source of trouble for Americans who wanted to decide for themselves whether or not to join a union.

Secretary Dunlop threw his support to the common situs bill immediately, using that old war-horse argument, the need for "industrial peace." Even with the Supreme Court's ruling against common situs picketing, the autocrats of the construction unions never stopped trying to use any means at their disposal to harass, intimidate, and drive away merit-shop contractors. Highlighting the problem, the CBS program *60 Minutes* on January 18, 1976, devoted one segment of its broadcast to the repeated violence directed against a merit shop contractor in Philadelphia, Altemose Construction. Leon Altemose and many of his workers had been beaten up and threatened by union thugs. Property damage in one infamous raid ran to the hundreds of thousands of dollars. It was all because Altemose wouldn't buckle under to union demands that he force his workers to become union members and pay dues for "representation" they didn't want. Such violence was of course illegal, but many construction union bosses resorted to it as their business continued to decline. In the 1970s they were turning the construction industry into a virtual war zone.

Rather than condemning the lawlessness fomented by the union bosses, Dunlop cited it as the reason for backing Thompson's common situs bill. He argued that if the bill became law, the union bosses would be pacified and tranquility would reign in the construction industry. The idea that appeasement of the power-hungry is the way to peace has proven to be just as delusional and destructive with regard to labor bosses as it has with dictators, but it resurfaces again and again. For Dunlop and many politicians in both parties, the supposed need for "peace" was a smokescreen for their willingness to help Big Labor monopolize the construction industry.

Dunlop even went so far in distorting the truth as to say that the common situs bill was supported by both the construction unions and the *construction industry.* There was a tiny grain of truth in the latter claim. A few of the huge construction firms, most notably Bechtel Construction, were happy to support the bill because they benefited from a cozy relationship with the construction union bosses. In return for their commitment to using only union subcontractors, these firms received union favors that helped them get an advantage over rivals who had not given in to the demand to freeze out merit-shop contractors. The union bosses would, for example, use their clout in certain segments of the industry to curtail delivery of construction supplies or jack up the prices for contractors who resisted their control. There was a symbiotic relationship between Big Labor and a few of the biggest construction firms— they scratched each other's backs. But it was emphatically untrue that there was widespread support for the common situs bill in the construction industry. Most of the firms vigorously opposed it, since they wanted to retain the freedom to do business with union shop or merit shop contractors based on cost and efficiency, not the threats of union bosses to shut down their construction sites if they made a "wrong" choice.

PRESIDENTIAL SUPPORT FOR THE BILL

As usual, Representative Thompson rammed his bill through committee and it came up for a floor vote in the House on July 25, 1975. The Committee had not as yet taken a stance against the bill, and it sailed through on a vote of 230 to 178. There were two main reasons why the Committee had not weighed in. First, the battle against the bills to foist compulsory unionism on government employees was simultaneously raging in Congress. That was more directly a Right to Work issue than common situs, and it had been absorbing the Committee's energy and resources. Second, it was widely thought that President Ford would not sign the common situs bill because he had opposed such legislation throughout his career in the House. The Committee therefore was not in on the battle at this stage.

The political calculus changed dramatically on August 25, however, when President Ford announced to television reporters in Milwaukee that he *would* sign the common situs bill if it came to his desk. Echoing Secretary Dunlop's "labor peace" argument, Ford called it "an acceptable solution to this longstanding conflict." With the president's backing, the bill now became a great danger and the Committee weighed the pros and cons of entering the fight against it. The common situs controversy was one that was complicated and harder to explain to the broad base of Right to Work supporters than threats to repeal Section 14(b) or to expand forced unionism to government employees. But if the bill became law, the result would be that thousands of non-union contractors and their employees would be faced with the choice of either capitulating to the labor bosses or else being driven out of business. The Committee's leaders concluded that although it was not a clear-cut issue of compulsory unionism, passage of the bill would mean that tens of thousands of construction workers would lose their Right to Work without paying a union boss for the privilege. Thus, the decision was made to enter the fight.

On September 9, Reed Larson wrote to Committee supporters, "With President Ford now backing away from earlier commitments to veto this dangerous bill, there is a serious prospect of its becoming law. While stopping this bill in George Meany's rubber-stamp Congress will be difficult, we believe that an aroused public can persuade President Ford to veto it if necessary."

Stopping the bill *would* be difficult. It had already passed the House. The Senate, where the effort to repeal Section 14(b) had been stopped with the filibuster ten years earlier, was different than it had been in 1965. Many of the solid Right to Work southern Democrats had retired and been replaced with "moderates" who could not be counted on to sustain a filibuster. The Committee concluded that the best chance for success was to mobilize grassroots opposition to the bill. That was the only way to get President Ford to change his mind and veto the bill that he had already promised to sign. Doing that would not be easy, and time was short.

THE COMMITTEE ATTACKS THE COMMON SITUS BILL

The campaign to enlighten and arouse the public over this latest quest for legal privileges by the union autocrats kicked off on September 17, when the Committee began running full-page newspaper ads in many of the nation's largest newspapers. The ads cut right to the heart of the issue—that the bill would, as its proponents admitted, be used to drive non-union workers off construction jobs. This was in keeping with the long-standing Committee approach of simplifying the question to one of freedom versus coercion. The ads led to a fine harvest of editorial commentary opposing the common situs bill as newspaper editors were alerted to its menace.

Also, the Committee launched a massive direct mail offensive, sending more than a million letters to the Committee's own mailing lists as well as other lists that were borrowed or purchased. Reed Larson concluded that it would be most effective to focus the attention of the recipients on the White House rather than on Congress, since the bill was already through the House and he figured that the likelihood of filibustering it to death in the Senate was low. Therefore, the letters asked people to call or write to President Ford, telling him that the common situs picketing bill was unfair and should be vetoed. Letters also went out to the owners and managers of merit-shop construction firms, linking the Committee's concerns with theirs and alerting them that they needed to pull out all the stops to create pressure on President Ford to veto the bill.

The direct mail campaign produced results quickly. Letters, cards, and phone calls began to pour into the White House, protesting the common situs bill. Many of them came from merit-shop contractors, the kind of businessmen whom Republicans regard as part of their "base." When top advisers in the White House took note of the outpouring of opposition to the bill from construction firms, they were first puzzled, then began to panic. Secretary Dunlop had said that the bill had industry support—but where was it? One of President Ford's aides reportedly concluded that support within the industry was limited to "Bechtel, Bechtel, and Bechtel." And from the general public, there was a veritable tsunami of protest against the bill. By October, the Committee's grassroots campaign had brought more than 200,000 letters and postcards into the White House—more mail than it had ever received on any piece of legislation in history.

Many of the letters to President Ford (with copies to the Committee) expressed intense, bitter opposition. A plumber from Arkansas wrote, "If you could know the Hell you go through if you don't join their corrupt and crooked unions . . . (you would) veto these bills." An Illinois electrician told Ford, "My son and I are both members of the International Brotherhood of Electrical Workers. . . . A little over a month ago, my son . . . had a disagreement with a steward, and an appointed Business Agent. Several days later, he was transferred 25 miles from home, hoping he would quit. He did not, so he was fired. . . ." A resident of the President's home state of Michigan said, "What we need is another item for our Bill of Rights which would outlaw forever compulsory unionism and GUARANTEE FOREVER that all citizens of these great United States will always have the Right to Work and not be subject to forced, compulsory unionism. For our citizens, for our government, for our children, for our future, please veto these bills, or any other bills which would legalize situs picketing."

Reading stacks of letters like that impressed on Ford's advisers a crucial fact: If he were to sign the common situs bill, he risked alienating a very large number of Republican voters. They might well decide to support the expected candidacy of former California Governor Ronald Reagan, who was gearing up to challenge President Ford for the nomination in 1976. If he were to sign the common situs bill, Ford would put his political survival in grave danger.

Putting further heat on the president (and any members of the Senate interested in the state of public opinion), on October 10 the Committee released a poll that had been done by the Opinion Research Corporation. The poll showed that 68 percent of the public, including 57 percent of union members, agreed with the statement, "Trades unions should only be allowed to picket the work of the contractor with whom it has a dispute and not the whole building site." When the issue was put clearly and simply to the people, common situs was as wildly unpopular as the repeal of Section 14(b) had been a decade earlier.

Continuing to throw fuel on the fire, on October 21 the Committee published its second "Open Letter" addressed to the President. In it, Reed Larson reiterated the findings of the Opinion Research poll and asked, "Mr. President, what has happened to all that talk about 'two-way communication?' Why can't the American people get through to you? For example, the hundreds of thousands of concerned citizens who have written you protesting this outrageous special interest legislation don't even get the courtesy of an answer! They receive, instead, a 33-word form letter from a Roland R. Elliott, your Director of Correspondence, who says, 'The President welcomes the comments of concerned citizens . . . your views have been carefully noted.' . . . Mr. President, the 450,000 supporters of the National Right to Work Committee appeal to you to reassert the innate sense of right and justice which prompted you, as a Michigan Congressman, to squarely oppose any bill legalizing 'Common Situs' picketing." Larson knew that the White House's evasive reply letter indicated that Ford was still holding to his commitment to Dunlop to sign the bill. More heat was needed!

On October 31, the Committee published 49 full-page newspaper ads in 17 states, urging Senators representing the people of those states to support the impending filibuster against the common situs bill. Those ads were designed not only to put pressure on members of the Senate, but also to generate more editorial opposition to the legislation. The result was another rich harvest of independent writing in opposition to Big Labor's power grab. The *New York Times* said, "(the) measure, which would vastly increase the ability of any single construction union to shut down an entire project would simply encourage irresponsibility." The *Wall Street Journal*'s editorial colorfully opined that "the only way to deal with common situs is to spray it, swat it, stamp on it." The *Richmond Times-Dispatch* asked, "Why is President Ford, a long-time conservative who presumably favors a worker's freedom-of-choice willing to sign a bill restoring the secondary boycott?"

Despite tumultuous opposition from all corners of America, heading into November of 1975 President Ford was still officially committed to common situs. The reason, the Committee had learned from insiders, was that Big Labor had offered him a deal. If he would sign the common situs bill that the union bosses so badly wanted, they would instruct their congressional puppets to go along with another construction industry bill that Ford wanted, one to create a dispute resolution mechanism that would supposedly help avert strikes.[2] The President was an old hand at legislative dealing, but this would have been a disastrous bargain—a few crumbs for the construction industry in exchange for the power by labor bosses to monopolize building sites and drive independent firms and workers out of business. The union bosses thought they had that abhorrent deal in the bag as the date for Senate debate on the bill approached.

Opponents of the common situs bill got a boost when Ronald Reagan gave a nationwide radio address on November 5. Among other things, he said that if he were President, the common situs bill would receive a much-deserved veto. Reagan hadn't yet formally announced his candidacy—that would come on November 20 but at that point few doubted that he would run. Having Reagan on record as opposing the bill emphasized to Ford even more strongly that signing the bill would give Reagan a big political advantage with a sizeable block of voters.

THE SENATE: NO REPLAY OF '65

The Committee had never held out much hope of stopping the bill in the Senate, but was still happy to see that Right to Work advocates in the Upper Chamber were prepared to filibuster the bill. The main reason why the Senate seemed to be a forlorn hope was that the rules on "extended debate"—the filibuster—had been changed since the epic 1965 battle over the repeal of Section 14(b). President Ford's appointed Vice President, former New York Governor Nelson Rockefeller, had in March of the year used his powers as president of the Senate to force a rule change with profound implications. No longer would it require a two-thirds vote to shut off debate on a bill. The rule change reduced the fraction to three-fifths; only 60 votes would be needed to break a filibuster and bring a bill to a vote. That rule change plus the fact that the Senate was more hostile to Right to Work than it had been back in 1965 boded ill for the chance of stopping the bill there. Nevertheless, a filibuster would buy more time to pressure the White House, even if it were ultimately broken.

Events in the construction industry in the weeks preceding action in the Senate further blackened the already bad reputation of the construction union bosses.

- In Philadelphia, several members of Roofers Union Local 30, including its vice president, were indicted by a grand jury for their participation in an assault on non-union roofers. The thugs were charged with carrying weapons illegally, assault and battery, assault with a deadly weapon, and resisting arrest.
- Anthony Mulligan, business agent for the Colorado Building and Construction Trades Council, was convicted of arson and conspiracy in connection with a series of fires in the Denver area, which had destroyed condominium construction projects that employed merit shop construction workers.
- Edward Urioste, former executive of the New Mexico Building and Trades Council, pleaded guilty to transporting, shipping, and processing the explosives that were used by the goons in the Colorado condominium case.

Events like those showed the lawless, often-violent nature of the construction union bosses. The idea that allowing them to engage in common situs picketing would bring peace to the industry and would be the last of their demands for special privileges under the law was absurd. Unfortunately, many members of the Senate had sold their souls to the union bosses and were impervious to the arguments against this craven special interest legislation.

When floor debate began in the Senate on November 8, the battle against the common situs bill was led by Senators Jake Garn of Utah and Paul Fannin of Arizona. The first sign that the defense could not hold came on November 11, when the Senate voted 66 to 30 to shut off debate on a procedural matter that would have blocked further consideration of the bill. Big Labor's lobbyists had done their work well—the bought senators were staying bought. Garn, Fannin, and their allies then launched a filibuster against the bill itself, but the handwriting was on the wall. On November 18, the cloture motion came and 62 senators voted for it, a sufficient number under the new rules. Among those voting to break the filibuster were fifteen Republicans, including Robert A. Taft Jr. of Ohio, the son of the author of the Taft-Hartley Act. Only fourteen Democrats voted to maintain the filibuster. The times had indeed changed.

The next day, the Senate voted its final approval of H.R. 5900 by a vote of 52 to 45. On the vote to shut off debate, 62 Senators had sided with Big Labor, so why were there only 52 votes for final passage? The answer is that politicians often vote one way on key procedural matters— in this instance, the cloture motion—and differently on final passage so they can tell diametrically opposed voting groups that they were on their side. By voting to shut off debate, Senators were doing exactly what the union bosses wanted, since it was certain that there were enough votes to pass the bill. That allowed ten of them to vote against the bill on final passage and thereby also be able to tell the great number of citizens who were loudly denouncing the bill that they had voted against it. Deception is the name of the game.

The House and Senate versions of H.R. 5900 were slightly different, so there had to be a conference committee to reconcile them. That was fortunate, because it bought a little more time for the Committee to increase the pressure on President Ford. In late November and early December, the reports coming from the White House were still that the President would sign the bill once it had cleared Congress. That occurred on December 11 when both the House and Senate passed the bill the conference committee had agreed upon. Now there was just one more thing the union autocrats needed in order to get their wish—the President's signature. Secretary Dunlop told the *Washington Post* on December 8 that he fully expected President Ford to sign his beloved bill into law.

GETTING TO NO WITH PRESIDENT FORD

By December the White House had received almost 700,000 letters and cards in opposition to the common situs picketing bill, thanks to the Committee's grassroots campaign. Between the flood of individual communications and waves of editorial denunciations of the bill as a foolish appeasement of construction union officials that would only drive non-union workers into unemployment, many members of President Ford's inner circle had come to the conclusion that the bill was a bad one. As David E. Rosenbaum wrote in the December 12 *New York Times,* "Among the President's advisers who are reported to be recommending a veto . . . are William E. Simon, Secretary of the Treasury; Alan Greenspan, Chairman of the Council of Economic Advisers; L. William Seidman, assistant to the President for economic affairs; Robert T. Hartman and John O. Marsh Jr., counselors to the President; Howard M. Callaway, director of the President's election campaign and Representative Louis Frey Jr., Republican of Florida, manager of the President's primary campaign in Florida."[3] All the heat generated by the Committee's all-out attack on the common situs bill had caused quite a few people to see the light, but would the President be among them?

Once a bill has passed Congress and come to the President, he has ten days to decide whether to sign it into law, or exercise his constitutional power to veto it. That clock had begun ticking on December 12. When there was still no signature on the bill by Wednesday, December 17, Secretary Dunlop issued an emotional statement, declaring that there would be "unmitigated hell" if President Ford vetoed his pet bill. The next day, the Committee responded with a statement of its own, saying that Dunlop "has taken leave of his senses" if he believed that non-union workers will allow themselves to be driven off their jobs without putting up a fight.

Going into the decisive weekend, President Ford's intentions were still unknown, but appearing on the program *Meet the Press* on Sunday, Bill Seidman gave a hint that a decision had been reached. When asked if the President was going to sign the common situs bill, he evaded the question saying, "unbelievable amounts of mail have come to the White House. People are very emotional about the bill ... very strident."

Sure enough, on Monday President Ford announced his decision: *He would veto the bill.* His statement said, "My reasons for vetoing the bill focus primarily on the vigorous controversy surrounding the measure, and the possibility that this bill could lead to greater, not lesser conflict in the construction industry." His formal veto of the common situs bill came after the Christmas holidays, on January 2, 1976.

The veto was hailed in much of the nation's press, and credit for pressuring President Ford to do the right thing was widely given to the Committee. For example, on December 24, the *Shreveport Times* editorialized, "Ford's reversal will undoubtedly be viewed as indecisiveness by his political adversaries ... probably more influential was the enormous campaign mounted by the National Right to Work Committee." And the *St. Louis Globe-Democrat* of December 27–28 said, "In large part, the mail, the largest outpouring to a president since the Vietnam war, appears to have been stimulated by an organization called the National Right to Work Committee, which contacted 4 million Americans ... (and) sought to draw citizens' attention to their stake in the measure."

On the other hand, the union bosses and Secretary of Labor Dunlop were furious at losing this great, big goody that they thought was in the bag. Two weeks after President Ford's veto, Secretary Dunlop announced his resignation, effective February 1, 1976.

To stop Big Labor's effort to rewrite the law so that it could keep merit-shop workers and contractors off building sites and move toward a monopoly in the construction industry, the Committee had spent some $800,000 on direct mail, radio, and newspaper ads. That was a small amount in comparison with the millions that the union bigwigs had lavished on electing a Congress that would jump at their commands. The entire episode demonstrated that it was still possible for a good idea, well-presented, to defeat a bad idea, even if it is overwhelmingly backed by special interest money and power. As the *Canton Repository* editorialized on December 29, "Even with all that money floating around and the promise of more and the pressure to act that goes with campaign financing, we are struck by this fact: When voters were alerted to what was at stake in the legislation, enough of them attempted to do something about it at the highest level of government that they succeeded."

COMMON SITUS RETURNS

President Ford's veto of the common situs picketing bill did not, of course, cause the union bosses to give up on common situs. Like a besieging army, they can suffer many defeats in their efforts to take the fortress, but one defeat for the defenders and the battle is over. Big Labor's brass shook their fists in anger and said, "Wait until next time!" In the 1976 elections, they spent money like it was water to elect politicians who would jump to their commands.

The crucial result of those efforts was the election of former Georgia governor Jimmy Carter to the presidency. When he served as governor, Carter uttered no words against Right to Work, and even wrote to Reed Larson on January 29, 1971, "I stated during my campaign that I was not in favor of doing away with the Right to Work law, and that is a position I still maintain." During the campaign for the Democratic nomination in 1976, however, Carter changed his tune. He badly wanted the backing of Big Labor and knew that he wouldn't get it unless he came out against Right to Work. He told union audiences during the campaign that he would be glad to sign a bill repealing Section 14(b). Carter went on to win the general election with massive support from Big Labor. Strategists at the Committee knew that his election, along with a Congress that was hardly less union-friendly than the one that had passed the common situs bill easily in 1975, meant that their defenses were sure to be challenged repeatedly in 1977 and 1978.

On February 16, 1977, Frank Thompson reintroduced his old common situs picketing bill, this time as H.R. 3500. Big Labor's House martinets dutifully paraded the bill through committee. Speaker Tip O'Neill was confident of victory, saying on March 21, "In light of the support for this bill in the Congress, I would say the best thing to do is for the construction industry to prepare for its orderly implementation." The union lobbyists were backed up with a special "tax" that the AFL-CIO brass had ordered on 14.5 million members of their affiliate unions, bringing in almost $900,000 of additional funds to be spent in pushing through the common situs bill. The AFL-CIO detailed senior staff members to work exclusively on lobbying for the bill. *Business Week* magazine quoted a top union strategist, "This is our final chance—if we don't get it this year, we'll never get it. We're not going to give Congress a choice. We're going to take people to the wall."

This time, however, the Committee was prepared to make a full-scale effort to defeat the bill in the House. It countered the Big Labor offensive with one of its own, using the time-tested weapons at its disposal. First and foremost, the Committee alerted its supporters that their voices were again needed in the fight to preserve worker freedom. The result was similar to 1975, but instead of the people aiming their outraged letters at the White House, they aimed them at Congress. Letters, postcards, and phone calls began cascading into congressional offices. Representative Tom Railsback of Illinois told the *Chicago Tribune*, "The building trades leaders in Washington lobbied me strenuously but the opposition outpouring was overwhelming." The Committee also released its latest poll, conducted by the Roper Organization in late February. It showed that among the population in general, 77 percent agreed that a union should only be allowed to picket a contractor with which it had a specific dispute. Only 12 percent agreed with the idea that a union should be allowed to picket a whole building site, even if it stops work of all contractors and employees. Even among blue-collar workers and union members, support for common situs picketing was low—19 percent and 30 percent respectively. House members were thus put on notice that a vote in favor of the common situs bill would be highly unpopular back in their districts.

The Committee's fierce counterattack against the common situs bill made a world of difference. The same bill that had passed handily in

1975 and which Speaker O'Neill was certain would breeze through, went down to a stunning defeat by a vote of 217 to 205 on March 23, 1977. Many Democrats who had voted for the bill in 1975 voted against it this time around, thanks to the opposition that the Committee's efforts had aroused. For example, Oregon's Al Ullman explained his switch as a result of "the surprisingly strong expression of opposition. . . . It even came from rank and file members of organized labor."

The nation's newspapers understood what had happened and why. The *Detroit News* editorialized on March 25, "The House wisely sensed the public mood and reached the logical decision." In its March 26 issue, the *Arizona Republic* said, " . . . the construction industry and the Right to Work Committee launched a public campaign, calling on the public to make its voice heard. And the public did." The *Pawtucket Times* wrote on March 31, "The National Right to Work Committee and several contractors associations faced an uphill lobbying battle, but their intense efforts paid off in preventing unfair treatment of the majority of workers and contractors. We think the Right to Work people deserve a vote of thanks from the public."

The union bosses didn't take their defeat easily. The AFL-CIO Construction Trades Department whined that the defeat of the common situs picketing bill was due to "a massive array of forces that want organized labor knocked down and knocked out at any price." But the truth was that many of the citizens who registered their opposition to the bill and thereby swung the vote in the House, were not against organized labor and did not want to see it "knocked out." They simply did not think it was right to force unionization on construction workers who did not want it. By correctly framing the issue as one of freedom of choice versus compulsion, the Committee had turned public opinion strongly against this power grab by the union autocrats.

There was an unexpected side benefit to the defeat of common situs, too. Speaker O'Neill concluded that if the House would not pass that bill, there was no point in spending time on the bill to repeal Section 14(b). Two birds with one stone!

Fighting off the common situs picketing bills in 1975 and 1977 was some of the hardest legislative action in the Committee's history. The stakes were high and the odds were long, but Big Labor's quest for the power it wanted to monopolize the construction industry was defeated. The United States would today be a poorer and less free country if the Committee hadn't won both of those battles.

NOTES

1. *NLRB. v. Denver Building & Construction Trades Council,* 341 U.S. 675.

2. Columnist William F. Buckley Jr. described it this way: "(President Ford) has coated the pill for conservatives by coming up with a syndicalist-sounding plan devised by his Labor Secretary John Dunlop, which would set up a board of ten of us, ten of them, plus Dunlop and Shirley Temple and one androgynous labor mediator, to attempt to reconcile differences between contractors and unions if a strike threatens." "Beware: Common Situsitis," *National Review,* December 5, 1975, p. 1436.

CHAPTER SIX

PREVENTING LABOR LAW "REFORM"

One of the most overworked and abused words in politics is "reform." The poor word is routinely hijacked to be used as cover for political schemes that make matters worse, rather than better. For instance, we often get "tax reform" bills that manage to make the bewildering and unfair tax code even more bewildering and unfair.

The same is true in labor law. As we have seen, Big Labor keeps demanding new legal favors from its congressional lapdogs—bills that "reform" the National Labor Relations Act or some other statute by making the law still more accommodating to its coercive agenda. The first rule of legislating is to slap a nice-sounding label on a nasty bill to help conceal its true nature. That was the case with the "Labor Law Reform" legislation introduced in 1977, legislation that required all of the Committee's resourcefulness to defeat.

PREMONITIONS OF TROUBLE AND THE DEFEAT OF SENATOR MCGEE

In the fall of 1976, Reed Larson surveyed the political landscape. The Democratic candidate, Jimmy Carter, was well ahead in the opinion polls and presumably headed for the White House. Unfortunately, the former Governor of Georgia, a Right to Work state, was no friend of worker freedom of choice and was receiving massive support from the union bosses. It seemed inevitable that he would side with them when they came to the feeding trough for political favors. Furthermore, the elections for the House and Senate appeared to be heading for bad results. Congress was already lopsided with politicians who were beholden to Big Labor, as the common situs picketing battle of 1975 had shown. In the Senate, where the new rules made a filibuster easier to break, it would be impossible for the Committee to hold back the tide of bills Big Labor would demand—unless its composition were changed. Right to Work leaders drew the obvious conclusion: They had to defeat some pro-compulsory unionism senators.

Larson and his compatriots chose their targets carefully. At the top of the list was Wyoming's Gale McGee, a veteran who had been in the Senate for 18 years and was widely regarded as unbeatable. He chaired the powerful Post Office and Civil Service Committee, where bills that would shove compulsory unionism down the throats of government employees would be referred. He had always been friendly with Big Labor's chieftains, voting for repeal of Section 14(b) in 1965, despite the fact that Wyoming had adopted a Right to Work statute in 1963. Moreover, despite an unbroken string of anti-business votes, McGee had received the "Guardian of Small Business" award from the National Federation of Independent Businesses. He had also been named "Statesman of the Year" by the National Rifle Association, even though he had voted in favor of gun control legislation. McGee was one of those entrenched politicians who gain added strength from the perception that they are unbeatable. Lobbying groups support them and butter them up so as to have "access" on critical issues. Nevertheless, Wyoming was a Right to Work state with a strong grassroots base. Larson decided that it was imperative to take a shot at McGee.

The Republicans had nominated a little-known state senator, Malcolm Wallop, as McGee's opponent. The first baseline survey his campaign conducted in June had shown Wallop trailing the incumbent by 43 points. That certainly seemed to validate the "conventional wisdom" that McGee was untouchable, but Larson didn't know about the poll and it wouldn't have mattered anyway. He had a sense that the race was winnable and went ahead with the Committee's plans.

While the Committee never endorses or directly assists candidates, it does let voters know where they stand regarding Right to Work. Trumpeting the news that a politician was a supporter of compulsory unionism had led to the defeat in 1966 of many members of Congress who had backed the repeal of Section 14(b). The citizens of Wyoming were going to hear loud and often that Senator McGee was on the wrong side of the Right to Work issue.

The Committee began in July with a mailing to its list of more than 7,700 Wyoming households—slightly more than 8 percent of all households in the state—headed by a Right to Work member. As the election neared, it took out newspaper ads stressing the importance of Right to Work not as a "business" issue, but as one that affected Wyoming citizens as individuals, as consumers, and as taxpayers. By framing the issue that way, the Right to Work message appealed to the widest possible audience, reaching many people who would not pay attention to an appeal from "business" groups like the U.S. Chamber of Commerce.

Those communications hit hard on the crucial point—that Senator McGee had a terrible voting record on Right to Work issues. It was necessary to blow away the fog of positive PR that McGee's handlers had created for him so Wyoming citizens could see the truth: When it came to worker freedom versus compulsory unionism, he wore a black hat. Finally, the ads and mailings asked Wyoming citizens to ask both candidates to pledge their support for Right to Work. Wallop was sure to do so; McGee's silence or evasion could prove harmful to him.

Another part of the Committee's standard procedure is to send candidates questionnaires on their views regarding Right to Work issues. Wallop answered his survey 100 percent in favor of Right to Work. Senator McGee, however, refused to answer his questionnaire. Larson used those facts in subsequent mailings. He recounted McGee's votes against Right to Work and urged Wyoming citizens to contact him and ask that he apologize for and repudiate his past support for forced unionism. On the other hand, Wyoming voters were encouraged to thank Wallop for his pro-Right to Work stance and encourage him not to waver from it. If the election could be framed as the choice between a pro-freedom candidate and a pro-coercion candidate, there was good reason to believe that McGee would be defeated.

In August, polls still showed McGee leading by a wide margin—34 points. He was so confident of winning the election that he even answered mail from constituents who backed Right to Work with defiant letters telling them that he disagreed with them and would continue to oppose it. Most politicians have more sense than to let their hubris show. By mid-October, with only two and a half weeks to go, McGee's margin had been cut in half; defeating him still looked impossible to most observers. But that was precisely when the Committee's program went into over-drive, with a new barrage of mailings and newspaper ads. It placed ads in every daily newspaper in the state contrasting the candidates' stands on Right to Work. The ads used McGee's own words against him, quoting from a letter he'd written back in August to a Right to Work supporter boasting, "My stand on Right to Work is well known in Wyoming. I am opposed to state right to work laws and, therefore, would vote for repeal of Section 14(b) ... should the opportunity arise." Those words would come back to haunt him.

Another ad, placed in every daily paper on the Saturday before the election, reprinted an editorial from the *Philadelphia Inquirer* about union violence. The headline consisted of the words of the threat a union boss (quoted in the article) had delivered to independent-minded workers: "We're going to blow your head off!" Larson wryly called this his "soft-sell" ad. The race was tightening day by day, mainly due to the Committee's blizzard of attacks on McGee's anti-Right to Work record.

When the votes were finally counted, Malcolm Wallop had pulled off a shocking upset, receiving nearly 55 percent. Big Labor's well-known and heavily financed puppet Gale McGee was put out to pasture. There was no doubt about the issue that had catalyzed the dramatic turnaround in the race—Right to Work. In the incoming Senate, there would be one fewer vote for the union bosses' agenda and one more vote against it.

Malcolm Wallop's victory over Gale McGee was not the only big electoral success for Right to Work in 1976. Its efforts were critical in defeating Big Labor incumbents in Indiana, where Richard Lugar upset

Vance Hartke; New Mexico, where Harrison Schmitt sent Joseph Montoya into retirement and in California, where S. I. Hayakawa managed to unseat John Tunney. But for those four victories, the 95th Congress would have no doubt given union bosses most, if not all of what, they wanted.

BIG LABOR'S "REFORMS"—1977–78

The defeat of the "son of common situs" bill in 1977 (discussed in the previous chapter) didn't slow down Big Labor's legislative juggernaut. No sooner had the Committee broken that assault on worker freedom than new ones were being mounted. Although Speaker Tip O'Neill decided against trying to pass a bill to repeal Section 14(b), he was highly receptive to two "reform" bills that the union brass wanted.

First, there was a "campaign reform" bill. It's a fact of life that running for federal office is an expensive proposition—at least if you want to have a chance at winning. The amounts spent seem huge, even though as a percentage of our GDP, campaign spending is actually very small. Big Labor's strategists, however, thought they had a way to use the trumped up "issue" of campaign spending to their advantage. They kept pointing out in feigned sorrow how expensive campaigning was becoming and how much candidates had to rely on money from interest groups. As a "reform," the union bosses (assisted by various "good government" organizations) advanced the idea of a system of taxpayer funding for all federal campaigns that would prohibit monetary contributions from individuals or groups. That might sound appealing and "fair" to people who don't understand that union officials would still be free to support their favored candidates with hundreds of millions of dollars worth of "in kind" services such as phone banks and get-out-the-vote drives. Big Labor excels at those kinds of campaign support and its opponents have never had anything comparable.

If the "campaign reform" bill were passed, the electoral playing field would therefore be even more strongly tilted toward candidates whom the labor bosses liked. They would be free to continue to use forced dues money to pay for the salaries of union employees who would "volunteer" to assist selected candidates, and to pay for rent, computers, printing and mailing costs, telephones, carpools, door-to-door campaigning and other efforts. On the other hand, candidates not backed by Big Labor would be restricted in their spending and prohibited from raising money from contributors in order to offset the great advantage of the "in kind" campaign assistance the unions officials provide. This "campaign reform" bill was a cynical attempt to stack the deck further in Big Labor's favor, a "reform" that was special interest legislation pure and simple.

The bill was brought to the Senate floor in July 1977, having received the usual kid-glove treatment in committees chaired by senators who were in the hip pocket of AFL-CIO president George Meany. The Committee ran up the red flags with its members and urged them to voice their support for the filibuster against the bill. That pressure helped stiffen the opposition to the bill. On August 3, the cloture vote came and Meany's supporters found that they didn't have enough votes to break the filibuster. The first "reform" bill thus died a much-deserved death.

THE LABOR LAW "REFORM" BILL

Killing off the second of Big Labor's "reform" bills would prove to be much more difficult. The bill was a masterpiece of deception, crafted around the alleged need to make the National Labor Relations Board and its procedures faster and fairer. If ever there was a wolf in sheep's clothing, this was it.

As we have previously seen, the NLRA (the Wagner Act with its subsequent amendments) is an incredible attack on the freedom of Americans, employers and employees alike, which violates the Constitution in several ways. (The fact that the Supreme Court has chosen to turn a blind eye to those violations doesn't mean they aren't there.) The statute confers tremendous legal privileges on union bosses to coerce companies into negotiating with them and to coerce workers into paying money to them in order to keep their jobs. Although the Taft-Hartley amendments slightly changed the legal imbalance by adding certain union unfair labor practices and affirming the right of states to enact Right to Work laws, that was like giving a baby aspirin to someone with a migraine. Federal labor law remained heavily tilted in favor of coercion by union autocrats to force themselves on unwilling employers and workers.

Nevertheless, AFL-CIO president George Meany and his congressional yes-men had the astounding temerity to complain that the NLRA as it stood wasn't fair to "workers"—of course, Big Labor's rhetoric always equates the interest of workers with the interest of union bosses—and therefore it needed to be changed. The "problem" as Meany and company saw it was that union organizing drives were often being defeated, and the answer had to be a further stacking of the deck to ensure more victories. Employers were using what freedom remained to them under the NLRA to convince their workers that the kind of "lock them in" unionism of Big Labor was not in their interests. Meany's answer was not to make unionism more appealing, but to further tighten the straps on the straightjacket around employers. He saw the salvation of his fortunes riding on the most authoritarian, coercive bill since the Wagner Act itself.

Early in 1977, two of Big Labor's most dependable politicians, Representative Frank Thompson, whom we have met before, and his fellow New Jerseyan Senator Harrison Williams each introduced "reform" bills designed to accomplish Meany's objectives. (Although no one then knew it, the days in office were numbered for both politicians. Thompson and Williams would become ensnared in the FBI's 1981 "Abscam" operation where a number of politicians were caught on tape accepting bribes from agents posing as Saudi businessmen. Thompson was indicted on bribery and conspiracy charges in June 1980. Defeated for re-election in November and convicted in December, he was sentenced to three years in prison. Williams resigned from the Senate in 1982 rather than face expulsion for his actions.) Their bills would have made the NLRA significantly more lopsided than it already was, further empowering labor bosses to ram compulsory unionism down the throats of employers and workers. Key features of the legislation included:

- Requiring "quickie" union elections that would greatly reduce the ability of management to communicate to the workers the short-comings of unionization. Once the NLRB determined that there was enough support to hold a certification election—the evidence being signatures that are often obtained through underhanded tactics—it would have to be held within 15 days, as opposed to the 60 or more that had always been allowed. Union officials, however, could petition to have elections delayed for up to 45 days if they thought they needed more time to build up support.
- "Equal time" campaign requirements: If a company official addressed workers to argue against voting for union representation, then union officials would have to be given equal time to reply—*during company-paid working time.*
- Expansion of the NLRB from five to seven members, thereby allowing President Carter to "pack" the Board to put it in the pocket of Big Labor.
- Double back-pay awards for any worker fired allegedly for having pro-union sympathies. Therefore, employers would be fearful of terminating unproductive or disruptive workers if they had also espoused a desire for unionization.
- Companies found by the NLRB to have committed "willful violations" of the law could be barred from obtaining federal contracts for up to three years.
- New powers for NLRB bureaucrats to impose penalties on employers who had not "bargained in good faith"—an undefined phrase that the NLRB could interpret to mean anything it wanted. Amazingly, if an employer was held to have violated this vague requirement, the NLRB could then require wage increases so that the firm had to pay its workers equal to "major collective bargaining settlements" in the nation. In other words, if companies didn't bend to union boss demands, federal bureaucrats could rewrite their labor contracts.

All that and more was packaged as "reform."

The phony "reform" bills didn't fool people who understood Big Labor and looked under the benign "fairness" costuming. The Committee, of course, saw the danger immediately and denounced them as nothing more than an attempt to intimidate employers into meek silence when union organizers came around. Many others were critical, too. For example, in July 1977 the veteran labor columnist for the *New York Times,* A. H. Raskin, wrote, "Most unions have got out of the habit of organizing in the years since World War II. To the extent that they have acquired new members, outside of the civil service and health fields, it has been primarily through union shop contracts and other kinds of 'pushbutton unionism' in which the employer delivers over workers."[1] Similarly, Peter Nash, former General Counsel of the NLRB, said that the major purpose of this so-called "reform bill" was to enable unions to win "quickie elections . . . all with the effect of requiring an election before the employee can be lawfully informed of the possible adverse consequences of unionism." Regarding the bill's penalties on employers, Nash said they were harsh and unwarranted, "particularly for small businessmen who operate on slight profit margins." Columnist James J. Kilpatrick termed it "monstrous legislation" and warned of dire consequences if it were enacted.[2] The Committee was not alone in raising the alarm.

Big Labor was undoubtedly going to pull out all the stops to get this legislation enacted. It had a huge war chest and lobbyists swarming all over Capitol Hill. President Carter was on board and both the House and Senate had large Democratic majorities. The Committee's leaders knew that it would be extremely difficult to keep those "reforms" out of the federal statute book, but failure to do so would mean compulsory unionism for many more American workers. This was going to be another epic struggle.

"NO HIGHER PRIORITY"

The battle began in the House of Representatives. Frank Thompson rammed his bill, H.R. 8410, through the House in October 1977 with passage by the wide margin of 256 to 163. It was the same House that had voted down common situs picketing in March, but many congressmen who had "crossed" Big Labor then now felt the need to go along with a bill that was even worse. Union autocrats smiled—they were half way home.

Some of the business associations in Washington that had opposed the bill were shocked by the terrible defeat in the House and talked about trying to negotiate some compromise in the Senate in hopes of making the bill marginally less destructive. The Committee, however, entertained no such thoughts and braced itself for an all-out war in the Senate.

At the AFL-CIO conference in December 1977, Vice President Walter Mondale told cheering throngs of union bigwigs that the Carter Administration "has no higher priority next year than the passage of labor law reform in the Senate." Big Labor had thrown its enormous political weight behind the Carter/Mondale ticket in 1976 and expected a good return on its investment. But behind the cheering there was fear. The percentage of workers in the private sector who were unionized had been falling for more than twenty years. Union organizing drives were being voted down more and more often. Deep in their hearts, the union bosses knew that they would never turn their fortunes around by *persuading* workers that unionization was in their best interest. They knew that they needed this new layer of legal powers to accomplish through threats and intimidation what they could not accomplish through voluntary means.

If there was no higher priority in the Carter Administration than passing "labor law reform," there was also no higher priority at the National Right to Work Committee than defeating it. Putting those "reforms" into law would have meant forced unionism for huge numbers of American workers.

As usual, the Committee began attacking the legislation by unleashing one of its tried-and-true direct mail blitzes, calling on its members and the general public to write to their senators to say that the "push-button unionism" bill should be defeated. By this time, the Committee had a membership of 1.25 million and their voices were desperately needed. A sophisticated phone bank that the Committee had established in Virginia Beach, Virginia, augmented the mail campaign. The assault also included press releases sent to the nation's newspapers to inform editors of the real intent behind the bill and to refute the whining arguments of Big Labor that it was needed to "make things fair again." Instead of letting the union bosses have the advantage of their chosen "reform" label, the Committee used A.H. Raskin's more descriptive and accurate term— "pushbutton unionism" to describe the bill. Finally, Committee representatives began working on the Senate, persuading any members who would listen that Senator Williams' bill (S.1883) was the worst kind of special interest legislation, an unscrupulous attack on the freedom to resist union compulsion. Big Labor's pet bill was attacked from all sides and with all the strength the Committee could muster.

But would there be enough Senators who would stand up against the power of Big Labor? Union officials were twisting arms very hard to get the bill through quickly and threatened political reprisals against senators who impeded the bill's progress. Just as had been the case back in 1965 with the effort to repeal Section 14(b), this fight was going to be close. The question came down to this: Would 41 senators continue filibustering the bill?

Hearings on the Williams bill were held in the Senate Human Resources Committee in November. Speaking in opposition, Reed Larson said that the National Right to Work Committee would enthusiastically support *genuine* reform of the National Labor Relations Act—reform that would restore to Americans the rights and liberties that had been taken away by the NLRA. However, the bill was emphatically not true reform since, as Larson said, "it fails even to address the most glaring inadequacy in the NLRA—namely those provisions that promote contracts which force workers to pay money to unwanted unions in order to work."

During his testimony, Larson discussed the widespread problem of union violence, citing numerous cases. Real labor law reform would deal with that ugly problem, he argued, but S.1883 said nothing about it at all. Of course, sound arguments against the bill bounced off the Senators who were under orders from the labor bosses to shepherd it through to a quick vote on the Senate floor. The bill was reported out of the committee and union lobbyists hoped to get the Senate to pass it early in 1978.

THE MAIL WARS

Once the Committee's campaign against the "pushbutton unionism" bill hit its stride, mail began to pour into Washington opposing the bill. Senate offices reported being "buried in sacks of mail" from constituents who were against it. Texas Senator John Tower said that his office received more than 125,000 pieces of mail on the bill. With opposition mounting daily, co-sponsor Jacob Javits (New York Republican) conceded to the *Washington Post* that the bill needed more grassroots support. The trouble was that there just wasn't much grassroots support for this Big Labor power grab.

Victor Kamber, director of the AFL-CIO's task force on labor law "reform" denigrated the outpouring of opposition to S.1883, calling the mail flooding into Washington against it "a tremendous proliferation of waste." Further demonstrating his "public-be-damned" attitude, Kamber bragged that the AFL-CIO was running a "pool" that enabled him to send "a couple of thousand pieces of mail every week" to "members of the Senate who like to weigh their mail." He even admitted to stockpiling "signed postcards" at AFL-CIO headquarters. "When a Senate office calls and complains about a lack of mail from us, we'll deliver," he said. Pushbutton "support" for the pushbutton unionism bill, in other words.

Loads of phony cards might matter to senators who "weigh their mail," but more perceptive ones prefer to know whether a communication is genuine or just part of a bogus publicity drive. Senator Orrin Hatch of Utah said that the union postcards "have all the earmarks of a strictly phony boiler room operation run by union professionals who can't even motivate their members to buy stamps, let along fill out the cards." Senator Hatch had hit upon the truth. While the union bosses were desperate to pass the bill, the workers they claimed to represent, hard-working auto workers, bricklayers, machinists, and so on, stood to gain nothing from the bill and weren't motivated to support it.

In contrast, the Committee had tapped into a strong vein of deep and genuine opposition to this new power grab by Big Labor. Senators who were not bought and paid for by the labor bosses could tell the difference.

There was further evidence that Big Labor's campaign for the bill was dishonest. Senator Strom Thurmond of South Carolina received numerous cards from citizens who said they wanted him to vote for the "reform" bill. He wrote back to explain why he was not in favor of it. Surprisingly, Thurmond then received letters from several of those people informing him that they had never written to him about the bill. Their names had been used by someone else. The story was picked up by the Columbia newspaper *The State,* which reported that "A close examination of the cards shows a striking resemblance in the handwriting on many of them. On some, personal printing is similar, leading an observer to believe that the same person signed two different names to two cards." No doubt about it—Big Labor was forging names on cards to make it seem that there was more support for "pushbutton unionism" than there really was.

DELAY IN THE SENATE

In January 1978, Senate Majority Leader Robert Byrd of West Virginia announced that floor action on S.1883 was going to be delayed until after the Senate had acted on the controversial treaties in which President Carter wanted to relinquish U.S. control over the Panama Canal. Given the strong opposition that the treaties were encountering, Byrd's decision meant that consideration of "labor law reform" would not begin until March at the earliest. That was a tremendous break for the Committee, giving it added time to press the case against the bill in the media and to further inundate Washington with sacks of mail.

Announcement of the delay, however, provoked a volcanic reaction from union bigwigs who knew that some of their Senate votes were wavering. The president of the International Association of Machinists, William "Wimpy" Winpisinger, announced bitterly, "If Mr. and Mrs. Main Street America don't want to stand up for the rights we got back in 1935, then we will go back to 1934 and have it out on the streets. And we're fully prepared to do that." In other words, pass the bill or expect violence! If Winpisinger really believed his foaming, blustering threats to have mobs in the streets if the bill didn't pass, he was entirely out of touch with reality. Few ordinary Americans, even union members, thought that the nation's labor law was in need of the "reforms" contained in the bill and scarcely any were ready to "take to the streets" just because seething union bosses like Wimpy Winpisinger didn't get their way.

One thing that was really bothering the top brass at the AFL-CIO was that the Committee's media blitz was working beautifully. In addition to the numerous mailings to newspaper editors, the Committee took the additional step of sending spokesmen on whirlwind tours to personally discuss the bill with editors across the nation. The response was overwhelming, resulting in a fresh barrage of editorials against the bill in early 1978. Here's a small sample:

- The *Arizona Republic:* "The economy and the worker will suffer in the end. Labor could cry 'unfair practice' or threaten to make a wide range of charges before the NLRB, hoping management would lie down and roll over, and come to terms to avoid penalties. This kind of power is frightful, and has a parallel in England where the labor-run economy is in dismal shape."

- The *Oklahoma City Oklahoman:* "One of the hoariest strategies in our system of lawmaking is to cloak a thoroughly obnoxious and self-serving bill under the guise of 'reform' legislation.... [This bill] bears the tag of 'labor law reform' but it really wears a union label."

- The *Los Angeles Examiner:* " ... the proposed changes are a thinly veiled attempt to increase the size, financial strength and political power of organized labor.... Unionism, while right for many, should never be forced down the throat of every American worker."

- The *Chattanooga Free Press:* "President Jimmy Carter is calling for adoption of a new 'labor law reform' bill. He says it's supposed to increase workers' rights. But it doesn't do that at all. Actually, it seems to be a political payoff to the big union bosses who supported Mr. Carter's presidential campaign with lots of money, manpower, and muscle."

In total, more than 800 daily newspapers ran editorials against the bill. Hardly any came out in favor of it.

Besides powerful editorials against the bill, Americans were reading full-page ads that the Committee placed in key newspapers. It was little wonder that union bigwigs like Wimpy Winpisinger were going ballistic: Thanks to the Committee's efforts, their darling bill was taking a sustained bombardment of criticism, and the more the public learned about it, the more they wanted it to be defeated.

THE SENATE REPUBLICANS

Getting the public and the press worked up over the outrageous pushbutton unionism bill was actually the easy part. Far more difficult was the task of catalyzing opposition to it among Senate Republicans.

Knowing that most of the Republican voting base was solidly opposed to compulsory unionism and the efforts of labor bosses to dominate the economic and political life of the nation, the Republican National Committee had been raising money by emphasizing its opposition to Big Labor. A typical fundraising letter from 1978 read in part, "Because I know how concerned you are, I am writing to tell you about the all-out effort Big Labor is making. It is trying to push through legislation that will do irreparable damage to our free enterprise system that will be felt everywhere." That letter, no doubt, hit a nerve with Republican donors, who would expect that the party leadership was prepared for a pitched battle against S.1883 and other bills in the union bosses' agenda. But the three top Republicans in the Senate, Minority Leader Howard Baker of Tennessee, Minority Whip Ted Stevens of Alaska, and Senatorial Campaign Committee Chairman Bob Packwood of Oregon had all refused to take a firm stand against the pushbutton unionism bill when contacted by the Committee in October 1977. (Stevens would later straddle the fence on the bill; Packwood would vote with Big Labor to shut off debate.)

As we have seen before, there are a substantial number of Republican politicians who delude themselves into thinking that they will reduce or eliminate Big Labor's opposition to them by taking its side on key issues such as repeal of Section 14(b) or common situs picketing. It seldom works even in the short run. Big Labor's political machine nearly always backs Democratic opponents of such Republicans just as vigorously as it does Democrats who are challenging Republicans who have voted solidly with Right to Work. And in the long run, capitulation to the union bosses only strengthens their ability to elect Democrats who are loyal to their whole anti-capitalist agenda. Nevertheless, many elected Republicans want to try to get into the good graces of union officials and the Committee was running straight into that problem over "labor law reform." If the top Republicans in the Senate, especially Minority Leader Howard Baker, weren't committed to killing S.1883, it would surely pass.

Therefore, the Committee went to work on those senators—particularly Baker, whose father-in-law, Everett Dirksen, had been so crucial in the preservation of Section 14(b) back in 1965. After receiving tons of mail from Tennessee opposing "labor law reform," Baker agreed to meet with Reed Larson. The meeting was anything but smooth. A Tennessee newspaper had sent Senator Baker a copy of the ad that the Committee was going to run, an ad that put him in the spotlight. That wasn't where he wanted to be on this issue. After agreeing to back the filibuster against the bill, Baker said, "I have learned that when I get this mad, the only thing to do is to leave the meeting"—and then stalked out of the room. It was another successful application of Dirksen's adage that when politicians feel the heat, they start to see the light.

Baker wasn't happy, but announced that he would steadfastly oppose S.1883 and use his position to help ensure its defeat. With Senator Baker on board, the ranks of senators committed to a filibuster rose to 36. But 41 were needed under the revised Senate rules. Furthermore, there was the fear that Big Labor would pick off one or more of the coalition against the bill with its arsenal of political threats or promises.

It was absolutely necessary that the "labor law reform" bill die in the Senate. Some Republican senators and some Democrats from Right to Work states wanted to try to amend the Senate version to remove the most objectionable parts, but that would have been a recipe for defeat. If the Senate passed a less virulent version of the bill, there was a strong probability that in the conference committee that would follow to reconcile the House and Senate versions, any weakening Senate amendments would be stripped out. Besides, there were so many awful provisions in the bill that allowing any of them to become law would have been a great victory for compulsory unionism. The form of the bill in the Senate therefore didn't much matter. It had to be stopped cold. Only a filibuster could do that.

THE FILIBUSTER

Senator Robert Byrd, the Democratic Majority Leader and a master of Senate rules and procedure, finally brought the bill to the floor on May 16, 1978. He decided not to put the Senate on a "two-track" system, which would have allowed other bills to be considered and voted upon while the announced filibuster against "labor law reform" was going on. This was a move designed to increase the pressure on opposing Senators to cave in so they could proceed with other business. Leading the filibuster against it were two Republican freshmen—Orrin Hatch of Utah and Richard Lugar of Indiana. By their reckoning, the fight would depend on the votes of five Democrats who were keeping quiet about their intentions: Lawton Chiles of Florida, Dale Bumpers of Arkansas, John Sparkman of Alabama, Russell Long of Louisiana, and Edward Zorinsky of Nebraska. All were from Right to Work states, but undoubtedly the Carter Administration and the AFL-CIO would apply enormous lobbying pressure on them to pass "labor law reform."

On June 1, opponents of the bill suffered a terrible loss when Senator James Allen of Alabama died of a heart attack. He had been advising Hatch and Lugar on the intricacies of keeping a filibuster going. His expertise would be missed, but Senator Jesse Helms of North Carolina, then completing his first term in the Senate and already a master of the rules, stepped in to fill the void. Helms was optimistic and told Hatch that they would keep the filibuster going even if "they have to wear their pajamas and bedroom slippers."

Senator Byrd called for the first cloture vote on June 7. It received only 42 votes, well short of the 60 needed to stop the filibuster and bring the bill to a vote. That comfortable margin of victory, however, was deceptive. There were many Senators who had pledged to vote against cloture initially, but who would ultimately jump ship. A second cloture vote came the following day, with the number for it rising to 49 and the number opposing falling to 41. Byrd's strategy apparently was to allow the opponents to prevail on the first two votes, thereby allowing a number of Senators to save face by saying that they tried to stop the bill by supporting the filibuster, but then switching sides when some meaningless "concessions" were made. On the third cloture vote, June 13, the number voting to shut off debate rose to 54, with 43 opposed. The Big Labor forces were steadily gaining ground with relentless lobbying from the White House and the AFL-CIO. Senator Byrd announced that a fourth cloture vote would take place the following day.

On that fourth vote, four more Republicans defected to Big Labor: Ted Stevens of Alaska, Charles Percy of Illinois, John Heinz of Pennsylvania and Lowell Weicker of Connecticut. President Carter's Secretary of Labor, Ray Marshall, confident of victory, watched from the Senate visitor's gallery. But the champagne would have to be kept on ice for a little longer: The vote was 58 to 41. Still, George Meany was just two votes from a momentous victory.

Senator Allen's place had been taken by his widow, Maryon, appointed by Governor Wallace to fill out the remainder of her husband's term. On Thursday, June 15, prior to the scheduled fifth vote, she told Senator Hatch that Senator Byrd was trying to get her to switch and support cloture by threatening to remove her from all of her late husband's committees. But she would not give in. For that afternoon's vote, several filibuster supporters were missing, but it's only the number of votes in favor of cloture that matter. On the fifth vote, the result was 58 to 39. Never before in Senate history had a bill gone through more than four cloture votes. Undeterred, Senator Byrd announced that there would be a sixth cloture vote the following week. Lobbying to pick up the two votes that Big Labor still needed frantically continued.

The June 20 *New York Times* published an op-ed piece by Senator Lugar that summed the situation up nicely: "To say that there is no public enthusiasm for the bill is to understate the matter. In poll after poll, fewer than one in four Americans endorses any change that would ease the job of union organizers. . . . The majority leader's duty to the Senate, its rules, its traditions and to the country was to withdraw this bill last Friday, secure in the knowledge that he had done his best for the President and for George Meany. Regrettably, he has chosen to proceed."[3] But so close to a victory for "the President and for George Meany"—it would have been more accurate to have put Meany first—Senator Byrd was not about to give up. He scheduled the sixth cloture vote for June 22.

THE SIXTH CLOTURE VOTE—A CLOSE CALL

On the morning of June 22, Senator Hatch went to see Minority Leader Baker, and just as he arrived, Senator Long was leaving. Baker gave him the bad news: Long was going over to the other side and Byrd had devised a strategy to send the bill back to committee for some cosmetic changes, then quickly bring it back for final passage. He expected to pick up the remaining vote needed to break the filibuster that way. Hatch then called Senator Zorinsky to see if he was going to succumb to the pressure from Byrd and the White House. Zorinsky said that Byrd had worked him over hard, saying that "They promised me everything." He told Hatch that he was still a "mushy no" on cloture but would call to let him know if he changed his mind. The fact that Zorinsky was still even a "mushy no" had much to do with the constant stream of calls, letters, and cards he was receiving from Right to Work constituents back home in Nebraska.

When the Senate convened in the afternoon, Senator Long announced his switch, angling for one more opponent to join with him. But Fritz Hollings of South Carolina then took the floor and said, "Well, the distinguished senator from Louisiana has always been the *fifty-ninth* vote for cloture and we have always known it." The implication was crystal clear—the *next* senator to switch would be *the one* who gave Big Labor its enormous victory. For a moment, the Senate chamber was quiet. Then Senator Stevens, who had jumped ship back on the fourth cloture vote, rose to say, "If Senator Long is going to cross over and vote for cloture, then I am going to cross back and vote *against* it." Pandemonium broke out. Byrd's gambit had failed. The final cloture motion was defeated, 53 to 45 and Byrd then sent the bill back to committee. Although Big Labor spokesmen talked about bringing the bill back to the Senate floor, they were never able to get their sixtieth vote. Their beloved bill was dead, at least for the 95th Congress.

Their high hopes dashed, Big Labor's autocrats finally admitted defeat, but promised to come back again. "Wimpy" Winpisinger said bitterly at an AFL-CIO conference in August, "If it's crumbs they [the Senate] are offering us, they can take it and jam it . . . and we'll go to the polls in November." But his hopes for a filibuster-proof 96th Congress that would rubber stamp his "reform" bill were smashed in the elections that fall. Instead of electing more sycophantic politicians who would do their legislative dirty work, Big Labor suffered a loss of fifteen seats in the House and three in the crucial Senate. Three incumbent Democrats who had backed "labor law reform" went down to ignominious defeat— Richard Clark of Iowa, Thomas McIntrye of New Hampshire, and Floyd Haskell of Colorado. The voters' reaction to Big Labor's attempted power grab was reminiscent of the 1966 elections, in which union puppets had also taken a drubbing after the attempt to repeal Section 14(b).

Once again, the Committee had saved the country from legislation that would have boosted the power of union bosses and led to a great increase in the number of Americans who would have to pay union dues in order to work. It had done so by grassroots activism that reminded politicians that most Americans dislike forced unionism and oppose laws that further the powers of Big Labor over our economy. The clamor from the voters back home was all that kept wavering senators from bowing to enormous pressure to support "labor law reform."

Even that clamor, however, wouldn't have been enough to stop the bill if it had not been for the Committee's work back in 1976 which caused the defeat of those four incumbents who were in the AFL-CIO's hip pocket. As the Duke of Wellington said of the Battle of Waterloo, "It was a very close-run thing."

NOTES:

1. A. H. Raskin, "Organizing Obstacles Are Not Just Legal," *New York Times,* July 24, 1977.
2. James J. Kilpatrick, "Tilting Toward Labor," *Baltimore Sun,* January 31, 1978.
3. Richard Lugar, "That Labor Bill," *New York Times,* June 20, 1978.

"To compel a man to furnish contributions of money for the propagation of opinions which he disbelieves and abhors, is sinful and tyrannical."
—Thomas Jefferson, 1779

"Americans must have the right but not be compelled to join labor unions."
—Reed Larson

Whiteford Blakeney, distinguished attorney and legal scholar, provided vital guidance and advice as founding board member and attorney for both the Committee and Foundation. He had carried one of the landmark Right to Work cases—*Railway Clerks vs. Allen*—to the U.S. Supreme Court before the founding of the National Right to Work Legal Defense Foundation

Nobel laureate F. A. Hayek, at Right to Work headquarters, reviews with Reed Larson his book, *The Constitution of Liberty,* where he declared, "It cannot be stressed enough that the coercion which unions have been permitted to exercise contrary to all principles of freedom under the law is primarily the coercion of fellow workers."

Forced dues payers take a stand against compulsory unionism outside the AFL-CIO lavish headquarters building in Washington, D.C.

Reed Larson, with Reps. David Henderson (D-NC) (right) and H. R. Gross (R-IA) (center) review their amendment to the Postal Reform bill of 1970. This amendment protected 750,000 postal workers from forced unionism. Both Henderson and Gross attributed this impressive "David vs. Goliath" victory over the alliance of Big Labor and the Nixon Administration to the work of the National Right to Work Committee.

Committee spokesperson Duke Cadwallader (a former voluntary union member) presents scroll to President Gerald Ford in appreciation for his last-minute decision honor public sentiment to oppose—and veto—"common situs" picketing—a measure to greatly expand compulsory unionism.

London, 1976: Britain's Margaret Thatcher, head of the Shadow Cabinet and soon-to-be-Prime Minister, expressed keen interest in Reed Larson's account of U.S. experience in mobilizing public support to curb union coercive practices. As Prime Minister, Thatcher greatly diminished the presence of compulsory unionism in the United Kingdom.

Committee Vice President Andy Hare (left) and Reed Larson (right) confer with Right to Work champion Sen. Jesse Helms (R-NC) on steps to curb compulsory unionism in 1976.

Journalist William B. Ruggles (1891–1988) coined the term "Right to Work" in his Labor Day 1941 editorial in the *Dallas Morning News*. His *Magna Carta* inspired citizen action to ban compulsory unionism.

Committee Vice President for Legislation Andy Hare and Sen. Orrin Hatch discuss the successful filibuster of the mislabeled "labor law reform" bill. The Committee-led battle—against overwhelming odds—turned back a major expansion of forced union membership.

Sen. Everett Dirksen, shown with pioneer Committee board members, led the battle which preserved the right of states to outlaw forced unionism. Dirksen praised the Committee's work to gain the support of wavering Senators, saying, "When I feel the heat, I see the light." Board members, left to right: Juanita Lamuel (KS), Father John Coogan (IL), John Martin (SC), Dr. Frederick Fowler II, Chairman (MN), Miriam Thompson (NC), Ted Clark (MT), Sen. Dirksen (IL), Tom Harris (OK), Raymond Losornio (OK) and Dr. Paul Brauer (MA). (Dr. Fowler II was father of current Foundation Chairman, Dr. Frederick Fowler III (TN).)

Board Chairman Tom Harris presides at a 1979 meeting of the Foundation's executive committee as it reviews the increasingly effective litigation program. Left to right: Rex Reed, Raymond Losornio, Chairman Harris, Reed Larson and John Davenport.

Ronald Reagan, a former president of the Screen Actors Guild union, pledged his opposition to compulsory unionism when campaigning for President of the United States.

Foundation attorneys Mike Merill (second from left) and Ray LaJeunesse (right) with Brotherhood of Railway, Airline and Steamship Clerks (BRAC) workers Alan Fails (left) and Howard Ellis after U.S. Supreme Court argument on use of compulsory dues for non-collective bargaining purposes. The court granted a victory to the employees in a ground-breaking win for worker freedom. (Ray LaJeunesse became Vice President and Legal Director of the Foundation in 2002.)

From groundbreaking to completion in 1980, Right to Work champions Wofford B. and Louise Camp played a key role in making possible the National Right to Work headquarters building, dedicated to worker freedom.

In 1984, U.S. Sen. Paul Fannin (R-AZ) paved the way for sweeping change in the makeup of the Labor Advisory Council. Sen. Fannin was fervently dedicated to protecting the rights of working people and demanded equitable representation by free-choice advocates on the Council. Since its formation in 1980, the Council had been a one-sided forum for Big Labor professionals.

In the opening round of an 18-year harassment campaign by hostile U.S. government officials, Reed Larson checks credentials of Federal Election Commission operatives demanding access to Committee and Foundation books and records. Larry Noble, shown second from left, later rose to become General Counsel of that over-reaching regulatory body.

Reed Larson helps load lists of Right to Work contributors into a Brinks armored truck for transport to courtroom. Right to Work attorneys offered the lists to a U.S. District Court judge under the protections of the court.

Foundation Attorney Robert Gore (right) won justice—and a million dollar judgement—for William Hinote after Hinote was shot down and gravely injured by union thugs simply because he had chosen to do his job during a strike.

Telephone worker Harry Beck's courageous stand against abusive union practices won basic changes in anti-worker federal policy. In the National Right to Work Legal Defense Foundation's landmark case, *Beck vs. CWA Union*, the U.S. District Court in Baltimore found that only 21 percent of Communication Workers of America Union's compulsory fees were being used for bargaining for the employees, while the other 79 percent apparently went for partisan politics and other non-bargaining purposes.

In 1993, Reed Larson (left) and Sen. Bob Dole (right) presented Charlton Heston (center) with an award for his invaluable help in fighting compulsory unionism. Heston was a powerful campaigner for passage of Idaho's Right to Work law in 1986. His influential voice for worker freedom has been heard in many states and in Congress. (Larson and Dole—both Kansans—had worked together for passage of that state's Right to Work law thirty-five years earlier.)

Charlton Heston and Reed Larson meet the press to mobilize opposition to the "Pushbutton Strike" bill, May 1994.

1995: Committee Vice President Mark Mix and Sen. Paul Coverdell (R-GA) review petitions asking Congress to end tax subsidies of compulsory unionism.

In 1995, a Right to Work Foundation court victory forced union officials to return more than $6 million illegally collected forced dues to Pennsylvania public employees. Ultimately, the class-action suit put more than $8 million back in workers' pockets.

(L to R) Former Attorney General Edwin Meese III, Reed Larson and Committee Vice President Stephen Goodrick conclude Congressional testimony in a conversation with Right to Work stalwart Sen. Jeff Sessions (R-AL).

Foundation Vice President Stefan Gleason stands by as President Reed Larson addresses the national media at a press conference outside Teamsters headquarters during its 1997 strike against United Parcel Service (UPS). Foundation attorneys had just served the union hierarchy with federal charges for bullying workers off the job.

(L to R) Rev. Frederick Fowler III, Foundation Board Chairman, with Rex Reed, Executive Vice President and Legal Director. (Mr. Reed retired in 2002.)

Foundation Vice President Stefan Gleason, a frequent spokesman on television, appeared with teacher Kathleen Klamut on FOX News' "The O'Reilly Factor." Foundation attorneys helped Klamut beat back the NEA union's systematic intimidation of religious objectors.

Labor Day 2003: Committee President Mark Mix, shown making a point during a Labor Day debate, knows union bosses would rather talk about anything except the Right to Work issue.

Union lawyers went to work immediately to undermine the constitutionality of newly enacted Right to Work protections in Oklahoma. U.S. District Court Judge Frank H. Seay upheld the will of Oklahoma's citizens, thanks in no small part to the leadership of Gov. Frank Keating (shown here) and the hard work of the Committee as well as Foundation attorneys.

Sylvester Petro (right) prominent labor law professor, author and one-time union organizer, was an advocate for Right to Work in Oklahoma long before the Sooner State became the 22nd Right to Work state in 2001. With him is Duke Cadwallader, one of the anti-compulsion union members who helped found the National Right to Work Committee in 1955.

Due in part to public pressure brought by Foundation-assisted workers and Congressman Charles Norwood (R-GA) at this Capitol Hill press conference, the National Labor Relations Board bureaucracy began to take notice and reconsider the permissibility of certain "card check" and top-down organizing methods.

Right to Work Committee Chairman Charles Serio (right) and President Mark Mix testified at Rep. Virgil Goode's 2004 hearing before an Ad Hoc Panel on Restoring Worker Freedom.

CHAPTER SEVEN

SEE YOU IN COURT

T he National Right to Work Committee began with, and has always had, a legislative focus. It has battled for Right to Work laws and against the enactment of laws that would give Big Labor more power to dragoon workers into union ranks. But the legislative arena is only one of two venues in the fight against compulsory unionism. The other is the courts. The judicial arena is just as important as the legislative in combating compulsory unionism. In 1971, Lewis F. Powell Jr.—who later became a Justice of the Supreme Court—told the U.S. Chamber of Commerce, "American business and the enterprise system have been affected as much by the courts as by the executive and legislative branches of government." The same can be said about the rights of individual workers. The Right to Work movement could no more afford to concentrate exclusively on legislative activity than a football team could afford to concentrate exclusively on its offensive team.

Federal and state laws allow workers some protection, however inadequate, against the assaults on their freedom to decide whether or not to associate with any labor union. Unfortunately, union officials regularly disregard the law when it gets in the way of their quest for money and power. What they cannot get legally, they often try to get illegally. Over the years, thousands of workers have suffered violations of their rights, including physical violence and even death, because they dared to put their own desires and welfare above the demands of union autocrats. The Rod Carter case, recounted at the beginning of this book, is just one of thousands of cases where workers have had their rights violated for going against the demands of imperious union officials.

Just having the law on one's side, however, is not enough. The individual worker is terribly overmatched if he or she tries to take on the union boss in court. As Archibald Cox, law professor and Solicitor General of the United States once wrote:

> Workers are unfamiliar with the law and hesitate to become involved in legal proceedings. The cost is likely to be heavy, and they have little money with which to post bonds, pay lawyers' fees and print voluminous records. Time is always on the side of the defendant. Even if the suit is successful, there are relatively few situations in which the plaintiff or his attorney can reap financial advantage. Most men are reluctant to incur financial cost in order to vindicate intangible rights. *Individual workers who sue union officers run enormous risks, for there are many ways, legal as well as illegal, by which entrenched officials can 'take care of' recalcitrant members.* (emphasis added)[1]

This David versus Goliath legal imbalance called for an organization that would provide workers who required assistance in fighting for their rights with free, high-quality representation. That is why, in 1968, Reed Larson catalyzed the creation of a new entity to fulfill that need—the National Right to Work Legal Defense Foundation—by going to the Committee's Board of Directors and convincing it that Right to Work had to have a litigation team on the field.

Larson knew that liberal legal aid organizations such as the NAACP Legal Defense Foundation and the American Civil Liberties Union (ACLU) were using tax-deductible funds to shape public policy through strategic legal action. The National Right to Work Legal Defense Foundation was expressly modeled after the NAACP's foundation. African Americans had long faced the problem of violations of their rights, both by official actions and by individual crimes. Without free legal assistance, the NAACP knew, very few of those injustices would ever be redressed. The famous 1954 case *Brown v. Board of Education* had been won by attorneys from the NAACP Legal Defense Foundation. American workers who had suffered at the hands of union officials needed exactly the same kind of organization to stand up for their rights. The National

Right to Work Legal Defense Foundation was the first conservative non-profit legal aid organization and it blazed the trail for the entire conservative litigation movement.

Prior to the formation of the National Right to Work Legal Defense Foundation, the Committee had attempted to secure legal representation for workers who were fighting against the oppression of union bosses. In the 1963 case, *Railway Clerks v. Allen* [2], for example, one of the Committee's founders, Whiteford Blakeney, had served as legal counsel to the plaintiffs, arguing their case all the way to the Supreme Court. The plaintiffs were railroad workers who objected to having their dues money used for political purposes they did not support. The Court's holding that dissenting union members did not have to prove "each distinct union political expenditure to which he objects; it is enough that he manifests his opposition to *any* political expenditure by the union," was an important victory. The Committee's leaders knew that there could be many more favorable precedents if a litigation shop was established that would concentrate exclusively on representing workers whose rights had been violated by union officials and employers.

The Right to Work Committee and the Legal Defense Foundation are separate organizations, each with its own staff and sources of funding. Like the Committee, the Legal Defense Foundation takes no partisan political positions. Its business is solely to assist workers who ask for help when union bosses have taken actions that force membership in, or payment to, an unwanted union.

Cases that the Foundation takes—and unfortunately, limited resources do not allow it to support the case of every worker who asks for help—fall into six categories:

1. Cases involving the misuse of compulsory union dues for political and ideological purposes.
2. Cases involving the violation of workers' constitutional rights of free speech, assembly, and other civil rights.
3. Cases involving violations of the merit principle in public employment and academic freedom in public education.

4. Cases involving injustices in the compulsory union hiring hall "referral system."
5. Cases involving violations of existing protections against compulsory unionism.
6. Cases involving union violence.

Whether or not the Foundation takes a case depends on the Legal Director's weighing of four factors: the magnitude of the injustice, the strength of the worker's legal position, the possibility of establishing good legal precedent, and the cost of handling the case.

The dedicated men and women who have comprised the Foundation's team of attorneys have repeatedly squared off in court against the high-priced lawyers hired by Big Labor and they have won a steady stream of cases. Some have set important legal precedents. Others have forced union bosses to pay for their vicious attacks on workers. The remainder of this chapter will give a "highlights reel" of the work of the Legal Defense Foundation.

RICHARDSON V. COMMUNICATION WORKERS

Dale Richardson worked for Western Electric Company in Omaha, Nebraska. He was, in fact, one of the best employees in the plant, having won three merit raises in his nine years there. He was a voluntary member of Local 7495 of the Communication Workers of America, which had won exclusive bargaining rights over the employees. However, Dale publicly questioned the use of union funds by the officials of Local 7495. That act, something he had a perfect right to do, would have serious consequences for him.

At a union meeting where he openly raised the issue of the misuse of funds, Dale was told that if he didn't like the way the union was run, he could get out. A union militant threatened to ram a beer bottle down his throat. Disgusted with the attitude of those who supposedly represented his interests, Dale resigned from the union. Using the protection afforded to him under Nebraska's Right to Work statute, he then stopped paying dues to a union he had come to regard as crooked and authoritarian. The contract between Western Electric and the Communication Workers contained a nondiscrimination clause, prohibiting discrimination against any worker due to his non-membership in the union, but that made no difference to the bosses of Local 7495, who wanted to make an example of Richardson.

What followed was a seven-month campaign of harassment against Dale and two other men who had also decided to leave the union. "Do anything short of murder," the union president told his goons. Daily, the three men were punched, pushed, spat upon, cursed at, and pelted with objects. Finally, the union officials figured out how to get Richardson fired—they concocted a story, supported by sworn statements of several union militants, that he had pushed a fellow worker in the plant. That gave Western Electric an excuse to remove this disruption from its workplace. The company fired Richardson, victimizing him doubly.

Dale refused to accept his mistreatment. In 1967, he brought suit against both the local and international union, and against Western Electric, claiming that the union had violated its obligation to give him fair representation. When the Legal Defense Foundation was formed in 1968, it offered to assist Richardson in his battle against the blue-chip lawyers of the union and the company. It was an offer he gladly accepted.

After the facts were put before them in the trial, the jury found that Richardson had been wrongfully discharged by Western Electric in breach of the collective bargaining agreement, and also that the discharge had been caused by the actions of the union, a breach of its legal "duty of fair representation." The jury awarded him $20,000 in damages. The case then dragged on for years, with appeals by both sides. Ultimately, he collected $96,000 in damages from his employer and the union.

The Richardson case set an important precedent, when the Eighth Circuit Court of Appeals ruled in 1971 that workers who had suffered harassment and discrimination by unions were not only entitled to compensatory damages, but could also collect damages for mental anguish. The Court's opinion said, " ... the law should not react niggardly as to the realization of his whole damages." The case was a tremendous victory for worker rights, and also served notice to unions and employers alike that when they violate those rights, they would have to contend with the National Right to Work Legal Defense Foundation.

KIRKLAND V. OPERATING ENGINEERS

Another early case in which the Legal Defense Foundation made union bosses pay for their mistreatment of a worker was that of Sammy Kirkland.

Kirkland was a backhoe operator employed by Deal Erection Company in Florida. He did not want to join a union in order to earn a living. A union official threatened Sammy with mutilation if he continued to work without joining his union, but Sammy ignored him. Union officials, as we have seen, usually won't take "no" for an answer, so on May 25, 1971, a gang of nearly 100 union thugs cornered Kirkland while he was operating a backhoe at a construction site and gave him a vicious beating. Three of his ribs were broken. Steel shavings were ground into his eyes. The mob's ringleader pulled a knife and threatened to cut off Kirkland's hands.

Sammy's life was probably saved when a deputy police officer came upon the scene and fired a shot—for which the deputy was then mobbed and beaten. Following the attack, the local union president openly bragged that the employer "will sign a union contract with us now . . . if he don't get right, it's going to get pretty wormy for him."

Several of the union goons who participated in the criminal assault on Sammy Kirkland were arrested, tried, convicted, and sentenced to five-year prison sentences in 1973. But that did nothing to help him get his life back or redress the terrible wrong that had been done to him by the union bosses who had ordered the brutal assault. Fortunately, Kirkland contacted the Legal Defense Foundation, which filed a civil suit on his behalf. Rather than face a trial, with all of its attendant publicity, Operating Engineers Local 675 agreed to an out-of-court settlement, paying Sammy Kirkland $165,000. (Local 675 also had to pay for its injuries to the deputy sheriff and for damage done to the company's equipment.) The violence had left Kirkland physically and emotionally scarred and, as his attorney said, "No amount of money can compensate him for the damage that's been done." Still, it was an expensive lesson for union bosses who were used to making examples of people at no cost.

ABOOD V. DETROIT BOARD OF EDUCATION

In 1969, the Foundation began the first of its many cases that have reached the Supreme Court, *Abood v. Detroit Board of Education,* which dealt with the rights of teachers who were forced to pay money to a union against their will.

The Michigan legislature had caved in to pressure from union lobbyists to pass a statute authorizing union representation and forced dues agreements for local government employees. Any worker who chose not to join a union still had to pay an "agency fee" equivalent to the full amount of dues paid by members if a local government and union so agreed. Failure to pay would, of course, lead to termination of employment under the supposed need for "union security." Numerous teachers employed by the Detroit Board of Education, including Louis Abood, Anne Parks, and Christine Warczak, objected to the Board's agreement which made their jobs dependent upon the payment of money to the Detroit Federation of Teachers—a union whose services they did not desire and which used some of their money for political and ideological activities they opposed. Their suit, filed in the Circuit Court of Wayne County, Michigan, argued that the agency shop requirement was unconstitutional, as it violated their rights under the First and Fourteenth Amendments. More than 650 Detroit teachers joined in the action.

Although things began badly, the entire case is a testament to the perseverance of the Foundation's attorneys. The Circuit Court granted a motion by counsel for the Board of Education for summary judgment, holding that there was no constitutional violation in the "agency shop" requirement. Undaunted by the setback, the Foundation appealed to the Michigan Court of Appeals. The Court of Appeals ruled that the use of compulsory "agency fees" by unions for political purposes having nothing to do with collective bargaining could violate the rights of the dissident teachers, but that they were not entitled to restitution of any money already paid since they had not disclosed to union officials *exactly which* political activities they found objectionable. That unsatisfactory decision was then appealed to the Supreme Court of Michigan, but the court declined to review it. Therefore, the Foundation attorneys appealed to the United States Supreme Court, which agreed to hear the case in 1976. The Court heard oral arguments on November 9, with the renowned labor law expert Sylvester Petro presenting the case for the teachers.

The Supreme Court's decision was handed down on May 23, 1977.[3] The majority opinion, written by Justice Stewart, while only a partial victory, gained important ground for worker freedom.

First, the bad news. Right to Work supporters were disappointed that the Court upheld Michigan's statute that provided for compulsory unionism among public employees. Despite Professor Petro's vigorous argument to the contrary, the Court saw no constitutional defect in forcing public employees to accept and pay for unionization.

But there was also significant good news in the decision. Stewart concluded that the teachers did have a constitutional right not to have any of their "agency fee" money used for political activities and ideological causes unrelated to the union's collective bargaining. He wrote, "The fact that the appellants are compelled to make, rather than prohibited from making, contributions for political purposes works no less an infringement of their constitutional rights. For at the heart of the First Amendment is the notion that an individual should be free to believe as he will, and that in a free society one's beliefs should be shaped by his mind and his conscience rather coerced by the State." The unanimous holding that public employees cannot be compelled to subsidize union political and ideological activities was extremely important. Workers trapped in unwanted unions at least have a constitutional right to avoid subsidizing the political action of the union bosses.

As to the idea advanced by the Michigan Court of Appeals that workers paying agency fees are only entitled to restitution to the extent that they can show that they objected to *specific uses* of money by union officials, the Supreme Court also disagreed. "It would place upon each employee the considerable burden of monitoring all of the numerous and shifting expenditures made by the union that are unrelated to its duties as exclusive bargaining representative," Stewart wrote.

But exactly what should the remedy be for the teachers? On that crucial point, the Court ducked. The teachers' union had, prior to the case reaching the Supreme Court, adopted an "internal remedy" that the union said provided "fair relief" for agency fee payers who did not want to support any union activities except for those directly involving collective bargaining. The Court chose to remand the case for further proceedings, leaving it to the Michigan courts to decide whether it was appropriate to defer further judicial proceedings pending the parties' use of that "internal remedy." Relying on the union's "internal remedy" was like throwing Brer Rabbit into the briar patch.

The case dragged on for another decade. Under the union's "internal remedy," the Detroit Federation of Teachers' self-appointed "Review Panel" determined that the dissenting teachers were only entitled to a rebate of six percent of the agency fee. Foundation attorneys fought on against the preposterous inadequacy of the rebate and unfairness of the procedure. After the Supreme Court's favorable 1986 decision in the Foundation's *Hudson* case (discussed below), which dealt with the problem of union internal remedies, the DFT finally agreed to pay the remaining 96 plaintiffs who had not left the bargaining unit. They would receive half of the fees they had been forced to pay from June 1973 through June 1986, plus interest, totaling more than $75,000.

The *Abood* case was a long, hard-fought battle to win the vital rulings that public employees cannot be forced to pay union dues or fees that will be used to finance political and ideological activities to which they object and that they cannot be required to bear the burden of stating exactly which union expenditures they oppose. The case opened the door for future court battles over two issues: What kinds of union expenditures can and cannot be charged to workers, and what procedures must a union follow to protect the rights of workers who object to paying for more than just their fair share of the cost of collective bargaining?

ELLIS V. BROTHERHOOD OF RAILWAY, AIRLINE, AND STEAMSHIP CLERKS

Howard Ellis and Allan Fails worked as ticket agents for Western Airlines in California. The union contract between Western and the Brotherhood of Railway, Airline, and Steamship Clerks (BRAC), compelled them to pay "agency fees" to the union in order to keep their jobs. They, and many other ticket agents, weren't happy about having to pay for the union's unwanted representation, but were utterly incensed that the BRAC then used a significant portion of their money for political activities they opposed. Therefore, in 1972, Ellis, Fails, and more than 200 other workers sent letters to the union that said:

> As an employee of Western Airlines, I feel that the Brotherhood of Railway, Airline and Steamship Clerks does not properly represent my interests and I protest the compulsory "agency fee" I must pay ... in order to retain my job. In addition, I hereby protest the use of these fees for any purpose other than the cost of collective bargaining and specifically protest the support of legislative goals, candidates for political office, political efforts of any kind or nature, ideological causes, and any other activity which is not a direct cost of collective bargaining on my behalf. I demand an accounting and refund from the (union) of all fees exacted from me by the so-called "agency fee."

BRAC officials simply ignored their request, so with the assistance of the legal staff of the Foundation, Howard Ellis brought suit individually and Allan Fails brought a class-action suit on behalf of the many other dissident Western Airlines employees.

The suits charged that the use of compulsory agency fees for purposes other than collective bargaining violated the rights of workers under the Railway Labor Act (which applied to Ellis and the others because they were employed in the airline industry) and also their rights under the First, Fifth, and Ninth Amendments to the Constitution. Moreover, the suits contended that the union's rebate procedure for workers who protested the use of their money was arbitrary and discriminatory.

The Supreme Court's decision in *Machinists v. Street*[4] in 1961 had already established that under the Railway Labor Act, unions could not use dues and fees for political activities. In *Ellis,* the judge granted the workers summary judgment on the question of the union's liability for compelling them to pay for several categories of activity in addition to politics, including lobbying, organizing, conventions, litigation not involving the Western Airlines contract, publications, social activities, and member death benefits. The case then went to trial to determine the amount of damages owed to the workers. The court found that more than 40 percent of the dues and fees paid to the union had gone for purposes that could not be charged to workers. Judge Nielsen ruled that in the future, the agency fee payments of protesting workers would have to be reduced by the amount the union spent on nonchargeable activities in the previous year. However, he found that the union's rebate scheme had adequately protected workers' rights in the past as to political expenditures.

Both sides appealed the decision to the Ninth Circuit Court of Appeals. Unfortunately, the presiding judge of the three-judge panel assigned to hear the case was Harry Pregerson, who had twice ruled against Right to Work in earlier cases challenging the misuse of union dues—and twice been reversed on appeal. To make matters worse, it appeared that lawyers for the BRAC were attempting to manipulate the panel to ensure a victory. One of the Foundation attorneys overheard a conversation in which a union lawyer said that he "could control the panel we get at the Ninth Circuit." Foundation attorneys asked Judge Pregerson to recuse himself from the case and when he refused, they attempted to get the Supreme Court to mandate that he step aside in favor of an unbiased judge. The Supreme Court denied that petition, however, so the case proceeded with what appeared to be a deck stacked against the workers. It soon proved to be.

In 1982, the Ninth Circuit issued a 2 to 1 decision largely siding with the union. The court held that the procedure of allowing dissenting workers a rebate was permissible, even though it allowed the union free use of their money for a year. Moreover, the union had appealed the lower court's decision as to the specifically challenged expenditures other than politics and lobbying. On those questions, Judge Pregerson's majority opinion kowtowed to the union, saying that the proper way to look at the matter was to ask whether an expenditure "can be seen to promote, support, or maintain the union as an effective collective bargaining agent." In his view, all of the expenditures at issue could be said to strengthen the union as a whole and were therefore chargeable to all workers. Foundation attorneys appealed that extremely adverse decision to the U.S. Supreme Court.

Justice White wrote the Supreme Court's opinion, which was announced on April 25, 1984.[5] The decision reversed the Ninth Circuit in part, significantly expanding worker rights.

First, the Court dealt with the union scheme of collecting full dues or fees but later refunding some percentage to workers who filed objections. Union lawyers had argued that it was more "convenient" for the union to handle things that way, but Justice White wrote, "the union cannot be allowed to commit dissenters' funds to improper uses even temporarily. A rebate scheme reduces but does not eliminate the statutory violation." So unions are not entitled to free use of dissenter's money—a major victory.

Justice White then turned to the question of the chargeability of union expenses. He concluded that "objecting employees may be compelled to pay their fair share of not only the direct costs of negotiating and administering a collective-bargaining contract and of settling grievances and disputes, but also the expenses of activities and undertakings normally or reasonably employed to implement or effectuate the duties of the union as exclusive representative of the employees in the bargaining unit." Applying that standard to the challenged expenditures, the Court's majority held that the cost of conventions was chargeable, as were expenses for social activities. On the other hand, the Court held that dissident workers could not be charged for the cost of litigation having no direct connection with their bargaining unit, the cost of union organizing efforts, and the cost of union publications to the extent that they were devoted to nonchargeable activities such as political advocacy. What about the argument that compelling workers to support union expenditures is a violation of their *First*

Amendment rights, rather than just their rights under the Railway Labor Act? Helpfully for worker rights in later cases, the Court recognized that "by allowing the union shop at all, we have already countenanced a significant impingement on First Amendment rights." Sadly, the Court also reiterated the musty old idea, deeply embedded in its jurisprudence, that "such interference with First Amendment rights is justified by the governmental interest in industrial peace." The supposed "industrial peace" interest was sufficient for the Court to hold that employees could constitutionally be compelled to pay for union convention costs, social activities, and publications to the extent that they deal with matters germane to collective bargaining. (As to convention costs, Justice Powell dissented, arguing that it appeared that a significant amount of the union's convention business was political in nature and that the case should be remanded for trial to determine the extent to which the costs of conventions were political.)

The Supreme Court ordered that the case be remanded for a recalculation of damages owed to the plaintiffs for having been forced to pay for extra-unit litigation, organizing, and publications, with the union being held to the burden of proof on a "preponderance of the evidence" standard. Ultimately, the BRAC agreed to refund to the plaintiff workers 31 percent of the fees they had paid between July 1, 1972, and July 30, 1980. In total, the union had to disburse more than $132,000 to satisfy the judgment against it.

Ellis was another significant, albeit partial, victory for worker rights. Although the amount of money involved was relatively small, the precedents it established were important. The Court made it clear that dissenting workers could not be compelled to pay full dues and then have to ask for a refund at a later time for union activities for which they could not legally be charged. Also, it specified additional expenditures that cannot be forced upon dissenters. One of those categories of nonchargeable expenses, organizing—i.e., marketing the cause of unionism—is particularly significant because unions typically spend as much as 40 percent of their budgets on it. Ellis marked another major milestone on the way towards fair treatment for workers.

WILLIAM F. BUCKLEY JR. V. AFTRA

Should you have to be a union member in order to speak your mind on television or radio? Amazingly enough, that was the position of the American Federation of Television and Radio Artists (AFTRA). It took the determination of two well-known Americans and nearly seven years of litigation to establish the principle that union membership cannot be a prerequisite for expressing your views on the public airwaves.

William F. Buckley Jr. and M. Stanton Evans were two nationally famous writers who often appeared on television and radio. Neither man wanted the services of AFTRA, but AFTRA wanted them—or at least their money. AFTRA had established contracts with many broadcasters specifying that they could employ only individuals who were "members in good standing" with the union. (This case harkens back to Cecil B. DeMille's fight with his union over the payment of a one dollar assessment and how his refusal to pay it led to the union's declaration that he was no longer a "member in good standing" and therefore ineligible to continue his radio work.) Buckley and Evans did not want to support AFTRA and sought the assistance of the Foundation in trying to establish that the union could not compel their membership.

Events began in September 1964, when Buckley received a letter from the New York AFTRA local, informing him that "Since AFTRA has a union shop in all its collective bargaining agreements, it is necessary that persons who appear on radio or television in AFTRA-covered employment be members of AFTRA." Evans was similarly told by a CBS vice president that he had to join AFTRA. Not only did the union demand that the two become members of AFTRA, but also that they, like all other AFTRA members, abide by the union's constitution, which gave union officials the power to expel from membership anyone who failed to observe any union rule or regulation. Thus, to appear on television or radio, Buckley and Evans were compelled to become members of and pay dues to a union they did not want—a union which would have power to deprive them of membership (and ability to broadcast) merely by finding that they had not observed every detail of the union's code. To escape from that Kafkaesque situation, both men filed suits in 1971 with the assistance of the Foundation.

Judge Brieant of the District Court agreed with Buckley and Evans and issued a decision in 1973 stating that because such requirements would violate the First Amendment, Congress had not intended to authorize agreements requiring commentators who express their views on the public airwaves to belong to or pay dues to a union for the right to speak.[6] A flat-out victory! But AFTRA then appealed Judge Brieant's decision to the Second Circuit Court of Appeals, which, unfortunately, reversed it in a complicated opinion.[7] The Second Circuit judges said that there was no First Amendment violation in the compulsory union dues requirement. Their ruling was based on the creaky old arguments that Congress was entitled to legislate so as to bring about "labor peace," and that if "free riders" were allowed, unions might not be able to fulfill their bargaining function. Therefore, the judges concluded, the mandatory dues system "serves a substantial public interest."

Judge Brieant had ruled that Buckley and Evans were not "free riders" even though they might derive some benefit from the union's pension plan, which neither man needed or depended upon. The Second Circuit took issue here, too, saying that "There is no rational basis for distinguishing between the degrees of benefit one enjoys as a result of a union's bargaining efforts on his behalf." So one becomes a "free rider" on the union's bargaining merely because it happens to produce some "benefit" that the individual had no need for! That point demonstrates the intellectual quicksand upon which our labor relations law is built.

The Second Circuit then went on to address the argument that compulsory union membership and compliance with union rules violated the plaintiffs' constitutional rights to be employed in the media. It declared that the district court did not have jurisdiction to decide that issue because it might be an unfair labor practice for the union to penalize Buckley or Evans with loss of employment for resigning from membership. It stated that when unfair labor practices are involved, the federal courts must "defer to the exclusive competence of the National Labor Relations Board." The court acknowledged that the union's conduct in telling Buckley that he had to become a "full fledged" member and obey all union rules arguably violated Section 8 of the NLRA, but said that the proper way for him to proceed would be to seek a declaratory order from the NLRB. In other words, take your argument elsewhere.

The Foundation appealed to the Supreme Court, but it declined to review the case, despite a dissent from Chief Justice Burger and Justice Douglas who thought that it raised important First Amendment issues.[8] Therefore, the Foundation did just as the Second Circuit had suggested, and filed for relief from the union's membership requirement with the NLRB. But the NLRB denied the petition on the grounds that the case was now moot—that is, no longer having a point of contention—because AFTRA had already admitted that it could not legally require anyone to become a union member. In its order, the NLRB stated that the law was clear that unions "cannot under any circumstances require 'full fledged membership' or any other type of membership; and a termination of employment for reasons other than nonpayment of dues and fees would be a violation of the Act."[9]

The Foundation kept up the litigation pressure until, on January 16, 1978, AFTRA agreed to mail a notice to all signatories of its collective bargaining contract telling them that no one they employed was obligated to maintain membership in the union and that employees must only pay money equal to the dues of members in order to keep their jobs. Summing up the case, William F. Buckley Jr. wrote in his syndicated column, "Thanks to the National Right to Work Legal Defense Foundation, which financed this case ... employees are precisely *not* bound to obey the union's rules any longer, and the First Amendment has won a significant victory."

SERITIS V. HOTEL AND RESTAURANT EMPLOYEES UNION LOCAL 28

The Foundation became involved in this shocking case in 1977 when two distraught young women sought its help, telling a most repulsive story. The secretary-treasurer of a union local was using his union's compulsory hiring hall to solicit partners for perverse and degrading sexual acts with himself, his buddies, and even with animals. Women who wouldn't go along with his demands were blackballed from getting decent work. It was an appalling case of the abuse of power that union officials can wield.

Karin Seritis and Teri DeLoache were college students trying to work their way through school as waitresses. Local 28 of the Hotel and Restaurant Employees Union in Oakland, California, controlled the highest paying and most desirable restaurant jobs in the San Francisco Bay area; if you wanted to work in any of the restaurants with which it had agreements, you had to go through the union's hiring hall. But when Karin and Teri went to the hiring hall, Ray Lane, the union's secretary-treasurer, made it clear what his terms were: No sex, no jobs. He tried to coerce Karin and Teri into working as topless waitresses, "entertaining" his union cronies at conventions, performing homosexual acts, and even performing on stage with a dog. Karin later told the Foundation's attorney that "He detailed a lot of sex for money ideas and said he wanted to test the merchandise."

When the two women refused to go along with Lane's "suggestions," he was furious and would give them no job referrals. Karin wrote a letter of protest to the union's international office, but instead of action against Lane's despicable antics, she received the advice that she should withdraw the complaint. A union member told her, "You're a pretty girl. I'd hate to see that ruined." So instead of finding good employment in the restaurant industry, Karin and Teri found pressure to become prostitutes and then threats for having the temerity to complain about it!

The two women retained a local attorney in 1976, who filed a complaint against the union for harassment and mental duress. Soon thereafter, the attorney's mother was savagely beaten by an attacker who warned, "Tell your son to drop this case."

Karin and Teri then contacted the Foundation, which entered the case in March 1977. After a hotly contested and dramatic trial, Judge Robert Kroninger awarded the plaintiffs $225,000 in compensatory and punitive damages—the largest award ever assessed against a union in California. But Ray Lane, then in prison on another criminal conviction, claimed that he was destitute and unable to pay. The union also sought to avoid paying by claiming that the award would bankrupt its health and welfare fund—an incredible argument from an organization that collected millions of dollars in compulsory dues every year.

Litigation then continued for two more years, with the Foundation attempting to discover the true financial worth of the union. Lawyers for Local 28 used numerous delaying tactics to prevent Foundation attorneys from obtaining the documents necessary, but they were all defeated, with the judge finally imposing financial sanctions on the union for its delays. The retrial concerning the union's financial condition took place on April 25, 1983, and Judge Kroninger ruled that Local 28 was fully able to pay his $150,000 punitive damage award to Karin and Terri.

Local 28 then appealed to the California Circuit Court of Appeals. Wanting to minimize the delay in getting the money paid to Karin and Teri, the Foundation attorneys asked that the case be assigned a priority basis. Arguments were heard on March 26, 1985, and the Court of Appeals soon thereafter announced its decision affirming Judge Kroninger's judgment against Local 28 in a 25-page opinion. The union appealed to the Supreme Court of California, which declined to review the case, but there was a strange twist at this point. Chief Justice Rose Bird (a highly political justice who would later be voted off the Court) issued an order forbidding the publication of the Court of Appeals opinion. That had (and still has) the effect of preventing it from being cited as precedent in other California cases.[10] The length to which some public officials will go to protect Big Labor is astounding.

After trying one last, desperate measure to get out of paying—an appeal to the U.S. Supreme Court, which was denied—Local 28 finally had to pay up. Karin and Teri received a total of $270,000 in damages—an expensive lesson to union bosses who use their positions of power to abuse and degrade workers.

HUDSON V. CHICAGO TEACHERS UNION

Annie Lee Hudson was a teacher in Chicago. She had been a stalwart in the classroom for thirty years, but in 1982, her employer, the Chicago Board of Education negotiated away her freedom by signing a contract with the Chicago Teachers Union requiring the Board to deduct automatically a union agency fee from the wages of nonmembers such as Annie. Based on the union's "calculation," the agency fee was set at 95 percent of the full union dues. The Board of Education accepted that figure without any question. If any nonmember protested the fee amount, there was a one-sided procedure, which he had to use, culminating in arbitration—*with the arbitrator chosen by the union president.* With that procedure, protesters could hardly expect fair and impartial treatment

Annie Hudson and two other teachers who declined to join the union sent letters protesting the agency fee calculation, arguing that the union was using a substantial part of their money for purposes unrelated to collective bargaining. In response, union officials sent her a brief letter explaining the calculation and how the objectors could file their complaint. Hudson persisted, requesting detailed financial information so she could verify the amazing claim that only 5 percent of the union's dues money was going into political activities. But the union merely replied that she could make an appointment for an "informational conference" at the union office where she could view its financial records. Exasperated, she and the other dissident teachers contacted the Foundation. With the help of Foundation attorneys, they filed suit in 1983, attacking the Illinois statute that permitted agency shop agreements within the public school system and the scheme that the union and the Board of Education had adopted.

The case began with a setback. The district court judge ruled on November 3, 1983 that the statute was not unconstitutional, that the agency shop clause was not objectionable, and that the union's rebate scheme was adequate to protect the First Amendment rights of dissenting teachers.[11] Naturally, the Foundation attorneys appealed this horrendous decision.

Writing for a unanimous Seventh Circuit, Judge Richard Posner reversed the district court.[12] He stated that the union's rebate/arbitration scheme was unconstitutional, a violation of the First Amendment and due process rights of objectors. The union was admonished to devise a new system for collecting agency fees that protected the First and Fourteenth Amendment rights of nonunion teachers. Now the union appealed, and the Supreme Court agreed to review the case.

The Supreme Court issued a unanimous decision affirming the Seventh Circuit.[13] Justice Stevens' opinion for the Court declared that a union must provide nonmembers from whom it collects agency fees with advance notice of the basis for the fee, showing the costs that the union claims are valid collective-bargaining expenses and having those costs verified by an independent auditor. Furthermore, he said, disputed fees must be held in escrow, pending a prompt determination of their legitimacy by an *impartial* decision-maker, not one chosen by the union. The Court's decision pulled the rug out from under union officials who want to use agency fees for their political empire building, and then use kangaroo court proceedings to quickly and officiously dispose of any protests.

Supreme Court decisions set precedents, but they don't enforce themselves. Often, union officials will continue to do things as they please and prefer to engage in further litigation with those who protest rather than comply with judicial guidelines, such as those set forth in the *Hudson* decision. When the case was remanded, the union set up a new system for dealing with objections to its agency fee determination. When Foundation attorneys scrutinized the new scheme, they concluded that it was constitutionally inadequate for numerous reasons, including the fact that it included as chargeable expenses union organizing and public relations that were clearly not chargeable under the *Ellis/Fails* decision. Despite that and other serious defects, the district judge again ruled completely in favor of the union. When the case was appealed again to the Seventh Circuit, that court now ruled that the nonunion teachers had to exhaust the union's new "impartial decision-maker" scheme before they could return to federal court to challenge the procedures. Unfortunately, that played right into the hands of union officials and their lawyers, who are capable of devising a maze of procedural steps designed to wear down dissenting workers. Litigation dragged on until 1992, when the union agreed to return to objecting teachers all fees collected for the 1991–92 school year rather than litigate the validity of its "fair-share" agency fee.

The Supreme Court's rulings in *Hudson* have resulted in favorable judgments against many unions in scores of subsequent cases brought for workers by Foundation attorneys. For all of its important precedents, however, perhaps the key lesson of *Hudson* is that as long as union bosses can make workers pay them money at all, they will do the very least they can get away with in complying with the law requiring fair treatment for dissenting workers.

BECK V. COMMUNICATION WORKERS OF AMERICA

One of the most momentous of all the Foundation's cases involved Maryland telephone lineman Harry Beck. His employer had a collective bargaining contract with the Communication Workers of America (CWA), but Beck had exercised his right to decline to become a union member and only pay an agency fee. He was, however, certain that the CWA's fee calculation was grossly inaccurate and its procedures were unfair to those who questioned it. With the assistance of Foundation attorneys, Beck filed suit in U.S. District Court in Maryland.

After almost three years of procedural sparring, the district court ruled that the collection and disbursement of agency fees for purposes other than collective bargaining violated the First Amendment rights of workers.[14] The judge appointed a "special master" to investigate the union's spending and determine the lawfully chargeable and nonchargeable portions. After months of poring over the union's books, *the special master reported that it was spending approximately 80 percent of its income on political activities and other matters having nothing to do with collective bargaining.* Based on that information, the court ordered the Communication Workers to refund all excess fees that Beck and his co-plaintiffs had paid since 1976 and required it to establish a record keeping system that would distinguish between its collective bargaining expenditures and other, nonchargeable expenditures.

Union officials, horrified at what that decision would do to their power to squeeze money out of unwilling workers, appealed to the Fourth Circuit. In two decisions, the second with all ten judges of the court sitting, the court held that it was a violation of the National Labor Relations Act for unions to compel workers to pay for more than the cost of collective bargaining, rather than the *constitutional violation* the district court had found.[15] Instead, the Fourth Circuit held that unions breach their "duty of fair representation" when they compel workers like Beck to pay for activities such as political lobbying, organizing of workers in other companies and various "community services." The Communication Workers then appealed to the U.S. Supreme Court.

Beck's case was ably briefed and argued before the Supreme Court by labor law expert Edwin Vieira Jr. and the Foundation's Hugh Reilly. To the great surprise of many, President Reagan's Solicitor General, Charles Fried, submitted a friend of the court brief *opposing* Beck and supporting Big Labor's forced dues scheme. Nevertheless, the Court, in an opinion by Justice Brennan, held in favor of Beck and affirmed the decision of the Fourth Circuit that a union breaches it statutory duty of fair representation by using objecting nonmembers' dues for political and other nonbargaining purposes.[16] After citing a precedent in which the Court had narrowed the obligation to support union activities to its "financial core," Justice Brennan wrote, "The statutory question presented in this case, then, is whether this 'financial core' includes the obligation to support union activities beyond those germane to collective bargaining, contract administration, and grievance adjustment. We think it does not." The Court's decision meant that, just as with public employees and workers covered by the Railway Labor Act (the *Abood* and *Ellis/Fails* cases), workers covered by the NLRA—that is, most of the American workforce—are also free from the obligation to finance union activities that aren't directly relevant to collective bargaining.

Although the Supreme Court's decision was a major victory for worker rights, the problem then became how to translate its words into actual freedom from the misuse of compulsory union dues and fees. It would be expected that union bosses would turn a blind eye to *Beck* and fight tooth and nail to continue skimming off as much money as possible for their political empire building. Astoundingly, they now received aid and comfort from the federal government itself.

The National Labor Relations Board has long been an accomplice in Big Labor's goals. Following *Beck,* it aided Big Labor by refusing to process cases where workers had clear-cut grievances over the misuse of their forced dues. Under both Republican and Democratic presidents, the NLRB has choked off cases where workers wanted to avoid paying dues to support union actions that the Supreme Court had ruled they could not be compelled to pay for. The situation is reminiscent of the "massive resistance" campaign mounted by officials in the South after the Supreme Court's desegregation ruling in *Brown v. Board of Education.* There is, however, a difference: After *Brown,* the weight of the executive branch was marshaled against segregation, but after *Beck,* the executive branch remained part of the problem, not part of the solution.

To be precise, the problem was that successive General Counsels of the NLRB have been hostile to the enforcement of *Beck* rights and have rejected out of hand or sat on worker complaints regarding the misuse of their dues money for years. The General Counsel has unreviewable discretion whether or not to prosecute unfair labor practice charges filed with the NLRB. Therefore, as a practical matter, it is the only forum available to most workers with *Beck*-rights grievances.

The Supreme Court's holding that it is a breach of the duty of fair representation to compel dissident workers to pay for costs beyond those of collective bargaining means that such workers can either take their cases directly into the courts or to the NLRB first. Litigation in court is protracted and costly, requiring workers to hire an attorney and, in many instances, an accounting expert—unless they're fortunate enough to have the Foundation's help. The administrative processes of the NLRB are supposed to be more expeditious and without cost to workers because the General Counsel's office prosecutes for them. But, if the General Counsel chooses not to upset Big Labor by undermining its power to squeeze money out of workers, the road to justice is effectively blocked for most workers.

The *Pirlott* case is a typical example of the stonewalling that workers have received at the hands of "public servants" who have the power to decide which laws they like and which ones they don't.

Dave and Sherry Pirlott worked for Schreiber Foods Company in Green Bay, Wisconsin. The company had a collective bargaining contract with Teamsters Local 75. Sherry was actually one of the union stewards, but she came to the conclusion that "the other union stewards did things for the betterment of the union, not for the betterment of the workers." Tensions mounted between Sherry Pirlott and the other union stewards to the point where she was threatened with bodily harm. That was enough. Sherry and Dave then announced that they were resigning their membership and would exercise their rights under *Beck*. A few months later, Local 75 sued them in local court to force them to pay their accumulated dues. The Pirlotts had to defend themselves in court because no attorney in the Green Bay area was willing to take on the Teamsters. The judge, who was friendly toward the union lawyers, refused to listen to Sherry's arguments and ruled that the couple had to pay their back dues. Only then did they learn about the Foundation.

Foundation attorneys filed NLRB charges in November 1989 to block the compulsory payment of dues and uphold the Pirlotts' rights under *Beck*. The administrative law judge who heard the evidence held that the Teamsters officials' claim that they spent only 1.1 percent of worker dues on politics and other nonchargeable items was "so implausible as to be a *per se* violation." But when the case was appealed to the full NLRB in 1992, the Board merely sat on the case. With the incoming Clinton administration in 1993, the new Board appointees continued stonewalling the Pirlotts' case. Finally, in 1999 Foundation attorneys took the extraordinary step of petitioning for a *writ of mandamus* in a U.S. Court of Appeals, which forced the NLRB to proceed with the case.

Amazingly, the NLRB then continued to drag its heels by remanding the case to the administrative law judge "for further record development." Another hearing was held in October 2001, and new appeals followed. In 2004, the Pirlotts' case is still pending before the Board, fourteen years after it was first filed!

The willingness and ability of NLRB personnel to ignore and evade the law when it displeases union autocrats is an appalling defect in our system of justice. Cases like the Pirlotts' explain why the Committee works so hard to prevent supporters of compulsory unionism from being appointed to the NLRB, something that has been an enormous task under both Republican and Democratic administrations.

Not only has the NLRB stonewalled enforcement of the *Beck* decision, thus enabling union bosses to continue raking in dues and fees from workers who want to pay for nothing more than the actual costs of collective bargaining, but it has even misled people about their rights. When the Foundation learned in the early 1990s that NLRB personnel were not correctly informing workers about their rights, it did a test, having individuals call NLRB offices to ask if the presence of a so-called "union security" clause meant that they had to join the union and pay full dues. Despite clear Supreme Court rulings that no one has to become a union member and pay for more than the cost of "core" union functions, the results were maddening. In the great majority of instances, NLRB personnel misinformed the callers, telling them that the law required union membership and full payment of dues. *They explained the law to callers as union officials wanted it to be, not the way it actually was.*

Legislation in Congress that would have put more teeth in workers' *Beck* rights was killed by Senators and Representatives beholden to Big Labor. At the time of this writing, 25 years after the district court ruling in Harry Beck's favor and sixteen years after the Supreme Court's decision, there are still numerous unresolved cases where workers are trying to escape from the financial grip of union bosses.

Beck and the many subsequent cases like *Pirlott* where workers have tried to assert their rights, show that we need a solution to this problem that cuts the Gordian Knot. Instead of fighting to get money back after union bosses have seized it, we need to change the law so that workers can just say "No" to their demands in the first place.

ROESSER V. UNIVERSITY OF DETROIT

Another facet of the battle between individual rights and union domination is that of employees' religious beliefs. Many workers are put in an unhappy situation because they find a conflict between compulsory unionism and their faith. The Foundation has helped to shape the law in this area through its assistance to such individuals. *Roesser v. University of Detroit* is a leading case.

Dr. Robert Roesser had been hired by the University of Detroit, a Jesuit institution, as an assistant professor of electrical engineering. Because the university had a collective bargaining agreement with the University of Detroit Professors Union, which was affiliated with both the Michigan Education Association (MEA) and the National Education Association (NEA), he either had to join the union or pay an "agency fee" to keep his teaching position. Roesser decided not to join the union, but authorized payroll deductions for his compulsory fees.

The dispute began when Roesser learned that the MEA and NEA were both engaged in activities promoting abortion. A strong Catholic, Roesser believed that the Church forbids members to in any way support the practice of abortion. He then informed the union that his religious beliefs were incompatible with continued support of the MEA/NEA, and said that he was withdrawing his authorization for payroll deductions for his agency fees. He offered to pay the entire fee amount to a charity instead, or to pay only the small portion that went to the University of Detroit Professors Union for its collective bargaining activities, with the balance going to charity. (Roesser did not believe that the local union was involved in pro-abortion activities.)

Union and university officials rejected Professor Roesser's offer. Instead, they would allow him to reduce his fee payment only by the percentage which the MEA and NEA claimed they spent on pro-abortion activities. That would still have meant that most of Roesser's money would flow to the MEA and NEA, and he found that unacceptable. He wrote back, saying, "The objectionable issues are supported not only by the budgeted amounts but also by the weight and influence of the entire

MEA and NEA. There is just no dealing with something that is inherently wrong."

Because Roesser and the union officials could not come to an agreement, the university then informed the professor that his employment was being terminated. Regarding the situation as completely unfair, Roesser contacted both the Foundation and the Equal Employment Opportunity Commission (EEOC). The EEOC filed a complaint stating that the university had engaged in an unlawful employment practice in violation of the Civil Rights Act because it discharged Roesser due to his sincerely held religious beliefs. The district court granted Roesser's request to intervene in the case, thereby allowing Foundation attorneys to participate in the litigation on his behalf.

In his affidavit filed with the court, Roesser testified, "I may not pay money to the union to support ... pro-abortion activities, nor may I associate with the union because of these activities." Nonetheless, the district court held in favor of the union, saying that its rebate accommodation was reasonable and that Roesser's proposed accommodation would be a "hardship" on the union.[17] Roesser's attorneys appealed that adverse ruling to the Sixth Circuit.

The Sixth Circuit unanimously reversed the district court.[18] Judge Norris observed that there were two elements of Roesser's complaint over having to pay agency fees to help finance the MEA-NEA political machine. His religious beliefs forbade him from paying money to organizations that worked to legalize abortion, and also from *associating in any way* with such organizations. The court stated that, "the district court erred in concluding that an accommodation offered by an employer which does not even address, let alone resolve, the employee's conflict is reasonable as a matter of law. The duty to accommodate cannot be defined without reference to the specific religious belief at issue. Here the employer was confronted with two religious objections, one of which was completely ignored." Judge Norris remanded the case with instructions to the district court to find a reasonable accommodation.

In the meantime, Roesser had found employment with General Motors, where his expertise in robotics was desired and he had no union dues or fees to pay. Although he was entitled to both back pay and rein-statement at the University of Detroit, he chose to take only the back pay and remain with General Motors because he foresaw future difficulties over tenure. Nevertheless, the Sixth Circuit's decision stands as a key prece-dent in the battle between union bosses intent on forcing all workers to finance their political and ideological activities and the consciences of workers who have religious objections to them.

ORR V. NFL PLAYERS ASSOCIATION

Using great teamwork and strategy, in 1993 and 1994 the Foundation assisted Washington Redskins players and defeated an attempt by the National Football League Players Association (NFLPA) to do an end run around Virginia's Right to Work law.

Forty-one members of the Redskins were fed up with the "represen-tation" they were receiving from the NFLPA. The players, like so many other Americans who have no choice but to put up with union bosses if they want to work, realized that the NFLPA officials were charging them far more than their "services" ought to cost. "I want to see the balance sheet. I want to see where the money is going," said star defensive line-man Charles Mann. Tight end Terry Orr, who contacted the Foundation and obtained its expert legal assistance soon after the NFLPA threatened to suspend the dissenting players for their refusal to pay their dues, blasted the union's massive increase in dues. "Some players don't like the fact that our dues went up 250 percent. You can talk about a rebate, but what's going to be rebated? Whatever's left over from big Super Bowl parties, or big pay raises for union officers, or what?" Orr said.

The key to the case was establishing that Virginia's Right to Work statute applied to the players and protected them against the union's demands and threats. Foundation attorneys immediately took the offen-sive by filing for a temporary restraining order in Virginia Circuit Court in Leesburg to stop the NFLPA from ordering that Orr and other protest-ing players be suspended from playing until they paid their dues. Lawyers for the NFLPA responded by trying to delay the state court's order and have the case removed to a federal court. Their plan was to buy time so that the NFLPA could bring in a union-paid arbitrator from the District of Columbia who would say that Virginia's law didn't apply and that the players must either pay up or sit out games. The union-picked arbitrator, Herbert Fishgold, determined that the predominant job situs for Redskin players was the District of Columbia because that was the location of the stadium where the team's home games were played. Very convenient for the NFLPA—the District has no Right to Work protection.

But the Foundation attorneys anticipated that play, and quickly obtained a hearing and a ruling from Federal District Judge Claude Hilton that the case was properly before the Virginia court. When Virginia Circuit Court Judge Thomas Horne heard the facts, he ruled on November 8, 1994, that "A Redskin player's primary job situs is where he spends the majority of his time working. In each case, as members of a team, that job situs is Virginia, where most of their working hours are spent."[19] Because Virginia is a Right to Work state, the NFLPA was forbidden to demand suspension of the players who had stood up to its enormous dues increase.

Cases of this kind come up repeatedly, with the issue being whether a state's Right to Work statute applies to a worker or not. Often the dispute involves workers who live in a Right to Work state, but do their jobs in a "federal enclave" in that state, such as a military base. In some cases, the Foundation has been successful; in others they have not. But as the NFLPA case shows, workers who receive Foundation assistance always get an expert legal team on their side.

AIR LINE PILOTS V. MILLER

One of the favorite tactics of union bosses who are intent on avoiding their legal obligation to deal fairly with workers who want to exercise their right to pay for only the cost of collective bargaining is to force them into arbitration. When the worker says, "I am dropping my union membership and will pay only my share of the cost of collective bargaining," union officials often say, "Fine. You're entitled to a minimal dues reduction, and if you don't like it, you'll have to go through our arbitration procedure." The arbitrators are rarely disinterested parties, however. They know that they would lose out on future union arbitration business if they were to forget who butters their bread. Compelling workers to go through a phony arbitration just raises the cost and frustration involved in challenging union officials.

Under ordinary principles of law, people are not bound to arbitration unless they have previously *agreed* to it. If dissident workers have not agreed to a rigged union arbitration procedure, should they have to waste their time with it? That was the question in *Air Line Pilots Association v. Miller.*

In 1991, Delta Airlines and the Air Line Pilots Association (ALPA) entered into a contract requiring that all Delta pilots either become union members or pay an "agency fee" to the union if they would not become members. Many pilots, including Robert Miller, decided not to become union members. For 1992, the union charged the non-members just 12.5 percent less than full dues, later revising the dues reduction figure to 19 percent and refunding the difference.

Dissatisfied with ALPA's calculations and procedures, Miller and more than 150 other non-member pilots took their case into federal district court, where they ran into a stone wall. The union announced that it was going to submit the pilots' objections to an arbitration under its "Policies and Procedures" before an arbitrator appointed by the American Arbitration Association *from a special panel of arbitrators approved by unions.* When the pilots asked the federal judge to enjoin the so-called arbitration, because they had never agreed to arbitrate and should not have to go through a sham procedure, the judge refused. As expected, the arbitrator sided with ALPA on almost all items that the pilots had challenged as not being germane to collective bargaining.

Back in court, when the pilots asked in discovery that ALPA produce documents identifying the nature of the activities and expenses in each "project code" it used to allocate its expenses as chargeable, ALPA countered by offering to let pilots examine all of its 1992 expense records—a mountain of paper that would have been very difficult for the pilots, as outsiders, to sift through. But then the judge cut off the dispute over documents by granting summary judgment in favor of the union. Relying on the arbitrator's "findings," he ruled that the pilots had to go through arbitration and that it had been done fairly. At that point, the Foundation agreed to represent the pilots and appealed the case to the U.S. Court of Appeals for the District of Columbia.

The Court of Appeals reversed the district court unanimously. To the union's argument that an arbitrator's decision was entitled to "deference," Judge Silberman responded, "(T)here is no statutory ground to defer to either the union or the arbitrator on any of the issues presented in the case. The only reason an arbitrator's decision is normally afforded deference in a federal court is because the parties have *agreed* to put their dispute to him or her." The union also tried to convince the court that its lobbying of Congress and government agencies concerning airline regulation should be regarded as germane to collective bargaining and therefore chargeable to dissenting workers. Judge Silberman also crushed that argument by writing that "it is hard to imagine (workers' First Amendment) interests more clearly placed in jeopardy than when the union uses the dissidents' money to pursue political objectives."[20] ALPA had lost big, and decided to appeal to the Supreme Court.

The Court agreed to hear only the arbitration issue. Oral arguments were presented on March 23, 1998, and the decision was announced barely two months later. Justice Ginsburg's opinion for a seven-member majority put the question this way: "When a union adopts an arbitration process to comply with *Hudson's* 'impartial decisionmaker' requirement, must agency-fee objectors pursue and exhaust the arbitral remedy before challenging the union's calculation in a federal-court action?" The answer was a clear "No." "ALPA," Justice Ginsburg wrote, "seeks exhaustion not of an administrative remedy established by Congress, but of an arbitral remedy established by a private party. Ordinarily, 'arbitration is a matter of contract and a party cannot be required to submit to arbitration any dispute which he has not agreed so to submit.'"[21]

Nor was the Court swayed by the union's argument that it was more "efficient" to force dissenting workers to go through arbitration first: "The answer to ALPA's efficiency concern lies in conscientious management of the pretrial process to guard against abuse, not in a judicially imposed exhaustion requirement," Justice Ginsburg wrote.

With the decision in *Miller*, one of the tactics of union officials in thwarting dissenting workers from vindicating their rights was taken away. Workers can point to a clear Supreme Court ruling whenever union bosses attempt to drag them through rigged arbitration procedures.

After the case was returned to the district court, a companion class-action suit was filed. In 2002, Foundation attorneys negotiated a settlement of more than $750,000 in damages and interest for 330 non-union Delta pilots.

This chapter has hit only some of the highlights of the National Right to Work Legal Defense Foundation's history. (See Appendix A for an overview of the Foundation's record and its Supreme Court cases.) Its expert staff of ten attorneys is currently handling almost 300 cases, representing workers from all over the United States whose rights have been violated by union officials. Some of those cases will establish crucial precedents, further protecting the rights of workers to be free from union coercion. There will always be an abundance of work for the Foundation as long as the laws of the United States permit compulsory unionism and labor union bosses refuse to respect the rights of individuals.

NOTES

1. Archibald Cox, "Internal Affairs of Labor Unions Under the Labor Reform Act of 1959" 58 *Michigan Law Review*, 819, 852.
2. *Railway Clerks v. Allen*, 373 U.S. 113 (1963).
3. *Abood v. Detroit Board of Education*, 431 U.S. 209 (1977).
4. *International Association of Machinists v. Street*, 376 U.S. 740 (1961).
5. *Ellis, et al v. Brotherhood of Railway, Airline & Steamship Clerks*, 466 U.S. 435 (1984).
6. *Evans v. AFTRA*, 354 F. Supp. 823 (S.D.N.Y.1972)
7. *Buckley v. AFTRA*, 496 F.2d 305 (2d Cir.1974)
8. *Buckley v. AFTRA*, 419 U.S. 1093 (1974)
9. *Buckley v. AFTRA*, 222 N.L.R.B. 197 (1976)
10. Chief Justice Bird was able to suppress official publication of the Court of Appeals decision, but it is available to interested readers: *Seritis v. Hotel and*

Restaurant Employees Union, Local 28, 213 Cal. Rptr. 588 or 119 L.R.R M. 2497.

11. *Hudson v. Chicago Teachers Union,* 573 F. Supp. 1505 (N.D. Ill.1983).
12. *Chicago Teachers Union v. Hudson,* 743 F. 2d 1187 (7th Cir.1984).
13. *Chicago Teachers Union v. Hudson,* 475 U.S. 292 (1986).
14. *Beck v. CWA,* 468 F. Supp. 93 (D.Md. 1979)
15. *Communication Workers v. Beck,* 800 F.2d 1280 (4th Cir.1986)
16. *Communication Workers v. Beck,* 487 U.S. 735 (1988)
17. *EEOC v. University of Detroit,* 701 F. Supp 1326 (E.D. Mich.1988).
18. *EEOC v. University of Detroit,* 904 F.2d 331 (6th Cir.1990).
19. *Orr v. National Football League Players' Association* 35 Va. Cir. 156 (1994).
20. *Miller v. Air Line Pilots Association,* 108 F.3d 1415 (D.C. Cir.1997).
21. *Air Line Pilots Association v. Miller,* 523 U.S. 866, 876 (1998) (quoting *Steelworkers v. Warrion & Gulf Nav. Co.,* 363 U.S. 574, 582 (1960)).

CHAPTER EIGHT

THE (BIG LABOR) EMPIRE
STRIKES BACK

J ust as union bosses frequently target companies and workers for
reprisals if they have the temerity to oppose them, so have they targeted the National Right to Work Committee and the Legal Defense
Foundation. Nothing would please Big Labor's autocrats more than to
weaken or remove the two foremost obstacles to its dream of spreading
compulsory unionism across America. In this chapter we will look at a
number of attacks launched by the union autocrats, or their governmental allies, designed to hinder and harass the Right to Work organizations.

THE MULTI-UNION LAWSUIT
Never was the "win at any cost" mentality of Big Labor put more con-
spicuously on display than by its lawsuit, initiated in 1973, against the
National Right to Work Legal Defense Foundation and the National
Right to Work Committee. Angered over the growing success of the
Foundation in advancing worker rights and forcing unions to atone for
violations thereof, the labor bosses and their legal advisers concocted a
nefarious lawsuit designed to sap the resources of both Right to Work
organizations. Reed Larson said of the suit to Right to Work supporters, "It is obvious that we have struck a sore spot in our successful liti-
gations on behalf of workers and against union officials who perpetrate
abuses and injustices under compulsory unionism." Big Labor wanted
such litigation to stop.

181

What had the Foundation and the Committee done that supposedly violated the law? According to the complaint of thirteen unions, including the AFL-CIO itself, the Right to Work organizations were financing workers' lawsuits against unions with funds provided by "interested employers," conduct which allegedly was prohibited by the Landrum-Griffin Act. Big Labor's autocrats knew that by bringing their suit, described as "the largest multi-union lawsuit in history," they would force the Foundation and the Committee to spend time and money on their own defense rather than defending the rights of union-abused workers. Moreover, there was a deeper purpose to the suit—to use the process of legal discovery to force the Foundation and the Committee to disclose the names of their contributors. *That* was something the Right to Work leaders were determined never to do. If Big Labor could identify Right to Work supporters, many of them would be targets for retribution.

The 1973 suit was not the first time that the Committee had been compelled to defend itself. Big Labor had tried a similar ploy in 1964 when President Johnson's Secretary of Labor, Willard Wirtz, instigated a suit against the Committee for allegedly having violated a provision of the law requiring organizations to file reports with the Secretary's office. The law applied only to organizations engaged in activities designed to "persuade employees to exercise or not to exercise . . . the right to organize and bargain collectively. . . ." The Committee had never tried to persuade workers not to form or join unions. The sole basis for the suit was a speech that Committee president William Harrison had given at the dedication of a new chemical plant in Virginia. In his speech, Harrison discussed the importance of Right to Work, but that was far from the kind of activity covered by the law.

Still, Wirtz contended that the Committee had violated the law by failing to file reports disclosing an agreement with the company to persuade workers not to unionize—an agreement that never existed! The Committee responded that it was unaware of any labor issues at the company at the time of Harrison's speech, which merely extolled the benefits of protecting the right of each worker to decide whether or not to join a union through Right to Work laws.

After three years of litigation and discovery, the Committee, eager to end the annoying and costly battle, offered to file the report *with the court,* but made out in a way that denied that the filing was legally mandated. U.S. District Judge Alexander Holtzhoff was glad to accept that resolution. He told the government's attorney that the Secretary of Labor could retrieve the report from the clerk of the court if he really wanted it, then dismissed the case, writing, "there has been a waste of government funds in filing this suit."

As we have already seen, Big Labor is nothing if not persistent. In 1972, the general counsel for the United Auto Workers tried to get the government to do its dirty work, asking the U.S. Department of Labor to compel the Committee to disclose the names of its contributors. This time, the Labor Department refused to cooperate with the union bosses, responding that it was not the intent of the law to require "a massive reporting program such as might result if all contributors to associations, or ... members of employer associations were required to report."

Hoping that the third time would be the charm in their drive to get their hands on the names of Right to Work contributors, Big Labor's top lawyer, Joseph Rauh, brought the multi-union lawsuit in 1973. The case was assigned to U.S. District Judge Charles Richey. Rauh's legal argument was that the Foundation was acting as a mere front for anti-union employers in violation of a provision of the Landrum-Griffin Act making it illegal for employers to assist union members in suing their unions. That theory was just as ridiculous as had been Secretary Wirtz's 1964 gambit over the alleged "persuader activities." The Foundation provided legal aid only in cases that were brought to it by aggrieved workers. In many cases, employers were named as co-defendants in Foundation lawsuits because they were just as culpable as the union officials in foisting compulsory unionism on employees. And in no case had any contributor ever influenced the selection or pursuit of Foundation litigation.

Despite the fact that the suit was based on nothing but empty accusations, Judge Richey denied a motion to dismiss the case and ordered that the Foundation disclose the names of more than 100 of its larger contributors so that the plaintiffs might seek evidence to prove their case.

This was just what lawyers call a "fishing expedition." The union lawyers had presented no evidence that the Foundation was in violation of the law, but wanted to make what they euphemistically called "discrete inquiries" of the contributors, hoping to find their evidence—or anything else of interest.

By ordering the disclosure of any of its contributors, Judge Richey in effect was putting in jeopardy the Foundation's entire litigation program. Release of any contributor identities to union lawyers would have virtually destroyed the Foundation's ability to raise the funds needed to carry out that program. Small business owners—who are a significant part of the Foundation's donor base—would clearly be loath to contribute if they learned that giving money to the Foundation automatically put their names on a target list for union organizers. Furthermore, individual union members and union-represented non-members—another significant group of Foundation contributors—would hardly give to the Foundation if they knew that doing so could mean suffering discrimination or retaliation by militant local union officials. Even though the Foundation's attorneys pointed out the extremely sensitive nature of the contributor list, Judge Richey remained adamant: Disclose or face the consequences.

The problem of protecting the freedom of people to contribute to organizations in privacy was not a new one. In 1958, the Supreme Court had dealt with the same issue when Alabama tried to force the NAACP to disclose its contributor list. In *NAACP v. Alabama,* the Court prevented the state from compelling disclosure of NAACP contributors, writing that "It is hardly a novel perception that compelled disclosure of affiliation with groups engaged in advocacy may constitute an effective restraint on freedom of association...."[1] Unfortunately, Judge Richey failed to see the parallel between the State of Alabama's interest in finding out who was supporting the NAACP and the interest of Big Labor in finding out who was supporting the National Right to Work Legal Defense Foundation.

In a last-ditch effort to avoid a contempt order, the Foundation offered to make the list available to *the court* for inspection, but only under conditions that would prevent the leaking of the names to the union lawyers. To show its good faith, the Foundation had the information boxed and shipped by armored truck to the court. But instead of seeing that as a way of resolving the matter, Judge Richey asked the union lawyers if it would satisfy them. Naturally, Rauh refused the offer, contending that his legal team needed to know who the Foundation's contributors were. That should have made it clear to Judge Richey that the point of the case was not the application of the law, but harassment and invasion of privacy. Richey, however, stuck to his disclosure order and the boxes of documents were returned to the Foundation.

Reed Larson, president of the Foundation, now had to decide whether to obey the order of a federal judge and violate the confidentiality of Foundation contributors, or refuse to disclose the information and risk going to jail for contempt of court. In the finest spirit of civil disobedience, he decided that he had to disobey the judge.

Finally, on June 2, 1977, Richey handed down his resolution of the case. He said that because the defendants had "steadfastly disobeyed the orders of this Court" and "refused to disclose to the plaintiff unions the names of their contributors," he would regard as proven all the factual claims made by the unions in their suit. But then came a surprise: He agreed with the Foundation's argument that even if the plaintiffs were correct that it had violated the law prohibiting employer associations from assisting union members in suits against their unions, *the law itself was unconstitutional.* Judge Richey wrote that the statute, "violates the first amendment rights of the Foundation and its contributors; the statute must therefore be deemed void and unenforceable as applied to the defendant Foundation."[2] After four years of legal wrangling, the Foundation had been found to have violated a law that was unconstitutional!

Joe Rauh and his union boss clients were furious at this defeat and appealed Judge Richey's decision to the Court of Appeals for the D.C. Circuit. That prolonged the case and succeeded in continuing the drain on the Committee and the Foundation, but otherwise accomplished nothing for Rauh's clients. The Court of Appeals, rather than deciding the issue of the constitutionality of the law, focused on the "interested employer" language of the statute and ruled that it "would not apply to legitimate activity of a bona fide, independent legal aid organization."[3] In that, the court was precisely correct. Whether constitutional or not, the law was not aimed at the sort of legal assistance to aggrieved workers provided by the Foundation. The D.C. Circuit vacated all of Judge Richey's orders based on the Foundation's refusal to produce the names sought by the unions, and sent the case back for further proceedings to ascertain whether the Legal Defense Foundation was truly "a bona fide, independent legal aid organization."

Richey then did just what the Court of Appeals had instructed him to do, and the case dragged on until 1984. In the end, he ruled forthrightly that, "Despite the large quantity of paper filed by the plaintiffs in this case ... plaintiffs do not present a single fact tending to dispute the following conclusions, supported by defendants' submissions: 1) Foundation participation in ... litigation is initiated by an employee request for assistance.... 2) Litigation decisions are made by the Foundation staff attorneys without any outside control.... 3) Contributions received by the Foundation are all placed in a general account and are not pledged for use in a particular case or for cases involving particular issues."[4] The exasperated judge therefore granted summary judgment in favor of the Foundation and the Committee and ordered that the case "be dismissed with prejudice."

Rauh wasn't quite through yet. The unions appealed once more to the D.C. Circuit. Strongly rebuffing Rauh's arguments, on January 21, 1986, the Court of Appeals affirmed Judge Richey's summary judgment for the Foundation and Committee. The Court's opinion pointed out that "(n)othing in the record even remotely suggests that employers involved in the Foundation have the power to cause any union members to bring harassing suits against labor organizations or otherwise to disrupt union harmony."[5] The thirteen-year ordeal was finally over.

Rauh and his union cronies had failed to silence the Foundation and had failed to pry loose the information they wanted—the names of contributors so that they could be harassed and intimidated. The time-consuming, vexatious litigation merely diverted resources away from cases that helped workers vindicate their rights under the law. In the smoke-filled offices where Big Labor makes its decisions, that was no doubt the silver lining to their loss—fewer workers (like those discussed in the previous chapter) were able to sue for the wrongs done to them because the Foundation was busy defending *itself* in this abusive and groundless lawsuit.

A LOW BLOW FROM THE IRS

Having charitable, tax-exempt status under the Internal Revenue Code is very important to the National Right to Work Legal Defense Foundation. Without it, donations made by individuals would not be deductible from their taxes and the level of giving would decline. Owing to an exceedingly strange ruling by the IRS, however, the Foundation's tax-exempt status was threatened for several years in the late 1970s.

When the Foundation was initially incorporated in the District of Columbia in 1968, it applied for and received from the Internal Revenue Service a ruling that it was a charitable organization and therefore exempt from taxation. The Foundation's articles of incorporation stated that its purpose was "to take all legitimate action to further the defense of the rights of workers who are suffering legal injustice as a result of employment discrimination under compulsory unionism arrangements, and to assist such workers in protecting rights guaranteed to them under the Constitution and laws of the United States without fee or charge...." That description of the Foundation's goals and activities satisfied the IRS that the Foundation was to operate exclusively for charitable purposes, and the IRS recognized the Foundation's tax-exempt status in a letter ruling dated January 20, 1969.

In 1975 the Foundation's trustees decided to move its operating headquarters from the District of Columbia to Virginia for a variety of reasons. At the same time, an application was made to reincorporate the Foundation in North Carolina, placing it in a jurisdiction much more favorable than the District to defend against the barrage of legal attacks on the Foundation coming from union officials. The trustees incorporated a new

National Right to Work Legal Defense Foundation, identical in all respects to the existing D.C. corporation, in North Carolina. To complete the maneuver, it was necessary for the new North Carolina corporation to apply to the IRS for charitable, tax-exempt status. No one thought there would be any trouble in that.

An application was made to the IRS on May 12, 1975. But rather than giving quick approval, as is typical in such cases, the IRS requested further information from the Foundation on June 27. The requested information was immediately supplied, but instead of promptly approving the application for tax-exempt status, the IRS then sat on the application *for two and a half years*. It denied the Foundation's repeated requests for action. Finally the IRS ruled on November 4, 1977, that the Foundation was *not* a charitable organization and therefore not entitled to tax-exempt status. It was a stunning blow.

Equally stunning were the reasons given by the IRS for its determination. The law provides that organizations are to be deemed charitable if operated for certain purposes, among them the defense of "human and civil rights secured by law." The IRS Commissioner gave that phrase a bizarre and unprecedented interpretation, saying, "We conclude that the phrase 'human and civil rights secured by law' refers only to those human and civil rights that can be clearly demonstrated to be of sufficiently broad public concern that their defense promotes the social welfare." That was an absurd idea—that IRS bureaucrats were entitled to decide which rights were "of sufficiently broad public concern" and confer tax-exempt status only on organizations defending those rights. The ruling went on to explain that "only those individual liberties, freedoms, and privileges involving human dignity that are either specifically guaranteed by the U.S. Constitution or by a special statutory provision coming directly within the scope of the 13th or 14th Amendment, [or] some other comparable constitutional provision. . . ." mattered as far as tax-exempt status went. The Foundation's defense of human and civil rights from abuse by union officials clothed with the coercive, government-granted power of exclusive bargaining representation, wasn't important enough for the IRS Commissioner, so tax-exempt status was denied.

The Foundation promptly sued to have the IRS ruling overturned, filing in federal district court in Raleigh, North Carolina. A trial without a jury was held before Judge Dupree, who gave the IRS a complete shellacking in his December 21, 1979, ruling.

First, to the IRS Commissioner's notion that the right to work is not among the "liberties, freedoms, and privileges involving human dignity that are specifically guaranteed by the United States Constitution," Judge Dupree pointed out that the Supreme Court disagreed. He cited the Supreme Court's opinion in *Truax v. Raich,* which held that "the right to work for a living in the common occupations of the community is of the very essence of the personal freedom and opportunity that it was the purpose of the [Fourteenth] Amendment to secure."[6]

Judge Dupree then took issue with the IRS's argument that the right to work is protected only "in the context of an individual versus the state" and is not a "generally protected constitutional right." His response was that the government's argument was "patently meritless" because "A fundamental right that would be protectable only against governments and not against private persons is fundamental in name only." Furthermore, he noted, the Thirteenth Amendment, which prohibits slavery, "is a direct prohibition upon individuals," not just the government.

The judge concluded his demolition job of the absurd IRS case by saying, "The defense of each citizen's right to work under the First, Fifth, and Fourteenth Amendments is a noble objective. The public has a paramount interest in insuring that compulsory union arrangements do not unnecessarily infringe upon each worker's freedom of thought, association or speech." He ruled that the Foundation certainly was a charitable organization within the meaning of the Internal Revenue Code. Seldom has the IRS lost a case so ignominiously.

But what was behind the case? It is extremely unusual for the IRS to take years to make a decision on an application for tax-exempt status. Moreover, the theory that an organization dedicated to providing free legal assistance to people whose rights have been violated is "charitable" only if it litigates solely constitutional claims was both unprecedented and a creative misreading of the law. Why did the IRS choose to try it out on the Foundation? It looks as though this was another of the many instances where the IRS has been used for political purposes. Syndicated columnist James J. Kilpatrick called the case "an IRS vendetta," saying, "The giants of labor complained that they were being impertinently trod upon by this pesky outfit, and they demanded that the IRS put an end to it."[7] While no "smoking gun" was found to prove that this case was concocted just to harass the Foundation (as the multi-union suit was) if it looks like a duck, walks like a duck and quacks like a duck....

THE FEDERAL ELECTION COMMISSION'S VENDETTA

The IRS is not the only federal agency that has tried to throw a noose around Right to Work. Almost since its creation, the Federal Election Commission (FEC) has been a thorn in the side of the National Right to Work Committee and the Legal Defense Foundation, costing them dearly in money and time.

The FEC is supposed to be a "watchdog" agency, preventing corruption in federal election campaigns. Unfortunately, the statute that the FEC enforces, the Federal Election Campaign Act, is vaguely written and therefore gives a great deal of leeway to its bureaucratic enforcers— much as the National Labor Relations Act confers power on the NLRB to "interpret" and enforce the law as its personnel see fit. To make matters worse, the original Chairman of the FEC, Thomas E. Harris, had once been a top lawyer to AFL-CIO President George Meany, serving as the AFL-CIO's associate general counsel. Harris had nothing but contempt for the Right to Work movement and referred to the National Right to Work Committee as "hypocrites and vultures" feeding on the "carcass" of Right to Work laws.[8] He used the powers of his office very selectively, turning a blind eye to flagrant violations of the Campaign Act by union operatives, but coming down hard on the Committee whenever his legal staff could manage to trump up some charges.

The first dispute between the FEC and the Committee erupted in 1976. The Committee, as well as Paul and Lore Chamberlain, two

Michigan teachers assisted by the Foundation, filed complaints with the FEC in October 1976. They alleged that the National Education Association, the Michigan Education Association, and the Garden City (Michigan) Education Association, were violating the rights of public school teachers by compelling them to pay money to the union's political purposes fund unless they requested a refund, and by soliciting contributions to that fund without informing teachers that they had a right to refrain from contributing without reprisal—all in violation of federal election law. This was the NEA's infamous "reverse check-off" political collection scheme: "We take your money first. If you don't like it, ask for it back." The unstated P.S., of course, was "We'll be keeping a list of you dissenters. . . ."

Instead of aggressively pursuing those complaints, however, the supposed watchdog opened one eye lazily and went back to sleep. Because the FEC chose to ignore the case, the Committee and the Chamberlains sued the FEC in March 1977, asking the court to declare the FEC's foot-dragging illegal and to order it to act on the complaints. (The law required the FEC to act on a complaint within 90 days, but it had done nothing for five months.)

The FEC defended by saying that it was engaged in "conciliation" with the unions, but the court held that engaging in "conciliation" was not enough, that "an expeditious resolution [was] essential to meaningful enforcement of the election laws." The judge also commented, "The long delay in these cases seems particularly egregious and unnecessary since the actions complained of are specifically prohibited by [the FEC's] own regulations." He then gave the FEC 30 days to proceed to a formal resolution of the case; failing that, the Committee and the Chamberlains would be authorized to sue the unions directly.[9]

Under that pressure, the FEC finally sued the NEA and 17 of its state affiliates. The court held that the "reverse check-off" was "per se violative" of the federal election laws and adjudicated the NEA and its affiliates lawbreakers.[10]

To say that the FEC and Right to Work got off to a bad start would be an understatement.

The next round in the fight began in November 1977. A part of the Federal Election Campaign Act, Section 441b(b)(4), declares it to be unlawful for "a corporation, or a separate segregated fund established by a corporation, to solicit contributions to such a fund from any person other than its stockholders and their families and its executive or administrative personnel and their families." That provision was meant to apply to campaign fundraising by businesses, restricting the people from whom a corporation could solicit contributions to a political action committee (PAC). An exception was made in the law to ensure that "membership organizations" and "corporations without capital stock" could solicit contributions from their members. Eager to find some basis for harassing the Committee, the FEC argued that the National Right to Work Committee had no "members" and thus had violated the law by soliciting contributions of money that were used in the Committee's Employee Rights Campaign Committee (ERCC), a registered federal PAC.

The ERCC had been established December 30, 1975, in accordance with then existing federal law, which had no "membership" restriction on PAC solicitations. A week later, on January 6, 1976, the Committee submitted an Advisory Opinion Request (AOR) to the FEC, wanting to know if the ERCC would be free to solicit contributions from Committee members. The law required the FEC to respond "promptly." But four months after submitting the AOR, there was still no answer from the FEC. Not wanting to wait indefinitely to obtain funds for ERCC in a crucial election year, on May 7 the Committee went ahead and solicited contributions. It did so again in June and September—still without word from the FEC on the AOR, which had now been gathering dust for eight months.

Congress amended the Federal Election Campaign Act on May 11, 1976, adding the "membership" restriction on PAC solicitations. The FEC adopted an unhelpful, circular definition of the term "member" in its regulations, i.e., "'Members' means all persons who are currently satisfying the requirements for membership in a membership organization...."

On September 27, 1976, the FEC's general counsel submitted a draft advisory opinion for the Commission's approval. That opinion would have upheld the Committee's interpretation of the law and the permissibility of its solicitation of contributions from Committee members. Chairman Harris, however, wanted to keep the Sword of Damocles hanging over the Committee and vetoed consideration of the favorable advisory opinion in a meeting with the FEC's legal staff.

The attack began on October 20, when a Big Labor front group called the National Committee for an Effective Congress filed a complaint with the FEC, charging that the National Right to Work Committee had violated the Campaign Act because it did not come under the "membership organization" exception. Now there was something that Chairman Harris liked, and the FEC filed suit against the Committee.

How could it possibly be said that the Committee had no members? The Committee was incorporated in Virginia, and under Virginia law, a "membership" organization had to have an annual meeting open to members. Holding such a meeting would be prohibitively costly, given that the Committee's supporters are spread across all fifty states. So for the purposes of Virginia incorporation law, the Committee said that it had no members. The FEC seized upon this as proof that the "membership organization" exception did not apply and therefore the ERCC solicitations were illegal and the Committee should be penalized and forbidden to continue to solicit PAC contributions. That eagerness to penalize the Committee over legal hair-splitting was inconsistent with the Supreme Court's landmark 1976 decision on election regulations in *Buckley v. Valeo,* where the Court said, "Our past decisions [concerning association for a cause under the First Amendment] have not drawn fine lines between contributors and members but have treated them interchangeably."[11] But Harris wanted a "fine line" in order to punish the Committee.

The case began in 1977 and on April 24, 1980, Judge Barrington Parker sided with the FEC, holding that the Committee had knowingly and willfully violated the law. He ordered that the ERCC could no longer solicit contributions, that all contributions made to the ERCC had to be refunded, and that the Committee pay a $10,000 fine.[12] Chairman Harris and his Big Labor allies had pulled off an incredible travesty of justice—if the court's decision would stick.

The Committee appealed that disastrous ruling to the Court of Appeals for the D.C. Circuit, which reversed the district court in a ruling issued September 4, 1981. Judge Homer Thornberry blasted the FEC and the district court, writing for the unanimous Court of Appeals, "We see absolutely no justification for applying a state law standard. State definitions of 'members' in nonstock corporations for purposes of state corporate or tax law are not likely to take into account the important first amendment considerations at the heart of any controversy surrounding the … Federal Election Campaign Act."[13] Looking to the purposes of the law, the court found that there was no potential for corruption in the activities of the Committee since "the individuals from whom NRWC solicits contributions, unlike employees of a corporation or members of a labor union, clearly are not subject to coercion." The Court of Appeals thereupon threw out the district court's penalties and refund order.

With lots of taxpayer money to spend on litigation and intent on harassing the Committee as much as possible, the FEC then appealed to the Supreme Court. The Supreme Court, abandoning its practice of treating members and contributors interchangeably for First Amendment purposes, concluded that the Committee's incorporation documents were dispositive and therefore it had violated the Federal Election Campaign Act by soliciting persons who were not its "members."[14] The Court remanded the case for a determination whether the violation was "knowing and willful."

With the case returned to it, the D.C. Circuit Court of Appeals decided on September 2, 1983, that the Committee had not "knowingly and willfully" violated the law. In fact, Judge Thornberry observed that the Committee had made reasonable efforts at satisfying the FEC, but had been rebuffed: "We note that during conciliation, NRWC offered to amend its articles of incorporation, but the FEC conditioned acceptance of that offer on the requirement that NRWC take additional undefined 'other steps' to become a membership organization. The position of the FEC was, in essence, to force NRWC to change its organizational structure with virtually no guidance and then to review the changes to determine if they were sufficient."[15] Judge Thornberry left no doubt as to where he thought the fault rested in the case, writing that "the FEC barricaded itself behind NRWC's articles of incorporation throughout this litigation and avoided the core problem of defining the terms 'member' and 'membership organization.'" Concluding that the Committee was innocent of deliberate defiance of the Federal Election Campaign Act, the court again rebuffed the FEC and tossed out the district court's penalty/refund order.

But just like a schoolyard bully, the FEC would come back again and again to pick on the Committee and try to hinder its opposition to compulsory unionism.

The next round with the FEC arose out of, ironically enough, efforts by the Committee to expose Big Labor's violations of the campaign finance laws. In response to media stories about cut-rate union phone bank services to Walter Mondale's presidential campaign, early in 1984 the Committee devised a plan to show conclusively that Big Labor illegally funnels campaign aid to its favored candidates. That plan involved placing detectives posing as campaign volunteers within various political operations, including union political operations supporting the Mondale campaign. The detectives would then be able to pinpoint illegal campaign assistance given by the AFL-CIO and the National Education Association, among others. The Committee ultimately spent almost $100,000 to hire those "volunteers," who gathered substantial evidence of campaign law violations. In one case, for instance, the Committee's sleuthing proved that 13 union PACs had violated FECA contribution limits and through allegedly independent but actually coordinated "delegate committees" had illegally aided the Mondale campaign by approximately $380,000. Union officials had been caught red-handed and were ultimately compelled to disgorge the money to the U.S. Treasury and pay a civil penalty of $18,500. The Committee was also able to document other violations of the Campaign Act stemming from the illegal use of compulsory union dues.

Based on its conclusive evidence that Big Labor and the Mondale campaign had violated the Campaign Act, the Committee made a formal complaint with the FEC in May 1984. But the FEC wasn't interested in wrongdoing by its friends and dragged its feet on the complaint. The Committee had to go to court and sue the FEC, trying to force it to act.[16]

Harris now used his power in a very creative way. The Committee's evidence was irrefutable, but under his direction, the FEC went easy on the Mondale campaign and the union officials. In the delegate committee case, for instance, while the Mondale campaign was ordered to disgorge the $380,000 in illegal campaign aid and was given a puny fine of $18,500, no action at all was taken against the union bigwigs who had violated the campaign law by making the excessive contributions to Mondale's campaign. Astoundingly, however, the FEC now chose to go after the whistleblower.

Early in 1985, acting on a retaliatory complaint filed by the NEA, the FEC concluded that there was "reason to believe" that *the Committee* had violated the law by spending corporate money in *opposition* to Mondale. The NEA's argument, on the other hand, was that because the "volunteers" had actually done work for the Mondale campaign in the course of gathering the evidence of the illegal campaign financing, by employing them the Committee had given *support* to the Mondale campaign, in violation of Section 441 of the election law. Either way, it was an amazing perversion of the law and the facts.

Not until 1989 did the FEC finally make a finding that there was "probable cause" to believe that the Committee's volunteer detectives had broken the law. It got around to filing a lawsuit against the Committee on March 13, 1990. The suit demanded an injunction against the Committee, forbidding it from ever engaging in such operations in the future, and the payment of a fine of $100,000. In the eyes of the FEC, exposing legal wrongdoing by Big Labor and its political cronies was more than five times worse than the violations themselves!

The case lingered for several years while the FEC "investigated." In 1994, the FEC dismissed 137 pending agency cases that had been initiated before 1990 in order to "prioritize" its bloated caseload—but decided to keep the court case against the Committee alive. It was finally resolved in 1996, when federal district judge Thomas Penfield Jackson threw the case out, ordering that it be dismissed "with prejudice"—a judge's way of saying that the case can't be re-filed. The reason for Judge Jackson's dismissal was that with all the FEC's delay before bringing the lawsuit, the statute of limitations had run out.[17] Therefore, the absurd theory that the Committee's undercover investigation and exposure of union campaign illegalities was itself illegal aid to a campaign was not tested in court.

Undeterred by its court defeats, the FEC has continued to harass the Committee, searching for ways to pin violations of the Campaign Act on it. In the process, the FEC has ignored Supreme Court precedents that the kind of communications the Committee makes regarding candidates for office—which never "expressly advocate" the election or defeat of candidates but simply tell the truth about their stands on Right to Work issues—are protected "issue discussion" under the First Amendment. In 1997, the FEC issued a subpoena demanding that the Committee turn over copies of "any communication" referring to federal candidates in the 1992 election. The Committee had to comply with that burdensome "witch-hunt" demand, but at least it did not lead to any new charges. Then in 2001, FEC bureaucrats proposed new rules that would have deemed the Committee (and other grassroots lobbying organizations) to be a political action committee and thus subject to strict contribution limits as well as disclosure of the Committee's donor list. The Committee filed comments arguing that the proposed rules were in violation of clear Supreme Court precedents on the First Amendment rights of American citizens and would undoubtedly be struck down if the FEC tried to enforce them. For once, the FEC backed off, deciding to put its new rules "in abeyance."

The FEC has also tried its hand at the old union-boss game of trying to pry loose the Committee's list of supporters. In the late 1970s, when the Committee was in the process of forming its political action committee, it needed to know how the FEC defined the term "member" so that it could be sure that it complied with the commission's rules. An aggressive young lawyer for the FEC, Lawrence Noble, replied that in order to determine whether the Committee was a "membership" organization, the FEC would have to have the names of all its supporters! Of course, the Committee refused to comply with that absurd demand and again the FEC was slapped down in court. But Noble's career with the FEC was not hurt in the least—in 1998 he was named the agency's top lawyer.

Passage of the Bipartisan Campaign Reform Act (BCRA) has given the FEC new authority to hinder the Committee in its efforts to inform Americans about Right to Work issues. No longer can issue organizations run ads in broadcast media within 30 days of a primary election or 60 days of a general election if the ads mention candidates by name. Such ads have played a crucial role in the Committee's efforts against compulsory unionism in the past, but under the new law, which the Supreme Court amazingly let stand in *McConnell v. Federal Election Commission*[18], the Committee will have to remain silent. Furthermore, the FEC began a new rulemaking project in March 2004 that threatens to bring the Committee and groups like it further into its regulatory web through the use of ambiguous terms like "election-influencing activities" to define a "political committee." If the FEC gets its way, it will have power to attack just about any Committee communication. Undoubtedly, the Committee's attorneys will have their hands full in the years to come, trying to protect what is left of the First Amendment from the FEC's desire to stifle all election-related speech that it doesn't like.

SPEAK OUT AND GET SUED

One of the Foundation's most shocking cases involved the near-murder of Bill Hinote. Bill worked at an oil refinery in Port Arthur, Texas, in 1982 and was "represented" by Local 4–23 of the Oil, Chemical, and Atomic Workers Union (OCAW). The union called a strike against the refinery, but after it had gone on for nine months, Bill decided that he had to return to work to support his family. Union militants take the crossing of a picket line as an offense against "union solidarity" that deserves violent reprisals, and they immediately began a campaign of terror against Bill and his family.

First there were telephoned threats to Mrs. Hinote. "Tell Bill we will get him," said anonymous voices. "You had better watch your little girl."

Then came drive-by assaults, with thugs hurling rocks and ball bearings at the Hinote's home. Windows were smashed. When all of that failed to keep Bill from doing what he had a perfect right to do—work—Local 4–23 moguls decided to escalate the level of violence and intimidation. On September 29, a large "dead man" weight was found on the driveway. Bill was followed home several times. Finally, on October 2, a lurking gunman pumped five bullets into Bill as he approached his car to drive to work. He barely survived the attack, thanks to heroic efforts by paramedics and surgeons.

Even the attempted murder of Bill Hinote wasn't enough to satisfy the militant thugs at Local 4–23. He had been crippled and wouldn't work again for many months, but they continued to harass *Mrs. Hinote* by repeatedly calling in threats to the Wal-Mart store where she worked, saying, among other things, "We didn't do a very good job on your husband, but we will make sure you are next." She had to take a leave of absence to escape from the union's campaign of terror. Hell hath no fury like a union boss scorned.

Local authorities never arrested the gunman or his accomplices. The Hinotes and many others believe that the thugs got away with attempted murder because of Big Labor's enormous political clout in southeast Texas. With the able assistance of attorneys from the Foundation, however, the Hinotes filed a civil suit against the union and officials and members of Local 4–23. After a dramatic trial, the jury found that Local 4–23 and some of its officers and members were responsible for the campaign of terror culminating in the attempted murder. The damages assessed against the defendants were nearly $1.2 million.

Lawyers for Local 4–23 succeeded in getting the trial court to overturn the jury's verdict and enter judgment for the defendants. That forced the Hinotes to appeal. The Texas Court of Appeals reversed the trial court and reinstated the verdict, stating, "the Union ratified these violent incidents, including the shooting, and was thus as responsible for them as were the individual appellees." The Texas Supreme Court declined the union's appeal. Two Texas courts were thus on record that Local 4–23 and some of its officials and members were responsible for a heinous crime.[19]

That was in 1989. Fast forward to 1997. The Committee sent a letter to its supporters that was designed to mobilize support for closing the loophole in the federal anti-racketeering law that exempts violence committed to advance so-called "legitimate union objectives." The letter, signed by Mrs. Hinote, presented facts about the barbaric violence directed against the Hinote family, as had been determined by the Texas courts. At this point, union lawyers for the International office of the OCAW saw their chance to get even with the Right to Work organizations. They filed a lawsuit in Jefferson County, Texas, claiming that the letter libeled the International union by not distinguishing Local 4–23, which had been found liable, from the International, which was not a defendant in the *Hinote* case. In reality, the union just wanted to harass the Committee and force it to spend resources defending against the suit. The entire case was absurd.

In August 1999, the case had reached the discovery phase. Before the boiling point was reached, however, the parties came to terms and settled. All the union lawyers had accomplished was to force the Committee to spend over $250,000 in defending itself.

DITTO

Several years after the end of the OCAW libel suit, another union that had been stung by a Right to Work *exposé* also sued for alleged "defamation" of its character. The case arose out of heavy-handed tactics of union officials to squeeze dues out of workers that they weren't legally obligated to pay.

A group of hospital workers in Anchorage, Alaska, who were represented by Local 341 of the Laborers' International Union of North America (LIUNA), had refused to pay their full dues. They were trying to avail themselves of the rights assured to dissenters in the Supreme Court's *Beck* decision, including an audit and accounting for financial core fees, but the union boss, Mano Frey, refused to acknowledge their rights. In a threatening letter to the workers in February 2000, he told them that unless they paid up, they would be fired. The workers then contacted the Foundation for help and its staff attorneys knew exactly what to do—they slapped LIUNA Local 341 with unfair labor practice charges.

Next, the Foundation's Legal Information Department contacted the local media in Anchorage, who jumped on the story. Faced with the prospect of a black eye in the media and of losing before the NLRB (which had found that the charges had merit), Local 341 officials quickly retreated and agreed to a settlement that gave the workers what they wanted. They also signed an NLRB notice stating: "**WE WILL** immediately refund any dues and fees paid by any Alaska Regional Hospital employee to us, if they have previously advised us that they wish to be a *Beck* objector." The union had to post that notice prominently to notify employees.

End of story? Not at all. The November/December 2000 edition of the Foundation's newsletter mentioned the case, and when Local 341 officials read that account, they called their lawyers. They concocted a lawsuit alleging that the story "defamed" the union, demanding $200,000 in actual damages, plus punitive damages, and a "retraction" of the allegedly defamatory statements.

The case was, just like the OCAW suit, mere harassment, and the Alaska court that tried the case saw it exactly that way. After more than a year of legal wrangling, the case went to trial. Judge Sen K. Tan heard testimony and both sides' arguments and then promptly dismissed the suit. Afterward, Stefan Gleason, Vice President of the Foundation, wrapped the case up this way: "This suit was simply an attempt to divert the Foundation's resources from its successful strategic litigation program that is increasingly cutting into union coercive power." So far, he has not been sued for saying that.

As much as they would like to use libel suits to silence the Right to Work movement, union bosses have little to show for their efforts.[20]

"AMERICAN RIGHTS AT WORK"

In 2003, Big Labor established an organization modeled after the National Right to Work Committee, designed to promote compulsory unionism and to "tangle" with the Right to Work movement. This group was orig-inally going to be called National Rights at Work Committee, but when the National Right to Work Committee threatened legal action because the name was too similar to its own, the labor barons settled on Ameri-can Rights at Work (ARAW).

ARAW vigorously promotes and defends compulsory unionism, while disingenuously denying that there is any such thing. Its Director, Jonathan Tasini, argues that there is no compulsion involved in unions because workers get to vote on whether to have a union.[21] That argu-ment mistakenly equates democracy with freedom. Just because work-ers were allowed to vote in an NLRB certification election (which some of them may not have wanted in the first place) does not mean that those who voted against the union have consented, not only to its representa-tion, but also to paying for it. If the citizens of a town held an election to decide which religion they would follow, no one would say that peo-ple who were thereafter compelled to stop attending their old church and attend the church picked by the majority had "consented" to that coercion. It's no different with compulsory unionism by majority rule. The fact of union compulsion cannot be hidden with verbal tricks.

Tasini and ARAW are perfectly within their rights to make clever but misleading arguments in favor of unionization, but they also make false statements about the National Right to Work Committee and the National Right to Work Legal Defense Foundation. Posted on the ARAW Web site, under a heading labeled "Union-buster Alert," is a document stating that "anti-union groups such as NRTWC and American Employ-ers for Free Enterprise . . . have assisted numerous employers with decer-tification campaigns."[22] The truth is that Foundation attorneys have on some occasions assisted *employees* in clearing legal obstacles to decertifi-cation elections raised by union officials, but neither the Committee nor the Foundation has ever assisted an employer in bringing about a decer-tification election, nor taken any part in a decertification campaign. The statement is simply incorrect.

Mr. Tasini is free and easy with false accusations against Right to Work. He claims that the Committee is merely "a front for the corporate world," which betrays his ignorance of the origins of the Right to Work movement (i.e., dissatisfaction among *workers* with compulsory unionism) and the fact that the Committee has never received more than a tiny fraction of its financial support from major companies. And Tasini continues with the calumny that, as a "front" for the corporate world, the Committee "doesn't want workers to have health care."[23] He clearly wishes to avoid the real issue that the Committee addresses—compulsory unionism—by trying to make people think that Americans must choose between having unions or having no unions. The true choice is between unions where membership and support is *voluntary* and the legal situation that prevails in non-Right to Work states, where workers are *compelled* to support unions that they don't want, and, throughout the nation, where exclusive union representation is forced on employees who would rather represent themselves or be represented by some other labor organization.

American Rights at Work is just the latest in Big Labor's campaign of disinformation, attempting to deceive Americans about what the Right to Work movement truly stands for.

NOTES

1. *NAACP v. Alabama*, 357 U.S. 449 (1958).
2. *International Union UAW v. National Right to Work Legal Defense Foundation*, 433 F. Supp. 474 (D.D.C.1977).
3. *International Union, UAW v. National Right to Work Legal Defense Foundation*, 590 F.2d 1139 (D.C. Cir. 1978).
4. *International Union, UAW v. National Right to Work Legal Defense Foundation*, 584 F. Supp. 1219 (D.D.C. 1984).
5. *International Union, UAW v. National Right to Work Legal Defense Foundation*, 781 F.2d 928 (D.C. Cir. 1986).
6. *National Right to Work Legal Defense Foundation v. U.S*, 487 F. Supp. 801 (E.D. N.C. 1979), citing *Truax v. Raich*, 239 U.S. 33, 41 (1915).
7. James J. Kilpatrick, "An IRS Vendetta," *The Augusta Chronicle*, Feb. 7, 1980.
8. *AFL-CIO American Federationist*, Feb. 1962, p. 14.
9. *National Right to Work Committee/Chamberlain v. Thomson*, Fed. Elec. Camp. Fin Guide (CCH) para. 9042 (D.D.C. 1977)
10. *Federal Election Commission v. National Education Association*, 457 F. Supp. 1102, 1110 (D.D.C. 1978).

11. *Buckley v. Valeo,* 424 U.S. 1, 66 (1976).
12. *Federal Election Commission v. National Right to Work Committee,* 501 F. Supp. 422 (D.D.C. 1980).
13. *National Right to Work Committee v. Federal Election Commission,* 665 F.2d 371 (D.C. Cir. 1981).
14. *Federal Election Commission v. National Right to Work Committee,* 459 U.S. 197 (1982).
15. *National Right to Work Committee v. Federal Election Commission* 716 F.2d 1401 (D.C. Cir. 1983).
16. *National Right to Work Committee v. Federal Election Commission,* Fed. Elec. Camp Fin. Guide (CCH) para.9225. (The court declined to order the FEC to act at that time.)
17. *Federal Election Commission v. National Right to Work Committee,* 916 F. Supp. 10 (D.D.C. 1996).
18. *McConnell v. Federal Election Commission,* 124 S. Ct. 619 (2003).
19. *Hinote v. OCAW International Union, Local 4–23,* 777 S.W.2d 134 (Tex. App.-Houston 1989, writ denied).
20. These are not the only libel cases the Right to Work organizations have had to defend. The earliest grew out of the 1976 campaign for enactment of Right to Work in Louisiana. Louisiana AFL-CIO president Victor Bussie sued for $1 million in damages over a letter signed by Reed Larson that had called for ending compulsory unionism in that state. The letter had referred to the notorious union violence in Louisiana (see Chapter 9) and Bussie claimed that the letter imputed responsibility for the violence to him personally. The case resulted in a precedent-setting decision that a "public figure" like Bussie would be held to the same standard as a "public official" suing a newspaper or television station, and would have to prove his case by "clear and convincing evidence." *Larson v. Bussie,* 501 F. Supp. 1107 (M.D. La. 1980). Shortly after the decision, the Committee's insurance company settled the case for a paltry $15,000, and it was dismissed with prejudice.

    Two libel suits were also filed against the Committee in 1987, both arising out of the Foundation's legal assistance to Bill Hinote. Both were filed just prior to scheduled trial dates in *Hinote* and were obviously attempts to divert public attention. Neither suit was successful.
21. Statement made on C-Span's September 1, 2003, "Washington Journal" broadcast.
22. John Logan, "Consultants, lawyers, and the 'union free' movement in the USA since the 1970s," available online at www.araw.org/unionbusters/.
23. C-Span broadcast, ibid.

CHAPTER NINE

BATTLES IN THE STATES

T he Right to Work movement began with efforts to enact Right to Work statutes in state legislatures and that is still a key objective today. While a Right to Work statute, as we have seen, does not eliminate the grip that a certified union has over workers due to the NLRA's exclusive representation provision, it at least permits workers who don't believe that union representation benefits them to stop paying for it without losing their jobs. That acts as an important check on union officials—if they behave in an arrogant, self-interested manner, they're apt to see more and more workers stop paying their dues. As a side-benefit, states that have enacted Right to Work legislation have a decided advantage in attracting new business, providing more jobs, and enjoying above-average increases in the growth of wages.[1]

Most of the Right to Work victories came in southern and western states after the passage of the Taft-Hartley Act in 1947. (See chapter 2 for the list.) This chapter will highlight some of the successes—and failures—of the Right to Work movement in state legislatures.

WYOMING—A MORALE-BOOSTING WIN

The reader will recall that 1958 had been a terrible year for the Right to Work movement, with bitter defeats in five of the six states where citizens had voted on Right to Work referenda. Union officials were gleefully pronouncing the movement dead. Reed Larson, who had come to Washington to work for the National Right to Work Committee from the one state where there had been success (Kansas), was eager to prove the doomsayers wrong. The best way of doing that would be to get a Right to Work bill passed in another state. Wyoming, where a state Right to Work committee had been formed in 1961, was the state that augured the best. Working closely with the Wyoming Right to Work Committee, Larson employed the same strategy he had used in Kansas back in 1954–55 to get the bill through the legislature. The state's Right to Work advocates began by identifying the politicians who were friendly, those who were opposed, and those who might be persuaded. From Washington, the National Right to Work Committee mobilized its members in Wyoming, calling on them to let their elected representatives know how they felt about compulsory unionism. The National Committee also made sure that Wyoming's newspapers were well-supplied with arguments in favor of Right to Work. The result was a raft of editorials in favor of making Wyoming a Right to Work state. Momentum was building.

Big Labor is not particularly strong in Wyoming, with only a small percentage of the state's workforce unionized. Nevertheless, the union brass reacts to a Right to Work campaign the way a bull reacts to a red flag. The concept of voluntary unionism is so mortifying to union bosses that they can always be counted on to wage all-out war against it, distorting the issue beyond any recognition. Wyoming was no different.

The AFL-CIO poured in its abundant resources in an effort to squash the Right to Work momentum by electing servile candidates to the state legislature. For all its slick campaign expertise, however, the 1962 elections produced a pro-Right to Work sweep of the governorship and both chambers of the state legislature. Many, but not all, of the Republican majority were Right to Work supporters, and when the new legislature convened, the Right to Work bill was at the top of the agenda.

Big Labor now pulled out all the stops in an effort to derail the bill, employing its arsenal of false and misleading claims designed to scare people. Senator Gale McGee, the Big Labor pawn who would later lose his Senate seat over his opposition to Right to Work, called the bill "a cover-up to completely do away with collective bargaining, leaving the working man completely at the mercy of the employer." That statement was, of course, blatantly and knowingly false. Right to Work laws do not do away with collective bargaining and they protect workers from being completely at the mercy of union bosses. When politicians get into bed with Big Labor, they lose their capacity to speak truthfully about the issue of compulsory unionism.

The union bosses also reached down into their bag of bullying tactics to harass individuals who were supporting the Right to Work drive. One of those individuals was Val Christensen, a dairy operator in Cheyenne who had publicly announced his support for passage of the Right to Work bill. Big Labor decided to retaliate against Christensen by targeting his business with a boycott. Customers were warned that they should stop buying from his dairy. The attempt to bully Mr. Christensen backfired, however, when newspapers picked up the story. Trying to coerce people just because they didn't hold the opinions that labor bosses liked didn't sit well with the independent-minded citizens of Wyoming.

Big Labor also tried frantically to browbeat legislators into voting against the bill with a costly campaign of TV and newspaper ads, telephone calls, and radio spots—all designed to sow fear over the prospect of Wyoming becoming a Right to Work state. Right to Work supporters matched the Big Labor campaign with newspaper ads refuting the false charges and documenting the economic gains made by other Right to Work states. Union lobbyists swarmed over the state capitol, cajoling and threatening members, but Right to Work backers kept up a steady stream of calls and letters to their elected officials to stiffen their backbones.

Despite Big Labor's all-out campaign against it, the bill breezed through both chambers of the state legislature and Governor Clifford Hansen signed it into law on February 8, 1963, making Wyoming the 19th Right to Work state. In his remarks upon signing the bill, Governor Hansen said, "The labor movement in America, which has done so much to raise the standard of living of our working men and women, will not be strengthened by making membership compulsory or obligatory." *There* was a politician who could speak the truth.

Wyoming was a morale-boosting win. After the successful fight to stave off compulsory unionism in the aerospace industry in 1962 (see Chapter 2), the defeat of bills in several states to repeal Right to Work laws, and the addition of a new Right to Work state in 1963, the idea that the movement was dead in the wake of the 1958 defeats proved to be nothing but wishful thinking by union officials.

INDIANA—ONE THAT GOT AWAY

Indiana is a state where compulsory unionism has long and bitter history, particularly in the heavy manufacturing companies there. A number of violent and highly-publicized strikes in the state in the mid-1950s—especially one by the United Auto Workers at the Perfect Circle Company in New Castle in 1956—outraged the citizens and gave a strong boost to the efforts of the Indiana Right to Work Committee. In the Perfect Circle case, UAW bosses had tried to force the company to sign a compulsory union-shop contract against the wishes of most of the employees. When they did not get their way, union officials unleashed an ugly reign of violence in the town. It was reminiscent of the taxi strike in Wichita in 1953 that had cost Deering Crowe his life, but helped trigger the successful drive for a state Right to Work law in Kansas.

Reacting to the violent strike, the *Indianapolis Star* editorialized, "Mayor Paul F. McCormack of New Castle has proposed that the Indiana General Assembly pass a Right to Work law to outlaw the union shop and protect the right of every worker to refuse to join a union. We already have laws that protect the right of a worker to join a union. Why is it not equally fair to protect by law the right of a worker *not* to join a union?"

That sentiment had an impact on the 1956 elections in Indiana. Many Big Labor candidates went down to defeat, paving the way for passage of a Right to Work bill in the 1957 legislative session. The bill readily passed both chambers of the General Assembly. Straddling the fence, however, Republican Governor Harold Handley allowed the bill to become law without his signature, and the statute took effect on June 25, 1957. (Handley thought that his dodging of the Right to Work issue would help him in a race for the U.S. Senate in 1958. It didn't. Handley went down to defeat, showing again that fence-straddling on Right to Work wins a politician no friends.)

Big Labor immediately set its sights on the destruction of the law. The strategy of the union bosses was to use the courts to override the determination of the General Assembly that Indiana workers should not be fired if they didn't want to support a union. Therefore, union officials in Indiana began negotiating "agency shop" contracts, hoping that friendly judges would say that the Right to Work statute did not ban such contracts. (The "agency shop," it will be recalled, does not require workers to actually become union members, but compels them to pay union dues in order to keep their jobs.) In 1959 the legality of agency shop contracts was challenged in a case that smelled of collusion. The ensuing legal battle played out just as the union bosses wanted. In *Meade Electric Co. v. Hagberg*[2] the Indiana Court of Appeals, in a unanimous decision, eviscerated the statute by ruling that contracts requiring compulsory membership were prohibited under the law, but not contracts requiring non-members to pay fees. Meade Electric did not appeal to the Indiana Supreme Court and the National Right to Work Committee was not in a position to do anything about it. *Meade Electric* punched a gaping hole in the law by allowing the payment of fees to become a condition of holding a job. The law was as good as dead.

Like a crippled ship, the Indiana Right to Work statute stayed afloat until 1965. Big Labor's candidates had swept up in the 1964 general election and a bill to repeal the already meaningless Right to Work statute was easily passed in the 1965 session and signed by Governor Roger Branigin.

The sad case of Indiana shows that no legislative victory is permanent. Right to Work advocates have to expect attacks from all sides—in the courts, the legislatures, and in the bureaucracy—as long as union officials continue to insist that unwanted union membership and support should be forced upon workers.

A measure of freedom was regained for Indiana workers in 1995 when the General Assembly passed—over a veto by Governor Evan Bayh—a bill making it illegal for local school contracts to include provisions that compel teachers who are not members of the state teachers' union to pay dues covering their "fair share" of union costs. And at the time of this writing a campaign is making progress to bring Indiana back into the Right to Work fold completely.

LOUISIANA—MORE UNION VIOLENCE

Louisiana was the last of the southern states to adopt a Right to Work statute, doing so in 1954.[3] But Big Labor has a strong presence in the state, especially around New Orleans, and union officials immediately set out to have the law repealed. They managed to do that in 1956 with a divide and conquer tactic—the repeal bill did not cover agricultural workers. Therefore, union strategists were able to find the votes they needed in representatives from agricultural areas to once again secure their power to force workers in other sectors of the economy to pay dues or lose their jobs.

The Louisiana Right to Work Committee worked for years afterward to build up support for re-enactment of a statute covering all workers. Its job was aided by some well-publicized union violence, particularly an attack in January 1976 on a construction site in Lake Charles that left one man dead and several others wounded.

Bob Kerley, a co-owner of Kerley Chemical Corporation, had figured out that the hydrogen waste material from local manufacturing operations around Lake Charles could be profitably turned into industrial ammonia. He put his life savings into the construction of a plant to do that, an enterprise he called Jupiter Chemical. Kerley was from Arizona, a Right to Work state, and never imagined the difficulty he would have in getting his project built in union-boss dominated Louisiana. He found that he had no choice except to deal with union construction firms in Lake Charles and instead of the rapid and orderly construction pace Kerley had envisioned, featherbedding slowed progress on Jupiter Chemical to a crawl. Union business agents sought under-the-table payments "to make things okay." Bob could see that he would go broke before the project was finished unless he solved those problems.

Desperate for some reliable workers, Kerley then contacted Shorty Landry, owner of a construction company that employed workers who were members of an independent union, Local 102. Kerley had heard that Landry's company was honest and efficient, so the two agreed that Landry's men would take on some of the work. But when the Local 102 men showed up for work, the union bosses of the big international AFL-CIO union ordered all other workers off the job. Landry, who knew the area well, feared that there would be trouble the next day, January 15, 1976. Early in the morning, he called the sheriff's office and asked that a car be dispatched to the construction site. A patrol car was sent, but finding things quiet, the officers left.

Shortly after 7 a.m., the morning calm was shattered as union militants raided the job site. The construction trailer was raked with gunfire as attackers burst through the gate with a forklift. Cars were overturned, equipment wrecked, and bullets continued to fly. One of the men in the trailer, Joe Hooper was hit and bled to death within minutes. The deadly message the union bosses had sent with the raid was the same as we have seen in many other cases: "Do business with us—or else!" (The business manager for the Southwest Louisiana Building and Construction Trades Council was later charged with crimes including manslaughter and first-degree murder. He was found guilty and sentenced to 22 years in prison.)

Owing largely to the Lake Charles violence, compulsory unionism was in bad odor when the Louisiana legislature met in 1976 and considered reenacting a full Right to Work law. As the *Minden Press-Herald* editorialized on March 1, "Recent labor violence in Lake Charles, which resulted in the death of a construction worker, underlines the fact that many unions have become as bad as the problems they were originally formed to solve." Right to Work proponents capitalized on that sentiment and also pointed to a new poll done by the Louisiana Association of Business and Industry showing that 76.9 percent of the state's residents favored passage of a Right to Work bill. They also noted the fact that Louisiana had been lagging behind neighboring Right to Work states Texas and Arkansas in job growth.

Conditions, in short, were ideal for the passage of Right to Work when the state legislature began its session in May 1976. Union bosses discovered that despite all of their bluster and threats to lawmakers who said that they backed Right to Work, they couldn't stop the bill from advancing. It passed the House 59–46 in June and the Senate 25–14 in early July. Governor Edwin Edwards signed it into law on July 9, making Louisiana the twentieth Right to Work state.

There was, however, a tragic postscript to the passage of the law. Right to Work supporters had enjoyed a victory celebration in Baton Rouge, the state capital, on the evening of July 8. Among those in attendance was Jim Leslie, a 38-year-old public relations expert from Shreveport who had handled advertising and media relations for the campaign. After the celebration, Leslie had parked his car and was returning to his motel when he was gunned down in the parking lot, killed by a shotgun blast in his back from a hidden assailant. Police described the murder as the work of a professional hitman. The case was never solved, but there is strong reason to believe that the murder of Jim Leslie was ordered by union bosses as retribution for his role in depriving them of their power to force workers to pay money to them as a condition of working.

Louisiana workers have enjoyed the freedom of Right to Work since 1976, but the killings of Joe Hooper and Jim Leslie serve as grim reminders that some union officials will stop at nothing to get their way.

IDAHO—THE WILL OF THE PEOPLE OVERCOMES PARTY POLITICS

Idaho's long struggle to enact a Right to Work statute is a great lesson in the power of perseverance and will be recounted here at some length.

Among the bitter defeats Right to Work suffered in 1958 was a narrow loss in Idaho. The campaign was so poorly managed that Right to Work supporters missed the deadline for submitting explanatory language on the ballot. As a result, voters read the paragraph submitted by Big Labor telling them why Right to Work would be bad, but there was nothing to counter that and explain why voting for Right to Work would be good. Not only was the 1958 referendum defeated, but anti-Right to Work Democrats won control of the Idaho legislature for the first time in decades. Republican candidates took a drubbing up and down the ballot with one exception. Gubernatorial candidate Robert Smiley, who had opposed Right to Work, was victorious. Republican Party officials in Idaho drew from that experience the same false conclusion that many others did: Right to Work had been the cause of their electoral debacle. They completely ignored the fact that 1958 was a disaster year for Republicans across the nation, whether Right to Work was an issue or not. But a scapegoat was needed and Right to Work was it. For decades afterward, many GOP politicians in Idaho held to the unshakable belief that the party needed to shun Right to Work as if it were the plague.

There were many staunch Right to Work advocates in the state, however, who were determined to prevail. Eventually they regrouped and late in 1976, the Idaho Freedom to Work Committee (IFTWC) was established by a young activist named Bill Wilson. Wilson succeeded in persuading a member of the state House to introduce a Right to Work bill in the 1977 session of the legislature. It passed the House, but then ran into trouble in the Republican-controlled Senate. Old-line party leaders were convinced that they had to derail the bill lest the voters punish them in 1978 just as they had (supposedly) done in 1958. The Republican Senate leader and future governor Phil Batt tacked on an utterly irrelevant amendment to the bill that made it unpalatable to Idaho's large agricultural community. That tactic succeeded in killing the bill that year, but Wilson and his associates doggedly went to work to eliminate the obstacles that Idaho Republicans had put in their way. Like a chess grandmaster who can see checkmate by removing just a few opposing pieces, Wilson formulated his strategy.

One piece that had to go was Senator Vern Brassey, an anti-Right to Work Republican who had played a key role in the sinking of the 1977 bill. Wilson recruited Boise attorney Ron Carter to oppose Brassey in the Republican primary in 1978 and pulled off the upset. Similar primary challenges and general election wins greatly altered the legislative landscape in Idaho—Brassey and eight other legislators who had opposed

Right to Work were out of office after the 1978 elections. Unfortunately, incumbent Democrat (and Right to Work opponent) John Evans defeated his pro-Right to Work Republican challenger, Allan Larsen that year. From that single defeat, and in a campaign with numerous issues, the Republican leadership in Idaho was quick to claim that once again Right to Work had caused their downfall.

Undaunted, IFTWC continued working toward its goal, now aided by a young staffer named Gary Glenn. In 1980, Wilson and Glenn further improved their position on the chessboard by replacing more members of the state legislature who opposed Right to Work with those who favored it. Especially notable were victories over two incumbent Senate Democrats in northern districts where Republicans had never won before. As the legislature convened in 1981, twenty of the twenty-nine members who had voted against Right to Work in 1977 were no longer in office. A Right to Work bill was again passed by the House, only to be defeated in the Senate due to the opposition of weak-kneed Republicans. The Republican establishment prevailed on popular United States Senator James McClure to personally call members of the State Senate and pressure them to oppose the bill by supporting a motion by Senator Brassey (who had succeeded in winning his seat back) to table it. Brassey's motion carried. The bill was again killed and the killer had again been the Republican Party.

Instead of quietly accepting the loss, IFTWC denounced McClure and the Republicans who had caved in under the "Right to Work hurts Republicans" chant, publicly calling them "traitors" to their own party's principles. The Republican establishment responded by attacking Right to Work activists. The war of words was bitter, but only hardened the resolve of Right to Work supporters to remove the rest of the pieces guarding the enemy king.

Later that year, there was an event in Idaho that had the political impact of a Force 5 hurricane—the closure of the Bunker Hill mine in Kellogg. The mine was owned by Gulf Resources and employed 2,000 workers who were represented by the United Steel Workers. Gulf announced that it was going to close the unprofitable operation, but three wealthy Idaho investors offered to buy the mine and continue in business, provided that the workers accept a new contract with wage and benefit cuts. Having somewhat less income was preferable to unemployment and the workers voted to approve the new contract.

At that point, officials from the Steel Workers intervened. Several of the union's top men flew in from Pittsburgh on a private jet and announced that the union would not honor the vote by which the workers had agreed to the concession contract. Under the union's constitution, that was enough to cancel the contract—distant union bosses were able to turn thumbs down on a deal that would have saved 2,000 jobs and the economy of the region, just because they didn't want to look weak and possibly set a precedent for other concessions at a time when much of the U.S. economy was struggling. The deal collapsed. Bunker Hill was closed down.

Idaho was outraged. Editorials across the state attacked the "Pittsburgh union bosses" who had sold out their own members. New life was instantly breathed into the Right to Work bill when Republican leaders suddenly saw it as a chance to hurt Governor Evans in the 1982 election. Early in the 1982 session of the legislature, the House passed Right to Work by a 50 to 20 margin and the Senate, this time without Republican obstructionism, passed it 21 to 14. Only two Senate Republicans opposed it. As expected, Governor Evans vetoed the bill. The House then voted to override the veto, but thanks to those two anti-Right to Work Republicans, the veto was not overridden in the Senate.

Setting their sights on electing a veto-proof legislature, IFTWC leaders now targeted the two Republicans who had enabled the veto to stand. Gary Glenn recruited political novices to challenge Brassey and Edith Miller Klein, who was a Republican establishment icon and considered unbeatable. Both she and Brassey were ousted in primaries, with the challengers winning almost 60 percent of the vote.

The 1982 election for the governorship matched anti-Right to Work incumbent John Evans against "moderate" Republican Phil Batt. Batt was the kind of politician who likes deal-making and compromise and abhors strong stands on principle. Throughout his campaign, he tried to avoid any discussion of Right to Work (if reporters really pushed, they could get him to express meek approval) and refused to attack Evans over the closure of Bunker Hill, even going so far as to defend him against charges that he was a "puppet of eastern union bosses." But with two weeks left before the election, Batt found himself trailing badly. Polling indicated that by embracing the Right to Work issue, he stood to gain three votes for every one he might lose. So for the last two weeks, Batt ran ads linking Evans to the Bunker Hill closing and emphasizing his newly-found support for Right to Work.

The result was a razor-thin election rather than the cakewalk Evans had expected—but Batt still lost by less than a percentage point. Immediately after the loss, Batt said that it was his support for Right to Work that had gotten him into a photo finish in the 1982 race. Amazingly enough, though, a year and a half later in his address to the Idaho Republican convention, Batt blamed his loss on the fact that he had embraced Right to Work in the campaign!

Not only had Evans been re-elected, but the 1982 elections failed to increase the pro-Right to Work balance in the Senate. IFTWC looked ahead to 1984, intending to elect a veto-proof legislature that year.

Idaho's legislature had to be redistricted and that issue was predictably contentious. Democrats wanted to redraw the lines to favor their party and Republicans wanted to do the same. Many plans were offered by party politicians. Many were also offered by a liberal college professor who had filed a lawsuit to force reapportionment. He set before the judge in the case a remarkable set of more than twenty plans, many of them with sub-options. Gary Glenn analyzed the plans and came to the conclusion that the plan that had the best chance of producing a legislature that would be veto-proof on Right to Work was, ironically, the one labeled Plan 14(b). Stranger yet, that was the plan that the judge eventually ordered into effect. Although Governor Evans was predicting that the plan would increase Democratic strength in the legislature, Glenn had done his homework and knew better. IFTWC then went about recruiting good candidates and preparing for a great battle in 1984.

By Glenn's reckoning, the House was a sure thing, but getting the two-thirds necessary to override a veto in the Senate would require winning five out of nine races that were expected to be close. On election night, the first eight of those contests split four and four. A computer problem delayed the results from the final race until the wee hours of the next morning, but when the results came in, Right to Work Republican Jerry Twiggs had ousted his incumbent Democrat opponent rather easily. Thus it appeared that Idaho had the veto-proof legislature that IFTWC had been working for so long to get.

Wasting no time, House Bill 2 in the 1985 session was the Right to Work bill. It passed the House 63 to 18. Then it passed the Senate 28 to 14. As expected, Governor Evans vetoed the bill, and both chambers promptly voted to override the veto. On February 1, 1985, Right to Work should have become law in Idaho, but a court order from a judge friendly to Big Labor declared that the bill could not have immediate effect because there was no true emergency, as the legislature had declared in passing the bill. Declaring an emergency was the necessary legal requirement for a law to take effect immediately. That was important for the following reason: Under Idaho law, a passed bill is held in abeyance if opponents can gather enough signatures to force a referendum on it at the next general election. There was little doubt that Big Labor would do that, but by declaring an emergency, the law would have immediate effect even if opponents forced a referendum. In telling the state legislature what was or was not an emergency, the judge was way out of line in stepping over the separation of judicial and legislative functions. The Idaho Supreme Court would later overrule him.

Big Labor had one last move to play in its effort to preserve compulsory unionism in Idaho—the referendum. Getting the necessary signatures to force a vote on the newly-enacted Right to Work statute was not hard for union officials and once they had secured the referendum, they began an all-out campaign to get the citizens of the state to defeat Right to Work in the 1986 general election. The anti-Right to Work campaign was heavily financed from Big Labor's deep war chest, and taking into consideration actual dollars spent and the value of in-kind services, the defenders of Right to Work were probably outspent by more than three to one. Making things still more difficult, the referendum was worded in such a way that citizens who wanted to preserve the Right to Work law had to vote "Yes." In referenda, voters who are uncertain or confused generally tend to vote "No" and Big Labor would take full advantage of that fact in the campaign.

On the other hand, IFTWC had a powerful weapon of its own. It made great use of one of America's most revered actors—Charlton Heston.

Gary Glenn had heard that Heston was a union member who adamantly opposed forced unionism, and on a hunch, wrote to his office to see if he would be willing to shoot a television ad for Right to Work. He was surprised and delighted to get a phone call a few days later from Heston's administrative assistant, who said that he would be glad to do the spot. She asked that he send a script to Mr. Heston, which Glenn promptly did. To do the filming, Glenn and a crew from Idaho flew to Los Angeles—even with the cost of airfare, that was less expensive than hiring a union-scale crew in southern California.

When Glenn and his crew arrived, they were courteously greeted by Heston, who then walked back into the woods behind his home to go over the script. After about ten minutes, he was ready. The filming went beautifully, with Heston powerfully delivering this message: "I've played men like Tom Jefferson, Andrew Jackson, Lincoln—all of them heroes defending American freedom. There are Americans still carrying on that fight in Idaho, where citizens want the Right to Work without being forced to join a union. Now, as a former union president, I believe Americans should be free to choose. We're all watching, Idaho. Strike a blow for freedom. Vote yes on Referendum One."

Throughout the campaign, that ad was shown repeatedly in all parts of Idaho. When he later discovered that the leftist officers of the Screen Actors Guild were planning to revoke his lifetime membership because he had spoken his mind in favor of Right to Work, Heston increased his support by scheduling a personal trip to Boise (the state capital) at a critical time of the fall campaign. Without Charlton Heston's gracious help, the campaign would probably have been lost.

There were many other important elements in the fight to keep Idaho's Right to Work law. One of the most important was "Union

Members for Right to Work," a group of union members who spoke up for the law. The public statements of that group helped to persuade many union members in Idaho that by giving them a choice, Right to Work was their friend, not their enemy. Black postal union president Tony Hodges also gave the cause a great lift in liberal areas around Boise, by arguing that Right to Work was a civil rights issue. On Election Day, while Republican candidates were losing badly in Boise, Right to Work garnered a whopping 60 percent of the vote.

Throughout the campaign, Glenn and his team stayed with the message that the issue in the referendum was freedom of choice. Occasionally, Right to Work advocates contended that the law would have good economic benefits and a small amount of time was devoted to refuting Big Labor's usual scare tactics. For the most part, though, the campaign hammered home the philosophical argument that allowing workers freedom to decide for themselves whether a union was worth supporting was consistent with the values of Idahoans. As we have seen, opinion polling has consistently shown that most Americans have an instinctive dislike for compulsory unionism. The "Yes on One" campaign capitalized on that fact.

When the votes were finally counted, Referendum One had won by more than 30,000 votes. Big Labor's last line of resistance to allowing Idaho workers freedom of choice had been overrun. Furthermore, the big turnout in favor of Referendum One saved the Senate seat of Republican Steve Symms. In an election where many GOP senators went down to defeat, Symms pulled out a slim 11,000 vote victory—smaller than the margin in favor of Right to Work. Most Idaho Republicans, who were quaking in their boots because Right to Work was on the general election ballot, didn't acknowledge the benefit of having the Right to Work vote, but U.S. Senator James McClure did. A solid conservative who truly favored Right to Work laws but feared that the referendum would be electoral disaster for the Republicans, McClure later acknowledged to Reed Larson that having Right to Work on the ballot had helped his party's ticket. Democratic National Committee Chairman Charles Manatt also understood the impact of the issue, telling Free Congress

Foundation's *Initiative and Referendum* that "Right to Work killed us in Idaho."

A CLOSE CALL IN GEORGIA

Georgia was among the early states to enact a Right to Work statute, in 1947. But the fact that a law has been on the books for a long time and is popular with the citizens of a state does not give it any protection when Big Labor's obedient politicians try to sneak through a bill to repeal or eviscerate Right to Work. In early 1995, that is exactly what happened in the Peach State and it took a whirlwind of activity by National Right to Work Committee leaders to save the day.

State Representative Sharon Beasley Teague introduced a bill in the Georgia legislature on February 9, 1995 (H.B. 668), that simply repealed the state's Right to Work law. The bill was referred to the House Industry Committee, where it was cleverly amended so as to no longer repeal Right to Work, but instead to destroy its effectiveness by allowing union bosses to demand that non-members pay "service and representation charges" to them if they wanted to keep their jobs. It was the same "agency fee" gambit that had wrecked Indiana's Right to Work law in 1959. The union bosses in Georgia knew that they would have a much better chance of success if they tried to punch a gaping hole in the state's Right to Work law rather than attempting a direct repeal.

This wolf in sheep's clothing bill breezed through the Industry Committee on a 21–1 vote and a week later cleared the House Rules Committee without even a recorded vote. Realizing the danger that H.B. 668 posed to freedom of choice for Georgia workers, the Committee launched a full-scale counterattack in late February. First, every member of the Georgia legislature was sent a letter on February 23 explaining that H.B. 668 was a stealthy way of destroying the Right to Work statute. In case that first letter was ignored, a second went out on March 1. Also, the Committee alerted all of its Georgia members and the media. Those efforts had the effect of turning the floodlights on to show a nighttime intruder.

Many Georgia newspapers responded with editorials against H.B. 668. For example, the *Albany Herald* called the bill "simply another shot fired by those who would adulterate the state's right-to-work law, which has been one of Georgia's major economic drawing cards."[4] Right to Work members flooded the offices of their legislators with calls telling them that they should not be deceived into supporting the bill. Mark Mix, the Committee's Vice President for Legislation, flew to Atlanta to coordinate the defense and meet with legislators who wanted to stop the bill. The crucial point, he knew, would be framing the debate so that it was clear to all members of the House that if they voted in favor of H.B. 668, they were voting to kill Right to Work in Georgia.

The bill came to the House floor on Monday, March 8. Debate began around noon and it was soon evident that Right to Work's efforts had paid off. Try as the proponents of the bill would to claim that they were only amending the law slightly to make things "fair" for unions, most of the legislators who spoke obviously weren't buying that line. Around 2 p.m., Speaker Tom Murphy entered the chamber and lingered near the rear entrance, listening to the debate. He listened for about twenty minutes and then sat down on a folding chair, rather than sitting in the ornate Speaker's chair. As soon as he did so, the Georgians with whom Mix was sitting burst out in smiles and congratulations. Perplexed, Mix asked what was going on, and one of the Georgians with him explained that the tradition in the House was that if the Speaker sat in his official chair, that was a signal that he wanted the bill to pass. By taking the folding chair, Murphy was indicating that his caucus could vote as they pleased. When the vote was subsequently taken, H.B. 668 was overwhelmingly defeated.

Sending H.B. 668 down to defeat was a big win, but a defensive one. Big Labor has tried similar tactics over and over again, by having its legislative martinets introduce bills that don't repeal Right to Work, but instead open holes that would sink the ship. The Committee's legislative team is kept busy monitoring bills that undermine Right to Work statutes and mobilizing to defeat them if they start to move. It is part of the AFL-CIO's strategy to stretch the Committee's resources by making it defend worker freedom on as many different fronts as possible. As we have seen, even though Right to Work laws are overwhelmingly favored by the public, Big Labor can often muster a lot of support in state legislatures for repeal or for amendments that are tantamount to repeal. Freedom of choice will always be endangered so long as union officials have the power to force the workers they "represent" to finance their political agendas.

OKLAHOMA—THE LATEST STATE TO GIVE WORKERS THEIR FREEDOM

On September 25, 2001, Oklahoma voters voted in favor of Ballot Question 695, a referendum on enacting Right to Work in the Sooner state. That made Oklahoma the 22nd Right to Work state. It was a long, hard struggle against the typical array of scare tactics and disinformation that Big Labor always employs against Right to Work.

A Right to Work referendum had been defeated in Oklahoma in 1964, with Big Labor resorting to astounding bits of scare-mongering and deception, such as a flyer distributed in black areas showing a civil rights protester being attacked by a police dog and bearing the caption "These are your civil rights in Right to Work Alabama." The defeat for that initiative was very narrow, but as had been the case in other states, after the defeat politicians decided that the issue was a sure loser that would be the death of any candidate who touched it—one of those "third rail" issues. For many years, the Oklahoma Freedom to Work Committee labored to change that perception and alter the political landscape so that Right to Work could once again be considered.

In elections from 1994 to 2000, Right to Work activists steadily pressed their case for having Oklahoma join bordering Right to Work states Texas, Kansas, and Arkansas in permitting workers the freedom to choose to pay union dues. In those elections, 28 pro-compulsion legislators went down to defeat and three strongly pro-Right to Work officials were elected to statewide offices—Governor Frank Keating, Lieutenant Governor Mary Fallin, and Labor Commissioner Brenda Reneau Wynn.

The climate in the state legislature had become far more favorable to Right to Work following the 2000 election, with majorities in both chambers. There were still two key legislators, however, positioned to block a Right to Work bill—House speaker Glen Johnson and Senate President Pro Tempore Stratton Taylor. Early in 2001, both maneuvered to prevent a vote on Right to Work bills. But then on February 6, Taylor announced that he would refer to a Senate committee SJR 1, a bill that would put a Right to Work measure on the ballot for the citizens to decide upon. In an open letter, he explained that he could no longer block passage of a Right to Work bill in the Senate, and was allowing SJR 1 to move forward because he wanted to give union officials "a fighting chance of defeating Right to Work at a statewide election."

Big Labor was confident that its usual anti-Right to Work campaign strategy of creating doubt through false, misleading, and inflammatory charges would defeat the referendum. Although a large majority of Americans favor Right to Work in principle, union bosses know from experience that they can cut that majority down substantially with a slick campaign of fear and deception. They were pleased at getting their "fighting chance." Maybe they would be able to snatch victory from the jaws of defeat.

The question is why Republican leaders in Oklahoma decided to give it to them. Initially, Republican leaders, who strongly favored the legislative approach, refused to take Senator Taylor's bait. The turning point came with an editorial in the *Daily Oklahoman,* the state's largest newspaper, contending that it was a great victory for Right to Work to have a chance to prevail at the polls and urging Governor Keating to back SJR 1. Several Republicans who were committed to Right to Work and whose votes were needed for passage preferred to avoid voting on the issue themselves and stated that they were going to support Right to Work in Oklahoma by "letting the people decide." Therefore, the Oklahoma Republican establishment agreed to throw Brer Rabbit into his favorite briar patch. The legislature passed SJR 1 and Governor Keating signed it, setting the date of September 25, 2001, as the date for the special referendum on what was designated Question 695. As had been the case in Idaho, Right to Work proponents would have to get citizens to vote "Yes" which, as we have seen, is usually a disadvantage in a referendum.

The Yes on 695 campaign began on June 20, 2001, with rallies in Tulsa and Oklahoma City. Governor Keating was an enthusiastic supporter, barnstorming the state to speak in favor of the referendum and to raise money. In all, the "Yes" campaign raised $6.4 million, with 84 percent of the money coming from within Oklahoma. In contrast, most of the anti-Right to Work funding came from out-of-state sources. Combining cash contributions with "in-kind" aid, such as union "volunteers" who helped the "No on 695" campaign with voter registration and turnout efforts, Big Labor spent an estimated $18 million in its attempt to defeat Right to Work. As has always been the case with referenda on Right to Work, this battle pitted a heavily financed opposition, ready and willing to use any tactic to create doubt about giving workers freedom of choice, versus a dedicated team of Right to Work advocates with much less money to spend.

Early polling showed Question 695 with strong support, 70 percent of voters surveyed saying that they favored Right to Work. Fortunately, that figure did not induce complacency among the groups working for 695. The Right to Work leaders in Oklahoma knew that Big Labor would unleash a vicious campaign against it that would cause their poll numbers to head downward. During the very hot summer of 2001, the Oklahoma Freedom to Work Committee concentrated on voter identification and mobilization, more than doubling its list of supporters, from 110,000 to 250,000. The State Chamber of Commerce and the Oklahoma City Chamber of Commerce worked to build support in the business community. Oklahoma Families for Jobs and Justice raised funds for the campaign and scheduled speaking engagements on behalf of Question 695 for Governor Keating and other officials.

Question 695's opponents remained remarkably quiet throughout most of the summer, causing some strategists to conclude that Big Labor was not going to run a public campaign against Right to Work at all, but instead would concentrate on getting its own identified voting core to the polls. That speculation was put to rest on Labor Day, when the anti-695 forces made the biggest media buy in Oklahoma history. Naturally, the ads tried to get voters to ignore the principle of Right to Work by fabricating charges against it, such as that it would cause wages to fall and workers to lose health insurance coverage. It didn't matter that the "research" behind the attacks was as phony as a three-dollar bill. Big Labor would say anything to create fear and doubt in the minds of voters. The expensive media campaign had a noticeable impact, though, driving down the poll numbers for Question 695 below 50 percent just weeks before the election.

The Yes on 695 campaign did not panic, and stuck to its message. First of all, backers kept hitting upon the moral case in favor of Right to Work, knowing that most people can see the fundamental wrong in forcing people to pay for union representation if they don't want it. The campaign also devoted some time and resources to refuting the economic scare tactics of the opposition, by demonstrating that neighboring Right to Work states were not suffering, and that Oklahoma was lagging behind them in job creation. Also, the campaign attacked the credibility of the out-of-state union officials who were bankrolling the opposition to 695.

Two late blunders by 695's opponents helped to turn the tide. One TV ad alleged that Idaho's economy had been depressed ever since enacting Right to Work in 1985. That absurd claim drew a lot of critical media scrutiny. Idaho's economy had in fact registered very impressive economic gains in the 1990s—fourth in the nation in growth of Gross State Product between 1992 and 1999. During that same time period, Oklahoma had ranked 34th in economic growth. Several newspapers criticized the false ads and the Oklahoma Freedom to Work Committee distributed a quotation from Idaho AFL-CIO president Dave Whaley, who had admitted, "Business has flocked to Idaho" in a 2000 op-ed piece in the *Idaho Post-Register*. In another instance, Oklahoma news media compelled the opposition to 695 to withdraw an ad that falsely stated that the *Tulsa World* had said that if Right to Work were enacted, 112,000 Oklahoma workers would lose health insurance benefits. In truth, the paper had merely quoted an economist on Big Labor's payroll who had made that ridiculous charge. Worker freedom to stop supporting unwanted unions is not connected in any way to the benefits that have been negotiated. *Tulsa World* executive editor Joe Worley said, "The ad was inaccurate and we are pleased that they recognized the fact." Those campaign mistakes helped to reinforce the impression among voters that the opponents of 695 would make up anything to get people to vote their way.

One more tactical error the opponents made was to continue their campaign in the days immediately following the September 11, 2001, terrorist attacks. Right to Work forces immediately suspended their efforts, but the opponents kept cranking out the lies and misinformation for three days after the attacks. The fact that Big Labor would not put aside politics during a national emergency was a public relations blunder of considerable magnitude.

On September 25, 2001, Oklahomans voted on Question 695. The result was a victory for Right to Work, with 54.2 percent of the voters casting their ballots in favor of 695.

As usual, Big Labor was not going to give up until it had exhausted every possible means of preventing workers from exercising their freedom to work without having to pay union dues. On November 13, just seven weeks after the vote, its team of lawyers filed suit to overturn the referendum on the grounds that it hadn't been conducted in accordance with Oklahoma law. The case went to trial in March 2002 before Judge Frank Seay of the U.S. District Court for the Eastern District of Oklahoma. Among other arguments, top AFL-CIO lawyer Lawrence Gold said that the referendum should be overturned because it failed to inform the voters of certain abstruse points of law, such as that workers in "federal enclaves" would not be covered and that Right to Work would not apply to workers in the railway and airline industries. Attorneys for the National Right to Work Legal Defense Foundation and the Oklahoma Attorney General's Office exhibited expert marksmanship as they shot down one desperate argument after another raised by Big Labor's lawyers. On June 6, Judge Seay handed down his ruling—the suit to overturn the voice of the people was dismissed.

That defeat, however, did not stop Big Labor from trying to get the courts to overrule the voice of the people. Its lawyers kept up desperate litigation to nullify the referendum. In one case, discovered by a Foundation attorney, a collusive lawsuit had been filed by a union and an employer with the evident intention of providing only a weak defense for the legality of the referendum. The Foundation promptly intervened in the suit to represent a worker who did not want to return to the days of compulsory union dues. After hearing the strong defense of the law that the Foundation gave, a state trial court tossed out the collusive suit. As of mid-2004, it seems that the litigation brushfires have all been put out. Oklahoma remains the 22nd Right to Work state.

At the time of this writing, Right to Work campaigns are progressing in several states, including Colorado, Indiana, Kentucky, New Hampshire, and Montana. Defensive efforts, however, are also necessary in several Right to Work states where Big Labor is pushing legislation that would undermine worker freedom of choice. Such battles will undoubtedly continue as long as Right to Work is only a state option. The solution that would cut the Gordian Knot would be to repeal the language in federal law that supports compulsory unionism. The next chapter will look at the Committee's goal of getting a national Right to Work statute.

NOTES

1. See W. Robert Reed, "How Right-to-Work Laws Affect Wages," *Journal of Labor Research*, vol. 24, pp. 713–730 (2003).
2. *Meade Electric Co. v. Hegberg*, 159 N.E. 2d 408.
3. The Louisiana legislature had passed a Right to Work bill in 1946, but it was vetoed by Governor Jimmie Davis.
4. *Albany Herald*, March 1, 1995.

CHAPTER TEN

THE CLINTON YEARS

T he election of Bill Clinton to the presidency in 1992 promised to create serious trouble for the Right to Work movement, much as the election of Jimmy Carter in 1976 had. Like Carter, Clinton had been the governor of a southern Right to Work state (Arkansas), and also like Carter, Clinton had abandoned all pretense of favoring worker choice when he sought the White House. In the campaign book Clinton and his running mate Al Gore produced, *Putting People First,* the candidates' opposition to Right to Work was made clear: "We support the repeal of section 14(b) of the Taft-Hartley Act." The union autocrats knew that the Clinton-Gore ticket was in their hip pocket and backed it full throttle to defeat George H. W. Bush in the 1992 campaign.

In fact, Big Labor had rescued Clinton early in the primary season when his campaign was on the ropes. In January 1992, just before the critical New Hampshire primary, it appeared that Clinton was going to be among the first candidates to throw in his cards and head home. Gennifer Flowers had gone public with her revelations of their extended affair while he was Governor of Arkansas and Clinton's shifty story on his avoidance of military service during Vietnam was playing badly with many voters. But just as his poll numbers were plunging, he received surprise endorsements from a group of government union officials. The National Education Association, American Federation of Teachers, and the American Federation of State, County, and Municipal Employees all threw their weight behind Clinton. The endorsements, money, and ground troops pulled Clinton's campaign out of its nosedive in New Hampshire, enabling him to finish a respectable second and call himself "The Comeback Kid." Bill Clinton owed Big Labor big time. Without its powerful assistance, he would never have gotten the Democratic nomination.

President Bush's term in office had been one of frustration and disappointment for Right to Work supporters. His chosen Secretary of Labor, Lynn Martin, boasted to talk-show host Larry King that she had always been opposed to Right to Work laws; in office, Martin tried repeatedly to appease Big Labor. Bush nominated Right to Work opponents for the National Labor Relations Board; sometimes the National Right to Work Committee was able to block the confirmation of those individuals, sometimes not. In 1990, for example, President Bush could have replaced NLRB Chairman James Stephens, but instead nominated him for another term. Among other things, Stephens insisted on writing regulations to implement the *Beck* decision that would "fit the needs" and "meet the demands" of union bosses. In another affront to worker freedom, the Bush Administration's Solicitor General Ken Starr intervened in a crucial court battle over the Boston Harbor project, siding with Big Labor in arguing that it should be permissible for Massachusetts to do that vast undertaking with a "Project Labor Agreement." Project Labor Agreements are the darlings of union officials because they require all contractors who work on the project in any way to use only union labor, thereby freezing out merit shop contractors—as well as raising the cost considerably. The sad fact is that the first three years of the Bush Administration were marked by one slap in the face after another for Right to Work advocates.

Throughout those years, Right to Work leaders repeatedly called upon President Bush for leadership on *Beck*. In the spring of 1992, he finally gave them a small morsel—an Executive Order (Number 12800, issued April 13, 1992) requiring that federal contractors post a notice informing their employees about their rights under *Beck*. That gesture did virtually nothing to slow the torrent of Big Labor cash flowing to Clinton's aid in the election; nor did it convince Right to Work supporters that President Bush was really on their side.

On November 2 Clinton won the election, capturing 370 electoral votes to Bush's 168. His victory was due in large measure to massive support from

Big Labor; the third-party candidacy of H. Ross Perot, and the fact that some of Bush's "base" stayed home on Election Day were also factors in the outcome. What would his administration bring?

CLINTON AND FRIENDS IN WASHINGTON

Despite his occasional "New Democrat" rhetoric, there was never much doubt that Clinton would do everything in his power to make his Big Labor benefactors happy, and he erased what little doubt there was almost immediately upon taking office.

One of Clinton's first official acts was to cancel Bush's Executive Order requiring the posting of notices about *Beck* rights, saying that it was "unfair." (Union officials want workers informed only of rights they approve of.) In addition, he issued an Executive Order barring employers who didn't force union membership on their workers from bidding on federal contracts. Political payoffs, pure and simple.

Furthermore, Clinton's chosen Secretary of Labor was Robert Reich, a Harvard professor who was a compulsory unionism enthusiast. Reich had famously said that union bosses need to have the power to "strap their members to the mast" during strikes, meaning that they should be able to force workers to remain on strike despite the fact that individuals might prefer to return to work. Big Labor was delighted to have a Secretary of Labor who was so solicitous of their "need" for compelled allegiance.

THE GUTTING OF THE HATCH ACT

An early payback to Clinton's union boss friends was his eager destruction of the Hatch Act. The Hatch Act had been enacted by Congress and signed into law by President Franklin Roosevelt in 1939. The bill had been promoted by New Mexico Democratic Senator Carl Hatch with bipartisan support, in reaction to instances of federal employees being pressured into supporting candidates with time and money. The Hatch Act addressed the problem of a politicized federal workforce by requiring that employees refrain from political activism. Of course, they could still vote and speak their minds, but federal employees could not go around soliciting campaign contributions, running for office, or otherwise actively participating in campaigns. As the *Providence Journal* wrote in an August 11, 1993, editorial, "The best way to guarantee the integrity of the Civil Service and to insulate federal workers from the dangers of the spoils system is to refrain from participating in political campaigns, from running for office, or from soliciting donations from fellow workers or the public."[1]

Big Labor, naturally, didn't like the Hatch Act. It saw in the federal workforce an untapped gold mine of potential activists for candidates and causes favored by the union autocrats. Early in 1993 bills were introduced in the House and the Senate to "reform" the Hatch Act by cutting back its coverage. Many newspapers saw the danger in such "reform." The *Wisconsin State Journal,* for example, wrote," Who wants to change the Hatch Act? Unions representing government employees. The union leaders believe their ability to win concessions for the members will increase dramatically when they can marshal an army of campaign workers for friendly lawmakers."[2] And the *Des Moines Register* said, "The only 'rights' this legislation gives three million government employees is the right to be exploited as cheap campaign labor and the right to collect money for their unions."[3] Nevertheless, both the House and Senate passed bills designed to gut the Hatch Act in the summer of 1993. The National Right to Work Committee lobbied hard to stop the legislation, but to no avail. In October, President Clinton eagerly signed the bill that came out of the conference committee, which kept the Act's rules against political involvement intact only for law enforcement personnel. With that victory under their belts, the labor barons licked their lips for more favors from Clinton and their minions in Congress.

THE PUSHBUTTON STRIKE BILL

Throughout the 1980s Big Labor's empire had continued to shrink in terms of the number of workers who were—voluntarily or involuntarily—paying dues. However, union officials had more money than ever to throw into politics, a feat they accomplished by squeezing more funds out of captive workers. Professor James T. Bennett of George Mason University calculated that the receipts of private sector unions, despite the fact that they represented an ever-decreasing percentage of the labor force, had increased by more than 115 percent from 1960 to 1987, after adjusting for inflation. Bennett concluded, "Simply put, falling membership has not resulted in a concomitant deterioration in the financial fortunes of organized labor in the private sector. Conventional wisdom about the financial decline of private sector unions is based on myth."[4]

Big Labor's declining market share certainly had not diminished its influence in Congress, where AFL-CIO bosses were riding high. They boasted that in the 1990 mid-term elections, 73.8 percent of their hand-picked House candidates and 60.7 percent of their Senate candidates had won. The 1992 election had given them a Democratic president who was beholden to them, as well as a Congress with Democratic majorities in both chambers and leadership in key committees that could be counted on to advance compulsory unionism. Predictably, the top union moguls turned once again to politics in an effort to obtain new legal powers that they hoped would reverse their declining market share and enable them to collect even more revenue.

The bill that they most wanted was one that Committee strategists dubbed the "Pushbutton Strike Bill." Co-sponsored in the Senate by two of Big Labor's most vociferous allies, Senators Ted Kennedy and Howard Metzenbaum, and in the House by another old antagonist, Representative William Clay, it had two main components. First, the bill required employers to fire all "replacement workers" as soon as a strike ended. Under the existing law, employers are free to hire replacement workers during a strike—people whom union militants invariably call "scabs" and often harass, threaten, and physically assault for the affront of "taking union jobs." (The fact that the jobs don't *belong* to the striking workers is immaterial to the labor bosses. It is effective propaganda to speak as if replacement workers were doing something wrong in agreeing to work under the terms that the union bosses had declared so bad as to warrant a strike.) When the strike was over, the employer was free to retain some or all of the replacement workers, hiring back strikers only as necessary. Naturally, that weakened the position of the union bosses since a large infusion of new workers who might want to retain their freedom to deal directly with the employer could lead to a decertification election, and in a Right to Work state, the new workers might be inclined to exercise their right not to pay union dues. To secure their grip on money and power, the labor chieftains wanted to make sure that striking workers "owned" their jobs, and could desert them but later reclaim them whenever they wished.

Secondly, the Pushbutton Strike Bill would have compelled employers to penalize workers who elected to remain on the job by rescinding any wage and benefit increases they had received while working during the strike. This brazen attack on freedom of contract fit in perfectly with the Big Labor mindset that nothing should be allowed to interfere with its orders. Besides, it would make it seem that the labor bosses weren't responsible for the disciplining of workers who chose not to strike—it would be done by the employer, who would be following "the law." This authoritarian legislation (S.55 and H.R. 5 were the bill numbers) would have propped up the sagging fortunes of compulsory unionism by making strikes more damaging—and probably more frequent. With their new strike powers, union bosses would undoubtedly have blackmailed many more employers into accepting their demands that all workers be forced to pay union dues.

That bill had already been fought over once in Congress. In 1991 it had passed the House easily, 247–182, and was beaten in the Senate only with a Herculean effort by the Committee to mobilize public opinion against the bill. Just as it had done in congressional battles going back to 1965, the Committee succeeded in getting huge numbers of Americans to flood Capitol Hill with cards and letters telling senators that they should not cave in to this outrageous power grab. The Pushbutton Strike bill was filibustered in 1992 with Senator Orrin Hatch leading the way; the closest that Majority Leader George Mitchell could come to breaking the filibuster left him three votes short. Big Labor's top brass promised to come back with a more "friendly" (that is to say, sycophantic) Congress in 1993 and pass their pet bill.

With the new 103rd Congress sworn in and President Bill Clinton ready to sign the Pushbutton Strike Bill, Senators Kennedy and Metzenbaum introduced it again on January 21, 1993. Many knowledgeable observers figured that it couldn't be stopped this time. For example, the respected *Kiplinger Letter* said unequivocally, "unions will win." Right to Work leaders were not about to concede anything to Big Labor, however. Reed Larson told Right to Work supporters that the Pushbutton Strike Bill could be defeated, but it would take an enormous effort to do so. Stopping the bill in 1992 had been extremely difficult and this time the lobbying power of the White House would be added to that of Big Labor. Undoubtedly the Committee was in for its hardest battle since the "Labor Law Reform" bill of 1977–78.

Congress went to work on the bill quickly, with simultaneous hearings in the House and Senate. The committee chairmen even went so far as to deny Right to Work spokesmen the opportunity to testify on the legislation. To get the Committee's views before the public, Texas Representative Dick Armey, then Minority Whip, joined Reed Larson in holding a news conference outside the hearing room. That accentuated the unfairness of the whole procedure, but Armey was openly pessimistic about the prospects for defeating this latest power grab by the union bigwigs, saying, "I expect Congress to pass it, the President to sign it, and the American people to suffer."

The bill passed the House in mid-June on a vote of 239 to 190. The only solace that Right to Work leaders could find in that was that the margin of victory for the bill was smaller than it had been in 1991. Perhaps the 1992 election had not strengthened the grip union officials had on the House, as had been widely assumed—and perhaps the Committee's resistance was more effective than the over-confident union bosses had expected. Still, the bill had cleared the House, and with Clinton eager to sign it, the only chance of saving the day was going to be in the Senate.

What about public opinion? Shortly before the House vote, the Committee commissioned Marketing Research Institute, a highly-respected polling company, to survey the public's views on the Pushbutton Strike bill. By a two-to-one margin, the American people were opposed to the bill. A poll done by Time and CNN came to the same conclusion. As had so often been the case in the past, Big Labor was trying to use its political muscle to force through legislation that most Americans disliked.

In mid-1993, top union officials flexed their muscles and ordered strikes against hundreds of small and mid-sized businesses. Those strikes served to remind people of the ugly face of union coercion and to strengthen the fears the people had been expressing to the pollsters. In two notable cases—West Central Turkeys, Inc., of Pelican Rapids, Minnesota, and Riverside Health Care Center nursing home in Missoula, Montana—union organizers delivered this ultimatum: "Fire all your workers who aren't paying union dues or we will strike until you're out of business." Such examples illustrated the Committee's point that giving Big Labor even more power with the Pushbutton Strike Bill would help it to eliminate freedom of choice for more workers.

Focusing attention on the Senate, the Committee launched one of its well-honed attacks on the Kennedy-Metzenbaum bill, sending out a targeted mailing to Right to Work members, asking them to register their opposition. In union offices, paid drones were already churning out bogus "constituent" mail—cards and letters telling senators to support the bill— so it was crucial that senators heard from real people who opposed it. The Committee also mailed to its special list of activists, asking for seed money to help ensure that the battle to show grassroots support would not be lost for want of funds. As always, they came through.

Furthermore, the Committee reached out beyond its current support base with mailings and newspaper ads designed to show people how dangerous the Pushbutton Strike bill was and why they should join in the effort to defeat it. The result was gratifying—tens of thousands of Americans who had never before supported the National Right to Work Committee financially sent in checks and became members. The union bosses' latest assault on freedom was having the beneficial side effect of increasing the grassroots muscle of the Committee. Now if only the bill could be stopped.

A number of senators had not committed themselves one way or the other and were keeping a finger to the political winds. The Committee targeted their states with newspaper ads and extra mail to supporters, explaining why the Pushbutton Strike Bill must never become law. Right to Work leaders wanted to make sure that the Senate fence-sitters felt a hurricane blowing against this reprehensible piece of legislation when they tested the political wind.

By the late summer of 1993, Committee personnel were traveling all over the country to inform the media, counter Big Labor's arguments, and to mobilize people to oppose the bill. Most of the effort centered on states where, as Senator Dirksen once put it, senators might see the light if they felt more heat. Most of the kindling was placed around a group of senators from Right to Work states who had bowed to Big Labor's pressure and supported the bill in 1992.

Reed Larson knew that it would be a great tactical stroke if Labor Day—usually a time when the union bosses crow about their supposed accomplishments and whitewash their use of compulsion to keep workers in their ranks—could instead be turned into a day for rallying workers who cherished their freedom. He wrote a column pointing out that the celebration was for Labor Day, not "Union Boss Day," and that eight out of ten Americans supported the right of an individual to work without being forced to support a union. That column was distributed to 1,340 newspapers around the country. Furthermore, Larson recorded an audio news release for broadcast by nearly 2,000 radio stations that exposed illegal activities by Big Labor's political machine. Right to Work Committee spokesmen also gave live interviews to CNN, CBS, and NBC. Labor Day 1993 turned out to be a very good day for Right to Work and not at all the big propaganda monopoly that the AFL-CIO had come to expect.

Television is, of course, one of the best ways to get through to large numbers of people and the Committee also made great use of it in the battle against the Pushbutton Strike Bill. Thanks to the generous support of Right to Work backers across America, the Committee was able to produce and air a series of hard-hitting ads featuring Charlton Heston. Heston, who had done so much to help Right to Work prevail in Idaho in 1986, again volunteered his time to help make the case against the bill.

Some of the ads took direct aim at those senators from Right to Work states who had gone astray on this bill in 1992—Senators Howell Heflin and Richard Shelby of Alabama, Dennis DeConcini of Arizona, and Charles Robb of Virginia—and others were directed at shoring up senators who might cave in under pressure from the Clinton White House, particularly Arkansas' two senators Dale Bumpers and David Pryor. The heat on all of them was then turned up another notch when the Committee held news conferences in the capitals of the states those men represented, pointing out how the Pushbutton Strike Bill was incompatible with the belief in worker freedom of choice that was enshrined in their state law.

Finally, Right to Work members responded to the call to arms with a stupendous outpouring of cards, letters, and other communications to Congress expressing their opposition to the bill—more than 2.5 million in all. The Committee's full court press against the bill was working. When the Labor bosses counted their votes in the Senate, they kept coming up several votes short of the 60 needed to stop a filibuster. The easy win they had envisioned when Bill Clinton moved into 1600 Pennsylvania Avenue was eluding them.

Therefore, the bill's supporters decided to resort to a subterfuge—a "compromise" that would somewhat dilute this witch's brew in hopes of luring in a few wavering senators. The bill was still poisonous, and in all likelihood the more onerous House version would have prevailed in conference committee, but Kennedy and Metzenbaum knew that there were several senators who were looking for any excuse to defect to their side. Oregon's Bob Packwood and Nebraska's Jim Exon and Bob Kerrey were the chief advocates of the "compromise." Packwood had never been with Right to Work on this or any other issue going back to the "Labor Law Reform" bill of 1978, but the two Nebraskans had been siding with Right to Work on this bill, owing to the pressure they were feeling from their freedom-loving constituents. Once the Committee's leadership got wind of the phony "compromise" bill, it dispatched spokesmen to Lincoln, Nebraska, where they attacked it and announced that Nebraska was going to be added to the list of the Committee's target states. As a result, Exon and Kerry pulled back and the "compromise" was quietly abandoned.

The union bosses were at the point of throwing a tantrum by the winter of 1994. Their pet bill was bogged down in the Senate, and neither lobbying nor deception was working. Next they resorted to public threats. United Auto Workers head Bill Casstevens called on union zealots to "take to the streets" to support the Pushbutton Strike Bill "and remain there" until the Senate passed it. Marshall Hicks, boss of the Utility Workers Union, demanded that the AFL-CIO hierarchy organize "a nationwide work stoppage" that would continue until the bill was passed. This sort of blackmail is common in Europe, where communist-dominated unions have frequently brought the economic life of countries to a halt until they got their way. Hicks was not shy in saying that he wanted the same thing to happen in America to force through the Kennedy-Metzenbaum bill: "the trucks don't roll, the trains don't roll, the planes don't fly, coal and oil doesn't move, the government employees are not on duty, and the machinery shuts down all over the country."

Heated rhetoric like that galvanized activists on both sides. The White House pledged to redouble its efforts to get the bill passed, which meant a combination of behind-the-scenes threats of political reprisals or promises of payoffs in the form support for bills for projects in their home states for senators who would go along. (That is one reason why the federal budget continues to mushroom—to get support for one costly program, the deal has to be sweetened with many others to round up enough support for passage.) On the other hand, though, Right to Work backers were enraged that Big Labor would threaten so much economic damage to the country over one special interest bill. Many of *them* redoubled *their* efforts to make sure that the Pushbutton Strike Bill would never become law.

Believing that raw force and violence would help his cause, hotheaded Mine Workers boss Richard Trumka orchestrated a series of strikes in the coal industry in 1993–94. The purpose of the strikes was to compel coal companies to fire any miner who wouldn't pay union dues—one of the ultimate goals of the bill. The strikes were notable for their destruction and brutality, with shots fired, property destroyed, and people injured. But Trumka had calculated incorrectly. His violence and intimidation had given Americans yet another reason to stand firm against the Pushbutton Strike Bill. Big Labor had once again overplayed its hand.

By the spring of 1994, the union bosses were growing very impatient and told Senate Majority Leader George Mitchell that they wanted the bill brought to the floor for a vote. Mitchell, perhaps believing that the storm of protest against S.55 had blown over, promised to do so by May 16. That was another miscalculation. Right to Work's pressure on the fence-sitting senators did not abate and Mitchell had to renege on his promise. After counting votes, he knew that he was still short of the 60 needed to stop the filibuster being led by Senator Orrin Hatch. Mitchell finally scheduled a cloture vote on the bill for July 12, 1994.

With the cloture vote set, the Committee ratcheted up its level of action. On July 8, its phone center in Virginia Beach went into high gear, mobilizing thousands of members in the key states to keep telling their senators not to vote for an end to debate on the bill. On July 11, nearly 20,000 Western Union mailgrams from Committee members flooded the Senate, while staff members alerted the media about the impending vote. The Charlton Heston ad played repeatedly on television in states with uncommitted senators.

When the cloture vote was held on July 12, the effectiveness of the Committee's attack on S.55 was apparent—Mitchell came up seven votes short of choking off the filibuster. He tried again the next day, but the lines held steady. After those defeats, he pulled the bill from the Senate floor. It still wasn't completely dead, though. Senator Metzenbaum, who was not running for re-election, tried desperately to find some way to sneak the bill through. He tried engineering yet another deceptive "compromise," and also to attach the bill as a rider to another piece of legislation. But alert sentries in the Senate and the Committee foiled every move Metzenbaum made to give himself an infamous going away present. The Pushbutton Strike Bill finally expired when the Senate adjourned in October prior to the fall elections.

Halting the charge of the Pushbutton Strike Bill was extremely important in preserving worker freedom and denying the union bosses yet another increase in their power to dominate the workplace. Without the perseverance of the National Right to Work Committee, that atrocious bit of special interest legislation would now be law.

In the November 1994 elections, the Democrats suffered a crushing rebuke, losing control of both chambers in Congress for the first time in forty years. Voters retired 37 incumbent members of the House and Senate who had voted for the Pushbutton Strike Bill, dealing Big Labor a staggering blow. While we have seen that Republicans are not sure-fire defenders of Right to Work (nor are Democrats sure-fire opponents), the turnover in Congress meant that many Democratic committee chairmen whom Big Labor knew it could count on to advance their agenda were replaced by Republicans who were somewhat less susceptible to its blandishments and pressure.

With Republicans in control of the House and Senate, an alluring new possibility opened up for Right to Work. Rather than just playing defense against Big Labor's efforts to wring from the government still more legal privileges, the National Right to Work Committee now had the chance to go on offense. The time was at hand to go for the big prize—a national Right to Work Act.

THE NATIONAL RIGHT TO WORK BILL

As we saw back in Chapter 1, compulsory unionism is a creation of the National Labor Relations Act. By destroying the common law as it applied to labor relations and replacing it with an authoritarian statute that took freedom away from workers and employers, the NLRA stacked the deck in favor of union bosses and gave them unprecedented powers. Enacting Right to Work laws in the states helps to mitigate the damage done by the NLRA, but Right to Work leaders have always understood that the only real solution to the problem is to have the federal government clean up the mess it has created. The way to accomplish that is through a National Right to Work Act that repeals the federal support for compulsory unionism and monopoly bargaining.

Almost all of the grand legislative changes that are proposed in Washington involve the writing of bills that add pages—sometimes thousands of them—to the United States Code and require the expenditure of billions of dollars. The National Right to Work Act, in contrast, would *subtract* from the U.S. Code by deleting 38 crucial lines from the National Labor Relations Act and would not entail the expenditure of *any money* whatsoever. The National Right to Work Act is truly a case where less is more—freedom, that is.

With a Republican Congress in place in 1995, the Committee began working toward a vote on the National Right to Work Act. It was sponsored in the House by Representative Bob Goodlatte of Virginia and in the Senate by Senator Lauch Faircloth of North Carolina. Everyone understood that success would neither be easy nor swift. Just because Republicans controlled Congress did not mean that the bill would even get a hearing, much less pass; and even if it did, Bill Clinton would undoubtedly veto it at the behest of his Big Labor backers. Legislative victories, as Right to Work advocates have learned in many state battles, often take years to bring about. The Committee's near-term objective was just to get a roll call vote on the Act in each chamber so that friends and foes would be clearly identified.

The great virtue of roll call votes is that they compel legislators to reveal their true colors. Many politicians like to say one thing and do another. In the case of Right to Work, that usually involves paying lip service to the idea of freedom of choice for workers—after all, more than three out of four Americans oppose forced unionism—while secretly making deals with union bosses to maintain or expand their empire. To make matters worse, many Republicans still labored under the delusion that to be seen as a supporter of Right to Work is political suicide because then Big Labor will "really be out to get them." Therefore, just getting a vote on the National Right to Work Act would take a great deal of effort.

Both the new Speaker of the House and Senate Majority Leader hailed from Right to Work states—Newt Gingrich of Georgia and Bob Dole of Kansas, respectively. Alas, neither was receptive to pushing through the National Right to Work Act for a floor vote, and without their help, the bill would languish in committee. Speaker Gingrich, who in his early days had been a Right to Work opponent until the Committee and his constituents brought him around, was preoccupied with other problems, including bad press and a group of rebellious freshmen who wanted faster action on many controversial items than the Speaker was willing to give them. Each time Committee strategists spoke with him about moving the Act for a vote, he hedged and squirmed. There never were hearings or a vote on Representative Goodlatte's bill in the House.

Senator Dole was also difficult. Throughout his long legislative career, he had proclaimed his support for a national Right to Work law, but now that the chance was at hand to bring about a vote on an actual bill, he hesitated. The main reason was that he planned a campaign for the presidency in 1996 and, like so many Republicans, feared the wrath of Big Labor if he should openly champion a bill that would drive a stake through the heart of its "your money or your job" racket. Senator Dole became evasive with the press. When asked his position on the Right to Work Act, he'd reply that he hadn't formulated one because there hadn't yet been hearings on the bill. But the reason why there hadn't been hearings was because he hadn't yet allowed any.

Reed Larson and other Committee leaders then realized that they could use Dole's planned race for the presidency to their advantage. He needed to be given an incentive to support the legislation he had always said he supported, and the competitive Republican contest for the nomination could be used to do that. The first two stops on the primary trail are Iowa and New Hampshire, states where many Republican primary voters strongly back Right to Work. The Committee budgeted $457,000 on ads in those states targeting Senator Dole. The ads did not attack him, but merely asked why he was not scheduling a vote on the National Right to Work Act. That started a wildfire. Soon cards and letters were pouring into Dole's office in Washington from Republican voters in those states, saying that they wanted action on Right to Work. Facing strong competition from other Republican candidates who unequivocally supported the Right to Work Act, Senator Dole was feeling the heat because of his evasion of the issue.

The Committee also applied leverage to Dole with a press conference in Des Moines, the capital of Iowa, on September 1, 1995. Reed

Larson said in that conference that one of the Republican candidates, Senator Phil Gramm of Texas, had given his support to the National Right to Work Act and then delivered the punch line: "If a politician wants the support of Iowans in his bid for the presidency, I suggest that he commit to enacting a National Right to Work law." Lest anyone miss the point, Larson then added, "Bob Dole is on record in the past in favor of this bill, but he has not taken a position yet as to what he is going to do about the bill this year."

Despite all of the pressure coming to bear on him, Dole still waffled on a vote on Senator Faircloth's bill throughout the fall of 1995. Therefore, early in 1996 as more and more attention was focusing on the upcoming Iowa caucuses, the Committee turned up the heat some more. It did so by running another Charlton Heston ad in which the distinguished actor—who could truthfully say, "I am a union man"—explained why America needed the national Right to Work Act and called upon Senator Dole to schedule an immediate vote on the bill. At the same time, the Committee ran full-page newspaper ads in the major daily papers in Iowa. Those ads said to Senator Dole:

> For decades, you have voiced support for Right to Work. And in 1992, you specifically endorsed the National Right to Work law proposal. The question now is whether the freedom to work is a priority you will fight for. How can the American people rely on you to make our Right to Work a priority as President—if you fail to make it a priority as Majority Leader?

Dole disliked the bind that the Right to Work campaign was putting him in. Like so many Republican politicians going all the way back to Senator Bricker, he wanted to dodge the issue in hopes that he would thereby soften Big Labor's opposition to him. And the Committee's leaders knew that if they eased up on Dole, he would let the National Right to Work Act gather dust until after the November elections.

The Committee was determined not to let that happen. AFL-CIO President John Sweeney had announced that Big Labor was going flat out to retake Congress in 1996. With its prodigious ability to throw money and manpower into races to elect politicians obedient to union boss desires, there was a good reason to fear that that might happen. If it did, the chance for action on the National Right to Work Bill would vanish. Getting a vote in 1996 was therefore critical. The Committee was not going to let Senator Dole out of the bind.

Still keeping mum on the National Right to Work Act, Dole managed to eke out a narrow win in Iowa—which was unimpressive given that he was from the nearby farm state of Kansas and that his opponents were far less known to voters than a senator who had been on the national stage since 1976 when he was President Ford's running mate. Dole had been widely regarded as the probable Republican nominee to face Bill Clinton in November, but with the New Hampshire primary the next stop along the primary trail and other candidates (including journalist Pat Buchanan, publisher Steve Forbes, and former Tennessee governor Lamar Alexander) cutting into his lead, he was clearly in trouble. If he did poorly in New Hampshire, Dole knew that his candidacy could be dealt a mortal wound in the next state, South Carolina, long a Right to Work bastion. So he decided to do the right thing, even if not for the right reason. He called Senator Lauch Faircloth and agreed that he would allow hearings and a vote on the bill if the Committee would pull its ad campaign against his waffling on Right to Work. Faircloth relayed the message to Reed Larson, who agonized over the decision. Just before the Iowa caucuses, Dole had lashed out against the Committee and Larson questioned his verbal commitment at that vital juncture. It was a sad turn of events. Forty years earlier, Dole, as a Republican leader in Russell, Kansas, had helped Reed Larson to get the Kansas Right to Work law passed. Now, against mounting campaign pressures, he seemed to regard Right to Work as an annoyance. Larson therefore asked Senator Faircloth to get Dole's commitment *in writing*. Faircloth sought to do so—on the Senate floor, with C-Span's camera's recording it all. Watching on TV at Right to Work headquarters as the drama unfolded, Larson and others could see Faircloth approach Dole and tap him on the shoulder. As the two spoke, their words could not be heard, but it was evident that Dole was angry. With a sweep of his arm, he waved Faircloth away.

It appeared that Dole had refused, but a minute later Larson's phone rang. It was Senator Faircloth, who simply said, "Come and get your letter."

After Senator Dole had managed to nail down the Republican nomination that spring, he instructed his Kansas colleague, Senator Nancy Kassebaum, who chaired the Senate Labor Committee, to give the National Right to Work bill a hearing. Dole then stepped down as Majority Leader to devote all his attention to the upcoming campaign for the White House. His successor, Senator Trent Lott of Mississippi, who had always been a strong advocate of Right to Work throughout his congressional career told Reed Larson that if he still wanted the bill brought to the Senate floor for a vote, he would do so. Larson said yes, and Lott kept his word. That was one of his first decisions as majority leader and it came at the cost of a great deal of flack from Republicans who wanted to avoid having to vote on the National Right to Work Act. For the first time in history, the U.S. Senate was going to vote on a bill to pull the plug on federal support of compulsory unionism.

Committee leaders were under no illusions that they had enough votes to pass the bill. There were too many weak-kneed Republicans and union-bought Democrats for that. But getting the roll call would still be useful in identifying friends and enemies and focusing attention on the issue.

When the bill was brought to the Senate floor, Big Labor's legislative lapdogs launched a filibuster against it. During the debate, Senator Faircloth said, "With this bill, not a single word is added to federal law. It simply repeals those sections of the National Labor Relations Act and the Railway Labor Act that authorize the imposition of forced-dues contracts upon working Americans." Opposing the bill, Senator Kennedy hypocritically declaimed, "We have no business telling the States that we know better than they how they should manage their affairs." That was an amazing statement coming from someone who had made a legislative career out of mandates to the states, but it wasn't even correct. Repealing the parts of the NLRA sanctioning compulsory unionism would not tell the states to do anything. Another opponent, Senator Dodd of Connecticut, called the bill "one more example of the Republican Party's systematic and unremitting attack on America's labor unions." That statement, too, was pure disinformation. Allowing workers the freedom to choose whether to support a union is no more an "attack on unions" than the freedom to choose whether to play golf is an attack on America's golf courses.

Senator Lott called for a cloture vote on July 10, 1996. That morning's edition of the *Wall Street Journal* stated the matter perfectly: "Compulsory union dues are not merely an esoteric issue of whether employers or unions hold the upper hand in federal labor law. The issue goes to the heart of individual freedom. Thomas Jefferson once wrote that 'To compel a man to furnish contributions of money for the propagation of opinions which he disbelieves is sinful and tyrannical.' Today we will learn how many Senators agree with Jefferson's sentiment."[5] When the vote was taken, only 31 did. (One pro-Right to Work senator, Thad Cochran of Mississippi was absent for the vote.) Sixty-eight senators had voted against the bill. That defeat stung, but it enabled Committee strategists to gauge the dimensions of the problem and focus attention on those senators who had voted to maintain compulsory unionism as a federal policy—despite the fact that polling consistently shows that more than three of every four Americans supports the Right to Work without having to join a union.

The greatest disappointments in that Senate vote were "conservative" Republicans including veterans Pete Domenici of New Mexico and Mitch McConnell of Kentucky, and freshmen Spencer Abraham of Michigan, Rod Grams of Minnesota, and John Ashcroft of Missouri. All voted against cloture, just as Big Labor wanted. (If they thought that they could mollify the union bosses with that vote and thereby lessen Big Labor's opposition when they ran for re-election in 2000, they were completely mistaken. The three were targeted by Big Labor and defeated.) In all, 21 Republicans had voted with the entire Democratic caucus in opposing the bill, and even Democrats such as Sam Nunn and Ernest Hollings who represented Right to Work states voted against it.

Despite the lopsided Senate vote, Right to Work supporters were not downcast. Senator Faircloth sat down next to Reed Larson in the gallery and said that he would reintroduce the National Right to Work Act in the next session of Congress. As the Chinese say, a journey of a thousand miles begins with a single step and Right to Work supporters knew that with the hearings on the bill and the Senate vote, they had taken the first steps on the journey toward the elimination of compulsory unionism.

NOTES

1. *Providence Journal,* August 11, 1993.
2. *Wisconsin State Journal,* August 9, 1993.
3. *Des Moines Sunday Register,* September 26, 1993.
4. James T. Bennett, "Private Sector Unions: The Myth of Decline," *Journal of Labor Research,* Vol. XII, Number 1 (Winter 1991).
5. *Wall Street Journal,* July 10, 1996.

LOOKING BACK, LOOKING AHEAD

At the beginning of the 21st century, what can we say about the Right to Work movement in America? Have the efforts of the Committee, the Legal Defense Foundation and alltheir supporters made any difference?

WHAT IF THERE HAD BEEN NO RIGHT TO WORK MOVEMENT?

Surveying the history that has been recounted here, we might begin by asking, "What would the United States be like if there had been no Right to Work movement? What if Big Labor had been able to push its agenda with only such opposition as traditional "business" groups and the small number of free-market organizations offered?

Had that been the case, it seems probable that:

- Today there would be no protection against compulsory unionism in any state because Section 14(b) of the Taft-Hartley Act would have been repealed in 1965.
- Compulsory unionism would be the rule for most, if not all, federal government employees.
- The National Labor Relations Act would have been amended on several occasions to give union officials yet more power to force workers into their ranks and command in the workplace.

- Workers who have been abused by union officials for seeking to remain independent would have had no particular place to turn to for help in obtaining justice.
- State and local governments would have lost their independence with regard to labor relations and would be following orders from Washington requiring them to engage in monopoly collective bargaining.
- The National Labor Relations Board would have been even more servile to the desires of union bosses than it has been, helping them to trample upon the freedom of workers and employers.
- With its might augmented by new legal powers and millions of additional dues-payers, Big Labor would probably have gotten far more of its socialistic, anti-competitive agenda in place, weakening the American economy and further eroding our liberties.

That frightening alternative history would probably have come to pass had it not been for the ability of the Right to Work movement to mobilize people and resources with the single goal of battling forced unionism. At many key junctures, all that stood between America and the self-serving, authoritarian agenda of Big Labor has been the grassroots efforts of the National Right to Work Committee, persuading millions of citizens from all walks of life to protest the manifest wrong of compelling workers to pay for union representation they do not want. No business-oriented or ideologically conservative groups could have possibly engineered the outpouring of protest that was essential in saving Section 14(b), in getting President Ford to veto the common situs picketing bill, in keeping "Labor Law Reform" from being enacted, and winning other razor's edge battles. Without any doubt, we would be a substantially less free and less prosperous nation today if the Right to Work movement had not been active for the last sixty years.

Looking back, the Right to Work movement has much to be proud of, but what about the future?

CHANGING LEADERSHIP AT THE NATIONAL RIGHT TO WORK COMMITTEE

Early in the new century, the National Right to Work Committee had to face the prospect of changing leadership. Reed Larson was approaching retirement and a new president would have to be named. With Larson's strong approval, the Board of Directors in July 2003 named long-time vice president Mark A. Mix to take the helm. All agreed that it would be far better to promote from within than to search for a new leader outside the Committee.

The key to continuity was to find someone who deeply understood the unique culture of the Right to Work movement and who recognized the danger posed by union coercive power to the preservation of our essential freedoms. Whereas many association executives are used to the "deal-making" that so often characterizes Washington politics, the Right to Work Committee has had the success it has had precisely because it refuses to make deals that compromise the principles on which it was founded. Mix, who had served the Committee in a variety of roles for seventeen years and understood perfectly the Right to Work formula for success, was the choice.

Born in upstate New York and raised in a union household, Mark Mix graduated in 1986 from James Madison University in Virginia. Having taken a strong interest in politics while in college, Mix accepted a job on the staff of Virginia Congressman Herb Bateman shortly after his graduation. He had marked success in turning out voters for Bateman in a year when many Republican candidates suffered from weak turnout. That demonstrated ability to motivate people came to the attention of the Committee's leadership and Mix was offered a position as a field coordinator working in Santa Fe, New Mexico, where a Right to Work campaign was taking shape. He continued to work on numerous state campaigns until 1990, when he was tapped to run the state legislation program at the Committee's national headquarters. In 1994 federal legislation was added to Mix's responsibilities and in 1998 he was made the senior vice president.

Interviewed in his no-frills office at Right to Work's headquarters—in contrast to the lavish offices of many Washington-area organizations, those of the Right to Work leaders are very spartan, reflecting their commitment to the cause rather than to their own high living—Mix explained to the author what he foresees in the years ahead.

BATTLES AHEAD—THE STATES

Mix is very optimistic by nature and foresees continuing success for the Right to Work movement in advancing its principles in the coming years. The fight against compulsory unionism will continue on several fronts.

The first Right to Work laws were enacted sixty years ago, and Mix regards the passage of statutes to extend the Right to Work principle to more states as a vital objective of the movement. Currently, 22 states are within the fold and others are within reach. Colorado is a good near-term prospect, where a Right to Work bill has several times passed in the House only to fall just short in the Senate. Governor Owens supports Right to Work, so the challenge is to elect just a few more senators who will go with the *vox populi* rather than the dictates of the labor bosses. Active Right to Work campaigns are also proceeding in Kentucky, Indiana, Montana, Delaware, New Hampshire, and Missouri.

Of course, it is never easy to pass Right to Work—the discussion in Chapter 9 of the fierce opposition by Big Labor to the campaigns in Idaho and Oklahoma should make that clear. The mindset of control and dominance that prevails among union officials guarantees that Right to Work legislation will always be met with ferocious opposition. Mix relates a story about New Hampshire Republican Congressman Bill Zeliff to make that point. Zeliff was running for the governorship of his state and met with Teamsters Union officials at a big political event. They told Zeliff that they would let him get by with anything else, but he had to announce his opposition to Right to Work. To Big Labor, supporting freedom of choice for workers is *the* unpardonable sin.

Not only will Right to Work forces have to fight tooth and nail to add new states, but they must continue to defeat attempts by Big Labor to repeal or eviscerate the statutes already in place. The AFL-CIO is pursuing a strategy of "stretching the defenses" by having its legislative allies introduce repeal bills in eight to ten states per year, hoping that sooner or later the Right to Work forces will be unable to stop one of them. A factor that works in Big Labor's favor is the fact that it has a lobbying presence in every state legislature, all the time; Right to Work is not a visible presence unless there is an active effort to pass Right to Work legislation or a bill that threatens to expand compulsory unionism. That asymmetry makes it possible for union lobbyists to hunt constantly for unprincipled politicians who will make a deal to back legislation to erode Right to Work in exchange for Big Labor's support. In recent years, Right to Work's defensive team has succeeded in repelling all the probing attacks (such as that in Georgia in 1995), but there is never a time when the guard can be let down.

BATTLES IN THE COURTS

The National Right to Work Legal Defense Foundation's current roster of cases includes several that could set crucial legal precedents in the fight against compulsory unionism. Mix, who is also president of the Foundation, is confident that we will continue to see successful action in the courts to protect and extend worker rights.

One such case, filed in 2003, aims to torpedo Big Labor's favorite tactic of "top-down organizing." As one union official boasted, "I don't organize workers—I organize companies." That clearly expresses the basic idea. Knowing that they fail half the time when they try to get *workers* to vote for their services, labor bosses have taken to pressuring *management* into forcing unionism on their employees whether they want it or not. Often, this kind of organizing continues even after workers have shown their lack of interest in having union representation in secret ballot elections, demonstrating that unionism today is less about improving wages and working conditions than about increasing the flow of dues money into union treasuries.

Foundation lawsuits attack the legality of this rapidly emerging trend in union organizing. In one case, the United Steelworkers of America had gotten Heartland Industrial Partners, an investment group, to consent to a deal whereby Heartland would remain "neutral" with regard to organizing drives by the Steelworkers at any industrial concerns that Heartland would acquire. In 2001, Heartland purchased the Collins & Aikman Corporation, an Ohio-based automotive parts manufacturer and soon thereafter the Steelworkers launched its organizing drives. Employees at the Holmesville, Ohio, plant—where union organizing drives had previously been defeated in secret ballots on several occasions—found themselves under pressure from both the employer and the union to sign cards saying that they wanted the Steelworkers union to represent them.

In return for Heartland's support for unionization, the Steelworkers union agreed to invest worker pension fund money in Heartland; to stifle efforts by employees to assert rights given to workers by federal law (including the right to strike!); and to limit employees' ability to influence wages, benefits, and working conditions. Naturally, workers would be compelled to pay dues if they wanted to keep their jobs. This is a most revealing deal—management conspiring to sell out the liberty of its employees to a union more interested in its revenues than in the workers it would supposedly "represent."

The Foundation's suit on behalf of Wanda Patterson and several of her coworkers at the Holmesville plant contends that the sweetheart pact between Heartland and the Steelworkers union is illegal, violating civil and criminal provisions of the Taft-Hartley Act designed to prevent corruption and conflicts of interest in labor representation. At the time of this writing, the case is at the discovery phase, with lawyers for the defendants stonewalling every attempt by Foundation attorneys to learn more about the deal between the company and the union. The opposing lawyers are trying to hide behind the assertion of novel claims of legal privileges that supposedly shield information they don't want to reveal.

In another case, involving the Thomas Built Bus firm in Winston-Salem, North Carolina, Foundation attorneys succeeded in June 2004 in getting the Regional Director of the NLRB to prosecute the UAW and Thomas Built's parent company, Freightliner, for having illegally coerced workers into signing union recognition cards. The company and the union had conducted a joint campaign to acquire enough signed cards to enable the company to declare that it would recognize the union as the exclusive representative of all 1,100 workers. Many workers complained that they were subjected to "captive audience" speeches at which UAW officials coerced them into signing the cards. More than 400 of the workers signed a petition demanding a secret ballot election to decertify the UAW after Thomas Built had recognized the union. If this case is brought to a successful conclusion, it would set an important precedent in the Foundation's ongoing efforts to put an end to abusive top-down organizing tactics that deprive workers of even a secret-ballot election.

So important is the battle against this kind of organizing that the Foundation has tripled the resources directed to its Top-Down Organizing Task Force. If Right to Work can stop top-down organizing, many thousands of workers will be spared from compulsory unionism. The Foundation's attorneys will no doubt be kept busy on this issue as well as all of the traditional areas of conflict discussed in Chapter 7.

BATTLES IN CONGRESS
Right to Work will also be active in promoting good legislation and fighting bad legislation in Congress.

As an egregious example of the latter, Mix cites a bill that was introduced in November 2003 by Senator Ted Kennedy and Representative George Miller. Misleadingly named the "Employee Free Choice Act," this bill would greatly *diminish* the freedom of workers to choose not to affiliate with a labor union. Like earlier bills to "reform" federal labor law, the Kennedy-Miller bill would attempt to stifle employer resistance to union demands by increasing the penalties for anything that might be deemed "interference" with worker rights, but the dangerous new wrinkle in the bill is that it expressly approves of unionization without a secret ballot vote of the workers.

Big Labor regards it as a terrible problem that it loses so many of the secret ballot certification elections conducted by the NLRB. While claiming to be in favor of free choice for workers, it hates the fact that in free elections, workers often turn thumbs down on union representation. The union bosses want to allow for the certification of monopoly unions simply on the basis of "card checks"—that is to say, signed cards that supposedly show a worker's support for a particular union. Why do the labor chieftains want to replace the secret ballot with this "card check" idea? That's easy—because they can use their well-known tactics of deceit and coercion more effectively if they can confront workers face to face and pressure them into signing the card. The secret ballot method of determining whether a union will represent the workers in a bargaining unit is a poor system in that it collectivizes what should be an individual choice, but at least the workers are free to vote without intimidation and after hearing arguments and counter-arguments. Under a "card check" rule, workers may sign away their freedom without understanding the implications of the card, or just to stop the pestering from union organizers.

Writing about the Kennedy-Miller bill, Mix pointed to the flagrant hypocrisy of Big Labor on the issue of elections. "(U)nion officials themselves vociferously oppose the decertification of unions without a secret-ballot vote. The AFL-CIO joined in a 1998 court brief insisting that unionized employees must be given a chance to cast a secret-ballot vote before the union is decertified, even if most have already signed a petition opposing the union. The brief said that a union's workplace status should not be the result of 'group pressure.'"[1] When it comes to workers choosing to *drop* union representation, therefore, Big Labor insists on the sanctity of the secret ballot, but it wants to be able to use a far less reliable method when it comes to imposing unionization in the first place.

Permitting unionization by card checks would enable the labor bosses to fasten the yoke of compulsory unionism on many more workers. The National Right to Work Committee is opposing this dangerous bill and supporting a competing bill, sponsored by Representative Charles Norwood of Georgia that would prohibit employers from recognizing unions without a secret ballot vote. In May 2004, the Committee held a press conference on Capitol Hill where workers from across the country appeared to tell their stories of threats, lies, and intrusive home visits by union officials to get them to sign cards. Right to Work will fight tooth and nail to prevent legalization of the flimsy and unreliable "card check" procedure.

THE FREEDOM FROM UNION VIOLENCE ACT

Fortunately, there is also good legislation stirring in Congress and the National Right to Work Committee is working to build support for bills that would protect workers against union coercion and abuse.

One such bill is the Freedom from Union Violence Act (FUVA), which would amend the federal Hobbs Act, clarifying its language so as to bring labor union violence under its control. In 1945, Congress passed the Hobbs Act, which provides that:

> Whoever in any way or degree obstructs, delays, or affects commerce or the movement of any article or commodity in commerce, by robbery, extortion, or attempts or conspires so to do, or commits or threatens physical violence to any person or property in furtherance of a plan or purpose to do anything in violation of this section shall be fined not more than $10,000 or imprisoned not more than twenty years, or both.

The Hobbs Act had been passed in reaction to a Supreme Court decision, *United States v. Local 807*[2] that had undermined the Anti-Racketeering Act of 1934. In that case, Teamsters Union drivers met trucks seeking to enter New York City and demanded under threats of force, the equivalent of a day's wages for driving and unloading "services" that were not wanted or usually even delivered. The Teamsters were simply extorting money, but a divided Court declared that the Anti-Racketeering Act did not apply, in essence saying that the end of "securing work on better terms" justified the use of coercion. Congress reacted swiftly to the horrendous *Local* 807 decision by passing the Hobbs Act and for many years, it seemed that the law was clear—union violence to extort money was a federal offense. But in 1973 the Court once again decided that Congress hadn't meant what it said, in a case named *United States v. Enmons*.[3]

In *Enmons,* Louisiana union officials had ordered acts of violence during a strike against the property of Gulf States Utilities Company, such as the firing of high-powered rifles at company transformers, draining the oil from a transformer to ruin it, and the dynamiting of a transformer substation. Those acts of violence were done to pressure the company into settling on a new collective bargaining contract with the union. The question before the Court was whether violence perpetrated by union officials in order to force employers to consent to their bargaining demands could be prosecuted by federal authorities under the Hobbs Act. Amazingly enough, the Court, in a majority opinion by Justice Stewart, held that Congress had not meant to outlaw violence during strikes where the purpose of the violence was the furtherance of "legitimate union objectives." Once again, the statutory language was tortured to bring about the conclusion that Congress had not meant to make it a federal crime for union officials to use violence. Four members of the Court—Chief Justice Burger and Justices Douglas, Powell and Rehnquist—dissented. Justice Douglas hit the nail on the head, writing, "The Court today achieves by interpretation what those who were opposed to the Hobbs Act were unable to get Congress to do."

The upshot of the *Enmons* decision is that violence orchestrated by union officials is not subject to prosecution by federal law enforcement agencies. It can, of course, be prosecuted by state and local authorities, but owing to the reach of union influence, such violence often goes uninvestigated and unpunished. Right to Work leaders know that it is imperative to have federal jurisdiction over cases of union violence if we are to effectively crack down on it and that is what the Freedom from Union Violence Act (FUVA) provides. Enactment of FUVA is one of the top legislative goals of the National Right to Work Committee.

On September 3, 1997, hearings on FUVA were held in the Senate Judiciary Committee, chaired by Senator Orrin Hatch. Hatch explained the need for the bill by citing statistics on the frequency of union violence.

From 1975 through 1996, there were more than 8,700 reported incidents of union violence across the United States, with at least one incident in every state. Of those, in only 2.9 percent were the perpetrators convicted of the crime. Testifying in favor of the bill, former Attorney General Edwin Meese stated, "The exemption that currently exists from the normal standards of the Federal criminal law is really foreign to American jurisprudence. In no other context does the statute put Congress essentially in the position of saying that the end justifies the means as it applies to a particular class of criminals or organizations." Pointing to the outbursts of violence that accompanied the coal and newspaper strikes of the 1990s, Meese argued, "to suggest that State law enforcement officials can adequately respond to mass violence that is sometimes involved in these labor disputes ignores the historical record."

Also testifying in favor of the bill that day was Reed Larson. He asked the members of the Judiciary Committee (and the C-Span audience), "Who here believes that union violence is acceptable? Who here believes that extortion is a legitimate tactic? Who here believes that union officials should be above the law? Union officials' immunity under the Hobbs Act is outrageous, lethal, and indefensible." The Committee also heard from victims of horrifying union violence.

Alas, FUVA does not yet have enough support in Congress to pass, which is itself an indication of the depth of the problem of Big Labor's control. While Congress has seen fit to federalize numerous areas of law enforcement, it has so far refused to do so for the widespread problem of violence by union officials. In the years ahead, Right to Work will continue building support for FUVA in Congress.

"SALTING"

One of the despicable tactics that Big Labor uses these days, particularly in the construction industry, is known as "salting." The idea behind "salting" is to create legal trouble for merit shop firms by having "workers" who are actually union militants apply for open positions. Whether these "salts" are hired or not, they cause trouble.

In a typical instance, the pro-union applicant makes it clear to the management when he is interviewed that he favors unionization. If the company decides not to hire him, then his union boss controllers use that as the pretext for a suit against the company for the "unfair labor practice" of "discrimination." The costs of defending against such litigation can be ruinous for a small company; if hit with a series of such charges, the result can be bankruptcy. On the other hand, if the company hires the applicant, it will find trouble anyway. The union "salt" tries to sabotage the company by looking for other grounds for bringing unfair labor practice or other charges against it. The law thus places merit shop contractors between a rock and a hard place, and union officials exploit the fact that the law can be used as a sword to damage companies that have not knuckled under to compulsory unionism.

Just like the "common situs picketing" tactic described in Chapter 6, "salting" is part of Big Labor's attack on companies and workers who choose to remain independent of its control. The Committee has helped to focus attention on this abuse of the law and backs legislation to amend the NLRA to put an end to "salting." A bill to do that has been introduced in the House by South Carolina Representative (now Senator) Jim DeMint. It would deny the protections of the NLRA to union saboteurs posing as legitimate job seekers. Hearings on the bill held in February 2003 highlighted cases of this nasty abuse of the law. For example, the subcommittee heard from Leonard and Carol Cloninger, whose Helena, Montana electrical contracting business was forced into bankruptcy by penalties slapped on it by the NLRB for "discriminating" against union "salts" on several occasions. Addressing the need to change the law, Mark Mix commented, "By removing union salts' privileges, H.R. 1793 would effectively shield independent employers and construction workers from salting abuses."

As is the case with all legislation that would chip away at the mountain of legal privilege that Congress and the courts have bestowed on Big Labor, passage of Representative DeMint's anti-salting bill will be very difficult, but the National Right to Work Committee will do everything possible to push it forward.

THE NATIONAL RIGHT TO WORK ACT—
AND BEYOND

Of course, Right to Work also remains firmly committed to the passage of the National Right to Work Act. The defeat in the Senate in 1996 has not taken their eyes off the prize—a bill that would repeal the provisions of the NLRA that give federal sanction to compulsory unionism. With far less difficulty than it encountered in 1996, the Committee was able to procure a hearing on Representative Bob Goodlatte's bill on May 3, 2000, before the Subcommittee on Oversight and Investigations of the House Committee on Education and the Workforce. Speaking in favor of his bill, H.R. 792 which had 134 co-sponsors in the House, Representative Goodlatte said, "Compulsory unionism blots the American tradition of individual liberty by stripping working Americans of their right to join, or not join or financially support a union. No other private organization in America possesses such power. By forcing independent employees to join or pay fees to a union, labor officials have embraced collectivism based on coercion, and discarded individual liberty."

Despite the compelling testimony of Representative Goodlatte, Reed Larson, and others who favor returning unionism to the realm of individual choice, that hearing did not lead to a roll call vote on the bill in the House. There has been no vote on the National Right to Work Act in either chamber of Congress since the July, 1996 Senate vote discussed in the previous chapter. Nevertheless, the Committee has been working to defeat senators and representatives who favor forced unionism and replace them with people who can see the moral and economic reasons for allowing workers to choose freely whether or not to join a union. Measured by the number of co-sponsors, support for the National Right to Work Act has been growing in each chamber, but it is impossible to say how long it will take to get the bill enacted. This much is certain— the Committee won't give up on this crucial objective.

Even passage of the National Right to Work Act, however, is not truly the ultimate legislative goal of the Committee. In its Statement of Principles, the Committee says that each worker "should be free to choose either collective or individual means of negotiating their wages and working conditions. No one should presume to act for another, speak for another, or control another person's wages, livelihood and future without the consent of the 'represented' worker." That view calls for more than just the enactment of the National Right to Work Act—it calls for the elimination of the entire panoply of legal privileges and immunities that enable union officials to force employers to bargain with them and workers to accept their representation. Accomplishing that requires repeal of the National Labor Relations Act, Railway Labor Act, Norris-LaGuardia Act, and other federal statutes that, as we have seen, create the legal asymmetry favoring compulsory unionism. The federal government should stop giving legal privileges and immunities to union officials. State legislatures should roll back any laws that foist compulsory unionism on state and municipal employees. Mark Mix readily admits that we are a long way from being able to correct all of the great blunders Congress and the states have made with special interest legislation empowering union bosses to trample upon the rights of others. He hopes, nevertheless, to see the day when legal support for compulsory unionism has been entirely uprooted.

WHY RIGHT TO WORK SHOULD BE (ALMOST) EVERYONE'S FIGHT

Compulsory unionism is so antithetical to the American tradition of liberty and individual choice that Right to Work should be a fight that almost every citizen supports. Opinion polls have consistently shown that roughly 80 percent of the public believes that workers should not be compelled to belong to a union in order to hold a job. In the author's view, that figure would rise well into the 90s if more people understood that compulsory unionism, far from strengthening labor unions and improving worker representation, actually works against those goals.

If worker allegiance were voluntary—if it had to be *earned* and *maintained*—union officials would have to be attentive to the interests of their members, just as business managers have to be attentive to the desires of their customers and clients. But because union officials represent workers who are virtual captives, they often cannot resist the temptation to feather their own nests and engage in political empire-building designed to further strengthen their position and promote their ideology. Rather than concentrating their efforts on improving conditions for their members—for example by improving workplace safety or providing financial support for those who need retraining—union officials have dumped those functions off on government so they can devote most of their revenue stream to organizing at other businesses, to political activism they find appealing, and to high living. The recent cases involving top teacher union officials in Miami and Washington, where it was shown that the individuals in question had been sucking the union treasuries dry to support their lavish lifestyles, are indicative of the corruption that compulsory unionism invites.[4]

The interests of workers are actually *harmed* by the institution of compulsory unionism. Americans who fear that the elimination of the legal powers and privileges that have been granted to union officials would diminish the ability of unions to improve working conditions for their members should consider the words of Professor Sylvester Petro on this matter. Petro, who grew up in a working-class household on the south side of Chicago, wrote in his book *The Labor Policy of the Free Society*:

> (T)here is no evidence tending to prove that private associations which enjoy the special privilege of coercing membership perform more effectively than those which do not enjoy that privilege. Indeed, such evidence as we have suggests the contrary. It suggests that associations which may compel membership tend ultimately to lose sight of the objectives which originally had been sought in forming them, and that the interests of the membership become subordinated to the institutional interests of the bureaucracy of the association. There is reason to believe ... that the defects of trade unions as we know them are largely a consequence of the privilege of coercing membership which unions have enjoyed.[5]

Americans of good will who believe that the coercive powers given to union officials is beneficial to the workers they claim to represent should reflect upon the fact (discussed in Chapter 2) that the first Right to Work organization in the U.S. was founded by *railroad union members* who did not want the right to accept or reject union membership taken away from them. Those workers understood that the essential character of a labor union changes for the worse once membership becomes mandatory.

Not only is compulsory unionism bad for workers, saddling them with representation they cannot escape if it turns out to be too costly or unsatisfactory, but it is also bad for taxpayers. As we saw in Chapter 4, growing government is very much in the interest of Big Labor. Expanding the size and scope of government means the hiring of more and more workers whose jobs do not depend on competition in the free market. Big Labor pushes incessantly, using its political power and alliances, for bigger government. It invariably opposes tax cuts or measures to streamline government operations, even though many dues-paying workers would like to see the huge burden of government spending and control lightened. In short, the labor union movement has been drawn into a marriage with those who philosophically oppose the ideals of limited government, free enterprise, and individual responsibility—people most accurately called "Statists."

What Big Labor brings to that marriage is its enormous power to influence elections through its resources of money and manpower. When top union officials decide that they want a certain candidate to win—as in the case of Bill Clinton, for example—their support often means the difference between victory and defeat. In every election cycle, spending by the unions, both in cash and with in-kind assistance, runs into the hundreds of millions of dollars. Professor Leo Troy of Rutgers University, who has studied Big Labor's political operations for years, testified before a House subcommittee in 1996 that it pours a half billion dollars into politics every election year.[6] The candidates who receive Big Labor's backing are overwhelmingly Democrats and a few big-spending Republicans; invariably, they are candidates who can be counted on to oppose Right to Work. Big Labor's political muscle strongly and incessantly pushes the United States in the direction of bigger government and less freedom. Everyone who wants to stop our statist drift should realize that the elimination of compulsory unionism would greatly weaken their adversaries.

People are undeniably free to make their own political choices, but for millions of Americans who have to pay union dues to keep their jobs, their dues go in large measure to back candidates whom they would never voluntarily support. Many individuals vehemently disagree with the political and ideological stances of "their" union officials, but are forced to help finance them. Even when workers agree with union politics, they would often prefer to put less of their money into politics and keep more for themselves—if they had the right to decide. One piece of evidence that union politicking would significantly decline if workers could make their own choices on contributions is that in the state of Washington, when a 1992 ballot initiative prohibited the withholding of wages for political "contributions," the state teachers' union found that the number of teachers who voluntarily made its suggested one dollar per month contribution fell to only 8,000, compared to 48,000 who had previously been compelled to turn over their money.[7] (Union officials compensated for the shortfall by the simple expedient of re-naming and allocating to politics funds which had been collected under compulsory unionism contracts; the measure thus had no practical effect, but does serve to show that if workers could really choose, union officials would see a great shrinkage in their political war chests.)

Just how much money Big Labor plows into political campaigns is a question that cannot be definitively answered because unions are subject to such weak reporting requirements. Knowing the exact amount, however, is not important. Whether or not to have a law against stealing does not depend on the value of property that is stolen. Similarly, whether or not to keep workers from being forced to subsidize union political activity does not depend on the magnitude of that spending. As a matter of simple morality, every person should be free to decide for himself how much money, if any, to contribute to political candidates or causes. If America could return to a regime of freedom in labor relations, the political influence of Big Labor, which always aligns with the growth of government, would substantially decline.

That is why *almost* all Americans should support the Right to Work movement's goal of restoring unionism to a question of individual choice and eliminating the many legal privileges and immunities that have been given to union officials. Those who want to see government stop growing apace—and perhaps even shrink back to a scope appropriate for a nation rooted in individual liberty—should want to see Right to Work's aims achieved because Big Labor's political machine is their mortal enemy. Those who want to see our competitiveness rise to meet global challenges should want to see Right to Work's aims achieved because inefficient union work rules would not long survive in an atmosphere of freedom. Those whose main concern is for the well-being of workers should also want to see Right to Work's aims achieved. Unions that have the power to force themselves on workers are prone to corruption as officials begin to take their members for granted. The truth of Lord Acton's observation that power corrupts and absolute power corrupts absolutely is proven out daily with regard to labor union officials. Taking labor representation out of the realm of individual choice has deflected the union movement away from the betterment of working conditions and the welfare of workers and into a quest for power and privilege for union officials.

Here we might resort to an analogy to religion: Are the spiritual needs of Americans better served by our regime of free choice in religion, or would we be better off with a state-mandated, tax-supported official church, as in some European nations? It is easy to see that the incentives of the clergy would be drastically different if people were not free to make their own choices. With captive church membership, clergymen would have far less reason to concern themselves with the needs of individual parishioners and would no doubt pay much more attention to the source of their livelihood—the government. Church administration would balloon and, under compulsion to pay for a monopolistic organization, many people would lose interest in participating. Scandal and abuse would become much more common and if discovered at all, would be dealt with less swiftly and effectively than under a system of free and voluntary religion. Worst of all, having an official, compulsory religion would compel millions to support ideas they didn't agree with.

Most people can easily see that the United States made a wise decision in rejecting the autocratic established church model that prevailed in Europe in the 18th century. The same arguments apply with regard to compulsory unionism. The performance of human institutions is always better when we have the freedom to choose among competing providers of goods and services, none of which can take for granted its source of revenue. Freedom to say "No" to a union that wants to give you labor representation services is just as important as the freedom to say "No" to a church that wants to give you religious services. The latter freedom we have wisely enshrined in the Constitution, but the former we foolishly tossed away with several pieces of ill-considered special interest legislation early in the last century. Abandoning legal neutrality with regard to labor unions was a blunder of enormous proportions. American conservatives and liberals should be able to agree on that.

Seeing that compulsory unionism is harmful in various ways, people have proposed many regulations of labor unions. A few have even been enacted into law, over the determined opposition of union officials. Some of those reforms have been intended to make unions more open and responsive to their members, but they've had little effect. Others have been intended to curb the abuse of dues money for purposes other than collective bargaining, but a union hierarchy bent on doing just what it wants to has evaded them. Attempting to regulate away the undesirable characteristics of compulsory unionism is futile. Rather than continuing to try, we should strike at the root of the problem, namely the legal privileges and immunities that allow labor union officials to act in ways that no other private citizens are allowed to. What has united the diverse Americans who have made up the Right to Work movement ever since the 1940s is the understanding that while labor unions can be good, allowing them to exercise coercion is necessarily bad.

Almost all Americans should support the Right to Work movement. It does, however, make sense for two categories of people to oppose it: Union officials who want to continue collecting dues from workers who would prefer not to pay for their services, and ideological proponents of Big Government who want to keep using the financial resources of dues taken from millions of workers to advance their socialistic vision for the nation. Those people will never agree to return the labor movement to voluntarism. Coercion of workers enables them to achieve their objectives. They are, however, vastly outnumbered by Americans who realize that compulsory unionism ill-serves workers and poisons our politics. The Right to Work movement's ability to mobilize those Americans has, in the past, defended against the efforts of Big Labor to expand its power; its ability to mobilize them will, in the future, lead to the restoration of freedoms that were taken away decades ago.

It is the author's conviction that in time, and perhaps aided in some measure by this book, the Right to Work movement will achieve its goal of removing all legal supports for compulsory unionism and restoring to our citizens the right to choose, but not to be compelled to join a labor union.

NOTES

1. Mark Mix, "Let Them Have a Secret Ballot," *National Review Online,* December 1, 2003, available at nationalreview.com/script/printpage.asp?ref=/comment/mix200312010928.asp.
2. *United States v. Local 807,* 315 U.S. 521 (1944).
3. *United States v. Enmons,* 410 U.S. 396 (1973).
4. See "Ex-Teachers Union Chief Gets 9 Years," *Washington Post,* January 31, 2004 for the Washington case and "Former teachers' union boss begins sentence at Kentucky prison hospital," *Miami Herald,* February 20, 2004, for the Miami case.
5. Sylvester Petro, *The Labor Policy of the Free Society,* The Ronald Press, 1957, p. 78.
6. The text of Prof. Troy's statement is found in House Oversight Committee, "Influencing Elections: Political Activities of Labor Unions," Hearings 104th Congress, 2nd session, March 19, 1996 (Washington: GPO, 1996). His subsequent Senate testimony is available online at http://rules.Senate.gov/hearings/2000/041200troy.htm. For a wide-ranging discussion of union political activity, with numerous documented instances of the disparity between reported and unreported spending, see "The Tip of the Iceberg," The Smith Center for Private Enterprise Studies, available at www.sbe.csuhayward.edu/'sbesc/tipoftheiceberg.html.
7. See "Fact & Fallacy," Employment Policy Foundation, December 19
8. Available online at www.epf.org/ff/ff2–11.htm.

APPENDIX

A LAYMAN'S HISTORY OF U.S. SUPREME COURT PRECEDENT CONCERNING COMPULSORY UNIONISM

1937—Virginian Railway v. System Federation No. 40, 300 U.S. 515 *NLRB v. Jones & Laughlin Steel Corp.,* 301 U.S. 1

The Court held that compulsory collective bargaining is constitutional, but declined to address the constitutionality of exclusive representation because these cases were brought by employers, not employees forced to accept a union as their exclusive bargaining representative.

1944—J.I. Case Co. v. National Labor Relations Board, 321 U.S. 332 *Order of Railroad Telegraphers v. Railway Express Agency, Inc.,* 321 U.S. 342

The Court interpreted the National Labor Relations and Railway Labor Acts as prohibiting individual employees from negotiating their own terms and conditions of employment where an exclusive bargaining representative has been recognized. Constitutional questions were not raised.

1944—Steele v. Louisville & Nashville R.R., 323 U.S. 192

The Court recognized that exclusive representation presents constitutional problems, but again ducks the issue by holding that exclusive representatives have a duty of representing nonmembers "fairly."

1949—Lincoln Federal Labor Union v. Northwestern Iron & Metal Co., 335 U.S. 525 *American Federation of Labor v. American Sash & Door Co.,* 335 U.S. 538

The Court ruled that state Right to Work laws are constitutional.

1949—*Algoma Plywood Co. v. Wisconsin Bd.*, 336 U.S. 301
The Court held that the National Labor Relations ("Wagner") Act permitted state Right to Work laws even before Congress passed the 1947 Taft-Hartley Act amendments.

1954—*Radio Officers' Union v. National Labor Relations Board*, 347 U.S. 17
The Court ruled that compulsory unionism agreements may not be used "for any purpose other than to compel payment of union dues and fees," that is, that employees may not be required to be formal union members and abide by internal union rules to keep their jobs.

1956—*Railway Employees' Department v. Hanson*, 351 U.S. 225
The Court held that "union shop" agreements authorized by the Railway Labor Act are constitutional, because the only condition of employment that the Act authorizes is "financial support" of "the work of the union in the realm of collective bargaining." The Court suggested that if compulsory dues are used "for purposes not germane to collective bargaining, a different problem would be presented" under the First Amendment.

1961—*Machinists v. Street*, 376 U.S. 740
Again ducking constitutional questions, the Court ruled that the Railway Labor Act prohibits unions from using objecting nonmembers' compulsory dues for political purposes. The Court did not clearly define political purposes, nor did it address whether unions could lawfully use objectors' monies for nonpolitical activities unrelated to collective bargaining. Dissenting Justice Black, predicting that the Court's rebate remedy would be ineffective, would have held the statute unconstitutional.

1963—*Railway Clerks v. Allen*, 373 U.S. 113
The Court found that, since unions hold all pertinent facts and records, they must prove the proportions of their expenses that are lawfully chargeable to objecting nonmembers. However, the Court reaffirmed *Street's* rulings that only nonmembers who notify their union that they object

are entitled to relief and that the appropriate remedies are refunds and reductions in future exactions.

1963—National Labor Relations Board v. General Motors, 373 U.S. 734
The Court reiterated that the "union shop" is "is whittled down to its financial core," that is, unions may require payment of initiation fees and dues as a condition of employment, but may not require formal membership.

1963—Retail Clerks Local 1625 v. Schermerhorn, 373 U.S. 746, 375 U.S. 96
The Court held that state Right to Work laws may prohibit "agency shop" agreements under which employees are required to pay fees to unions to defray the costs of collective bargaining. In a second decision in the same case, the Court ruled that the state courts, not just the National Labor Relations Board, can enforce state Right to Work laws. (The National Right to Work Committee financed this case in the Supreme Court for the nonmember plaintiffs.)

1968   **The National Right to Work Legal Defense Foundation was established. Unless otherwise noted, all subsequent cases listed were brought by Foundation attorneys.**

1976—Oil Workers v. Mobil Oil Corp., 426 U.S. 407
The Court held that the employees' "predominant job situs" determines whether a state Right to Work law applies, and that seamen employed primarily on the high seas are not protected by the Right to Work law of the state in which they were hired. The Foundation filed an *amicus* ("friend of the court") brief urging that Texas' Right to Work law protected the seaman.

1976—City of Madison Joint School District No. 8 v. Wisconsin Employment Relations Commission, 429 U.S. 167
The Court ruled that a state may not constitutionally require school boards to prohibit nonunion teachers from speaking against agency shop agreements at public meetings. The Foundation filed an *amicus* brief supporting the nonunion teachers' free speech rights.

1977—*Abood v. Detroit Board of Education*, 431 U.S. 209
A six-member majority of the Court rejected arguments that requiring public employees to pay agency fees to keep their jobs violates the First Amendment. The Court ruled that the agency shop as such is constitutionally
valid, but only "insofar as the service charges are applied to collective-bargaining, contract administration, and grievance-adjustment purposes." The
Court unanimously agreed that "a union cannot constitutionally spend
[objectors'] funds for the expression of political views, on behalf of political candidates, or toward the advancement of other ideological causes not
germane to its duties as collective-bargaining representative."

1983—*Knight v. Minnesota Community College Faculty Association*, 460
       U.S. 1048
Without an opinion giving its reasons, the Court affirmed a lower court
decision rejecting arguments that exclusive representation of public
employees by a union such as the National Education Association is
unconstitutional because it forces association with a political-action
organization.

1984—*Minnesota State Board for Community Colleges v. Knight*, 465 U.S. 271
The Court ruled that a state may constitutionally bar nonmembers from
participating in their public employers' "meet and confer" sessions with
the employees' exclusive bargaining representative on policy questions
relating to employment, but outside the scope of mandatory collective
bargaining.

1984—*Ellis v. Railway Clerks*, 466 U.S. 435
The Court held that the Railway Labor Act not only prohibits coerced
financial support of union politics and ideological activities, but also
coerced support of other activities unrelated to collective bargaining and
contract administration, such as organizing, litigation not concerning
objecting employees' bargaining unit, and the parts of union publications reporting on nonchargeable activities. The Court also ruled that a
"union cannot be allowed to commit dissenters' funds to improper uses
even temporarily," prohibiting "rebate" schemes under which unions col-

lect full dues, use part for improper purposes, and only later refund that part to the employees.

1985—*Pattern Makers v. National Labor Relations Board,* 473 U.S. 95
The Court recognized that the National Labor Relations Act guarantees workers the right to resign union membership at any time. The Foundation filed an *amicus* brief urging this ruling.

1986—*Chicago Teachers Union v. Hudson,* 475 U.S. 292
The Court unanimously held that First Amendment due process requires that certain procedural safeguards be established before compulsory union fees can be collected from public employees: adequate advance notice of the fee's basis (including an independent audit), reasonably prompt impartial review of nonmembers' challenges, and escrow of "amounts reasonably in dispute" while challenges are pending. Because the Court had earlier ruled in *Railway Employees' Department v. Hanson* that constitutional limitations apply to the Railway Labor Act, these procedural safeguards also must be established by railway and airline unions.

1988—*Communications Workers v. Beck,* 487 U.S. 735
The Court determined that Congress intended the substantially "identical" authorizations of compulsory unionism arrangements in the National Labor Relations and Railway Labor Acts "to have the same meaning." The Court, therefore, held that the former statute, like the latter, "authorizes the exaction of only those fees and dues necessary to 'performing the duties of an exclusive representative of the employees in dealing with the employer on labor-management issues.'" As a result, private-sector employees have the same right not to subsidize union non-bargaining activities as railway, airline, and public employees, and are entitled to the procedural protections outlined in *Chicago Teachers Union v. Hudson.*

1991—*Lehnert v. Ferris Faculty Association,* 500 U.S. 507
Summarizing its earlier decisions from *Hanson* through *Ellis,* the Court concluded that union activities are not lawfully chargeable to objecting nonmembers unless they *both* are "germane" to collective-bargaining activity" and do "not significantly add to the burdening of free speech

that is inherent in allowance of an agency or union shop." Applying this test, the Court ruled that objecting public employees may not be charged for litigation not directly concerning their bargaining unit, lobbying (except for ratification or implementation of their collective bargaining agreement), public relations activities, and illegal strikes. However, the Court also held that the First Amendment does not limit lawfully charge-able bargaining-related costs to the objecting employees' bargaining unit.

1998—*Air Line Pilots Association v. Miller,* 523 U.S. 866
The Court ruled that nonmembers who do not agree to union-estab-lished arbitration procedures cannot be required to use those procedures before bringing a federal court action challenging the amount of their compulsory fees for collective bargaining.

1998—*Marquez v. Screen Actors Guild,* 523 U.S. 866
The Court held that a union does not breach its duty of fair representa-tion "merely by negotiating" a compulsory unionism provision that says that employees must be union "members in good standing" as condition of employment without expressly explaining, in the agreement, that the National Labor Relations Act does not permit unions and employers to require that employees become formal union members. Importantly, for the first time, the Court declared that, if a union negotiates a compul-sory unionism provision, it must notify workers that they may satisfy the provision's requirement merely by paying fees to support the union's "rep-resentational activities" in collective bargaining and contract adminis-tration, without actually becoming members.

INDEX